D1796533

Psychology in the Light
of the East

Psychology in the Light of the East

Margot Esther Borden

ROWMAN & LITTLEFIELD
Lanham • Boulder • New York • London

Published by Rowman & Littlefield
A wholly owned subsidiary of The Rowman & Littlefield Publishing Group, Inc.
4501 Forbes Boulevard, Suite 200, Lanham, Maryland 20706
www.rowman.com

Unit A, Whitacre Mews, 26-34 Stannary Street, London SE11 4AB

British Library Cataloguing in Publication Information Available

Library of Congress Cataloging-in-Publication Data

Names: Borden, Margot Esther, author.
Title: Psychology in the light of the East / Margot Esther Borden.
Description: Lanham, Maryland: Rowman & Littlefield, [2017] |
    Includes bibliographical references and index.
Identifiers: LCCN 2016040322 (print) | LCCN 2016051220 (ebook) |
    ISBN 9781442260245 (cloth : alk. paper) | ISBN 9781442260269 (pbk. : alk. paper) |
    ISBN 9781442260252 (electronic)
Subjects: LCSH: Mental healing. | Mind and body. | Philosophy, Asian. |
    Alternative medicine. | Psychology. | Mental health—Religious aspects.
Classification: LCC RZ400 .B67 2017 (print) |
    LCC RZ400 (ebook) | DDC 615.8/51—dc23
LC record available at https://lccn.loc.gov/2016040322

Printed in the United States of America

Contents

Acknowledgments   xiii

Foreword   xv

Introduction   xix

Timeline of Psycho-Spiritual Belief Systems—East and West   xxix

1   Origins and Development of Western Psychology   1

    Ancient Origins   1

    Zeroing in on the Psyche   4

    Emergence of Semitic Religions   5

    The Birth of Psychology   6

    Early Medical Models of Psychiatric Disorder
    and Assessment   7

    Freud's Psychoanalysis   8

    Post-Freudian Psychoanalytic Thought—Jung, Adler, Rank,
    and Horney   9

    Limitations of Psychoanalysis   12

    Vignette—Fragmented Personality   13

    Vignette—The Ego as a Suit of Armor   14

    Stepping Stones Toward an Integral Psychology—
    Psychoanalysis   15

    Developmental Psychology—Piaget, and Vygostsky   15

    Behaviorism—Pavlov, Watson, and Skinner   16

    Cognitive-Behavioral Therapies—Bandura, Ellis, and Beck   16

    Limitations of Behaviorism and Cognitive Behaviorism   17

    Vignette—Contacting and Healing the Core Wound   19

Behavioral and Cognitive-Behavioral Stepping Stones Toward
an Integral Psychology   19
Current Medical Models   20
Vignette—Antidepressants   21
Limitations of the Medical Model   22
Medical Model—Stepping Stones Toward an Integral
Psychology   24
Conclusion   24
Annex I: In-Depth Case Study on Psychoanalysis   25

2   History of Modern Western Psychology   33
Humanistic Psychology—Maslow, May, and Rogers   33
Abraham Maslow   34
Vignette—Integrating Levels of Functioning   34
Rollo May   36
Vignette—Love and Will   37
Carl Rogers   37
Vignette—Person-Centered Presence   38
Limitations of Humanistic and Person-Centered Approaches   39
Vignette—A Directive Kick in the Behind   39
Conclusion   41
Transpersonal Psychology—James, Jung, Assagioli, Grof,
and Vaughan   41
William James   44
Carl Jung: Transpersonal Aspects   45
Roberto Assagioli   47
Stanislav Grof   50
Spiritual Emergency   51
Frances Vaughan   52
Limitations of Transpersonal Psychology   53
Stepping Stones—Humanistic and Transpersonal
Psychologies   55
Conclusion   55

3   Eastern Psychology   59
Hinduism   60
The Vedas   63
The Upanishads   65
The Bhagavad Gita   68
The Yoga Philosophy of Mararishi Patanjali   69
Indian Psychology   71

*Indian Views and Approaches to Mental Health—Traditional
and Modern* 72
The Challenge of Modernization 72
Hinduism and the West 74
Jainism 75
Buddhism 76
Zen Buddhism 78
Vignette—Meditation 79
Tibetan Buddhism 80
The Psychology of China 82
I Ching—The Book of Changes 83
Confucianism 83
Taoism 84
Vignette—Realigning the Will 85
Limitations of Eastern Psychologies 86
Stepping Stones for an Integral Psychology 87
Conclusion 87

4 Sri Aurobindo's Integral Yoga Psychology 91
Integral Psychology 92
Planes of Consciousness 92
Liberation vs Transformation 94
Practices in Integral Yoga 95
Karma Yoga: The Yoga of Works 96
Jnana Yoga: The Yoga of Knowledge 98
Bhakti Yoga: The Yoga of Devotion 99
Yoga of Self-Perfection 100
Psychic Transformation 101
Spiritual Transformation 102
Supramental Transformation 103
Psychopathology and Diagnosis 104
Mental Disturbances 105
Vital Disturbances 106
Disturbances of the Physical Consciousness 106
Disturbances of the Subconscient 107
Vignette—Spiritual Self-Delusion 108
Adverse Forces 108
The Role of the Psychic Being in Mental Health 109
*Vignette—Levels of Consciousness: Multidimensional
Diagnosis and Treatment* 109
Indian Schools of Integral Thought 111

Indra Sen	111
Haridas Chaudhari	111
A.S. Dalal	112
Limitations of Eastern Approaches to Integral Psychology	113
Stepping Stones for Integral Psychology	113
Conclusion	114

5 Ken Wilber's Integral Psychology — 117

The Great Nest of Being	118
Unity in Diversity	119
Spiral Dynamics	120
Premodernism, Modernism, and Postmodernism	120
All Quadrants—All Levels (AQAL)	121
Psychological Development and Integral Psychotherapy	122
Vignette—Healing: An Upward Spiral	124
Spirituality in Wilber's Integral Psychology	125
Personal Development—Integral Life Practice (ILP)	126
Vignette—Collective Healing	127
Diagnosis in Integral Psychology	130
Western Schools of Integral Thought	131
Limitations of Integral Psychology	131
Stepping Stones for an Integral Psychology	133
Conclusion	134

6 An Integral Approach to Psychology: Theoretical Considerations — 137

Evolution of Psychology "Developmental Issues"	138
Where Do We Go From Here?	139
Eastern Consciousness Perspective—Evolution of Consciousness	139
Sri Aurobindo's and Ken Wilber's Integral Psychologies: Eastern and Western Perspectives	140
Shift to an Integral Paradigm	141
Theoretical and Therapeutic Potential	142
Defining Integral	142
1. Unity in Diversity	143
2. Spiritual Worldview	143
3. Multidimensional Grasp of Consciousness and Human Potential	144
4. Levels of Truth	145
Where Should Psychology Bring Us? Why Not Shoot for the Stars?	145
Adjustment and Adaptation	146
Alleviation of Emotional Distress	146

Material and Affective Fulfillment   146
Elimination of Suffering   147
Peace with Oneself and Self-Acceptance   147
Integration   148
Spiritual Development, Transcendence, and Transformation   149
Dangers of Spirituality and Spiritual Approaches to
  Psychotherapy   151
Distraction by Physical, Emotional, Mental, or Astral
  Phenomenon   152
Spiritual Bypass   152
Vignette—Spiritual Bypass   152
Huxley Placed Much Emphasis on the Perils
  of Imbalanced Spiritual Development   153
Lack of Discernment   154
New-Age Fads, Pop Psychology, and Pseudo Gurus   154
Almighty Syndrome   155
Vignette—Almighty Syndrome   155
Halfway Up the Mountain   156
Insufficient Psychological Maturity   156
Spiritual Narcissism   157
Desire First, Truth Later   157
Spiritual Materialism   157
Reaching for the Low-Hanging Fruit   158
Spiritual Perfectionism and Other Spiritual Neuroses   158
Conclusion   159

7   The Making of an Integral Psychotherapist   163
  A Four-Leaf Clover   163
    Psycho-Spiritual Development   164
    GPS: Guru, Psychotherapist, or Self as Guide   166
    Going Solo   166
    Psychotherapeutic Accompaniment   167
    Choosing—or Being Chosen by—a Guru   167
  Taking Our Turn as Clients   169
    Creating a Safe and Healing Space for Ourselves   169
    Getting to the Core Causes   170
    Control vs Mastery   171
    Vignette—Control, Letting Go, and Mastery   172
  Life Hygiene   173
    Waltz or Slam Dance—Taking Care of Our Subtle Bodies   174
    Just Do It   175
    Getting to the Essence: Simply Being Our Authentic Self   175

Integral Ethos: Putting Our Ideals into Practice   176
Humility   176
Discernment: The Crown Jewel   177
Client Autonomy   177
*Vignette—Respect for Client's Worldview and Freedom
    of Choice*   178
Bring Our Ethics Up to the Mark   178
Consciousness Is Multidimensional   179
*Nonjudgmental Understanding of World Spiritual
    Traditions*   179
*Ability to Distinguish Between Healthy and Unhealthy
    Spiritual/Religious Experience*   180
Practice What We Preach   181
Contribute to Society and Planet   181
Take Off Our Helping Hat   181
Keep a Flexible Mind   182
Vignette—The Mind: Gateway or Gatekeeper   182
Supervision   182
Conclusion   183
Annex I: Healthy vs Unhealthy States   183

8 Integral Psychotherapy in Practice   185
The Journey of Integral Consciousness   186
Who Comes for Integral Psychotherapy?   186
The Therapeutic Relationship Begins   187
Creating a Safe and Healing Space for Our Clients   188
Client Dynamics—A Bicycle Built for Two   189
A Multidimensional View of Issues/What Issue,
    What Level?   190
A Word on Diagnosis   191
Physical Level—Medical and Intuitive Assessments   194
Vignette—Medical and Intuitive Assessments   194
Emotional Level   194
Vignette—Emotional Healing   195
The Emotional Body Is Like a Minefield   196
The Mind   197
Subtle Mind   197
Vignette—Family Secrets   198
Religious, Spiritual, and Subtle Issues   199
Vignette—Spiritual Emergency   200
Karma   201

Vignette—Past Life Recall	201
External Disturbances	203
Occult Disturbance	203
Vignette—Occult Disturbance	203
Conclusion	204
9 Techniques: An Integral Therapy Toolbox	207
Development of a Tri-Fold Approach	208
Person-Centered Dialogue	209
Vignette—Person-Centered Dialogue	209
Breathwork	210
Modern Perspectives on the Breath	210
Physical Benefits of Breathwork	211
Emotional Benefits	212
Healing Cellular Memory	213
Mental Effects of the Breath	213
Spiritual Dimensions of the Breath	213
What Happens in a Breathwork Session?	214
Vignette—Liberating the Root Cause	214
Vignette—Breathwork	214
Mindfulness	217
Mindfulness in Psychotherapy	217
Accept It	219
Vignette—Embodied Mindfulness	219
Cognitive and Behavioral Interventions	222
Journaling	222
Journaling as an Intervention	223
EMDR	223
Vignette—Post-Traumatic Stress Disorder	224
Dreamwork	224
Vignette—Dreamwork	224
Gestalt Role-Play	226
Inner Dialogue and Psychosynthesis	227
Flower and Plant Essences	228
Jin Shin Jyutsu (JSJ)	228
Vignette—JSJ "Attitudes"	229
Yoga Therapy	230
Psychogenealogy	231
Family Constellation	231
Prayer	233
Vignette—Prayer	233

Meditation   234
  Mindfulness Meditation   235
  Meditation as a Therapeutic Tool   236
  A Word of Caution   236
Which Type of Technique or Intervention and When?   237
Conclusion   239

References   241

Index   249

Acknowledgments

I thank my beloved Satguru Gurudev Paramahamsa Hariharananda Giri and his divine successor Guruji Paramahamsa Prajnanananda Giri who drew me into the mysteries of India, quenching the thirst of my seeker's soul with their infinite wisdom and compassion. Heartfelt thanks to all my predecessors in the field of psychology and inner inquiry who opened doors and kept me challenged on this adventure of self-knowledge. Thank you and dhaanyavaad to the many friends and colleagues who inspired me with hours of conversation on Eastern and Western spiritual traditions and psychology.

Sincere gratitude to Colin Ahern whose genius helped me begin to solve a sprawling jigsaw puzzle of scattered phrases and inspirations. Claude Le Saché for his friendship, tireless patience, big ears, wide shoulders, and a big heart. Ann Isik for her boxes, patience, humor, and beautiful country walks in times of trouble. Dinesh and Anuradha Rathi for their selfless time and help. Ashish Pant for our discussions and countless cups of cutting chai at the Prithvi Theatre Café in Mumbai, which brought out the essence of the most difficult to articulate observations and experiences, not to mention the countless bouts of laughter. Michael Burns who helped me bring my story to life. Michael Gelb for his boundless positive energy, support, and advice. And my dear mother, Diana Ruth Krohn, for dedicating tireless hours toward editing and fine-tuning the final work.

Foreword

Abraham Maslow wrote: "I suppose it is tempting, if the only tool you have is a hammer, to treat everything as if it were a nail." In this extraordinary book, Margot Borden guides therapists to develop a more balanced and complete toolkit. She describes the use of techniques ranging from breathwork and mindfulness to Jin Shin Jyutsu and flower remedies, but these modalities are explored in the framework of an exquisitely sensitive attunement to the needs of the client. Borden's application of a range of techniques, including some that may seem unconventional, is grounded in the fundamentals of therapeutic excellence as described by Carl Rogers. Rogers' *Client Centered Therapy* was predicated on three pillars for which Borden is an outstanding role model: Congruence, Unconditional Positive Regard, and Accurate Empathic Understanding.

Congruence: Therapists needn't be fully self-actualized and enlightened, but they do require an above average level of openness, integrity, and authenticity. Borden brings life to this text by sharing key elements in her personal journey. Her unwavering quest for truth and self-knowledge shines through every page, as does her tireless search to find the best ways to help others. The integrity and authenticity she brings to her own journey, and thereby, to her clients, will illuminate and inspire all practitioners aiming to deepen their own congruence.

Unconditional Positive Regard: Rogers observed that genuine caring has a profoundly positive therapeutic effect. When clients feel accepted they are better able to bring awareness to, and begin to change, behaviors that may be unacceptable. As he explains, "The curious paradox is that when I accept myself just as I am, then I can change."

The paradox for therapists is *How to be unconditionally loving, without attachment?* This is also one of the great questions contemplated by spiritual seekers. Borden is an excellent guide and example in this regard, offering readers valuable support in the quest to discover this balance.

Accurate Empathic Understanding: Rogers explains, "When the therapist does understand how it truly feels to be in another person's world, without wanting or trying to analyze or judge it, then the therapist and the client can truly blossom and grow in that climate." Gifted from childhood with a remarkable sensitivity to the feelings, needs, and energy of others, Borden has developed a sound structure for these talents through her own professional training. She shares vignettes abstracted from real client sessions that elucidate her gift for empathizing, thereby guiding us to develop our own capacity in this essential element of therapy.

More than just a toolkit and a guide to the author's journey, this book also aims to expand our understanding of the field of psychology by presenting a holistic, integrated theoretical framework. Borden elucidates the evolution of Eastern and Western approaches to psychotherapy aiming to show how we can apply the mystical, transcendent insights of the East in harmony with the pragmatism and results-orientation of the West. This is not an easy task. Borden acknowledges that psychology and spirituality are different, but she shows how they can be woven together both theoretically and in application. For example, she cites an ancient Hindu text that urges spiritual seekers to cultivate *The Crown Jewel of Discernment*—the ability to distinguish truth from untruth. Borden shows how this quality is essential to both the quest for Enlightenment and "for navigating our day-to-day experiences more gracefully." She notes, "Humility paves the way for Discernment."

Discerning readers who wish to navigate their lives and work with more grace will discover many gems of insight in these pages. These gems are polished by Borden's experience of living, studying, teaching, and working with clients in a global context. She is equally at home in an Indian ashram, a Parisian coffee house, or an American diner, and she brings together the best of all these worlds: mystical, transcendent insight, sophistication and *savoir-faire*, and down-to-earth common sense. It's a rare and precious combination. And so is the juxtaposition of wisdom from two of Borden's strongest influences—the Indian mystic and reformer Sri Aurobindo and Carl Rogers.

Aurobindo emphasizes, "Evolution is not finished. . . ." and Rogers observes, "The good life is a process, not a state of being. It is a direction not a destination."

Aurobindo states, "What the soul sees and has experienced, that it knows; the rest is appearance, prejudice and opinion."

And Rogers writes, "Experience is, for me, the highest authority. . . . Neither the Bible nor the prophets—neither Freud nor research—neither the revelations of God nor man—can take precedence over my own direct experience."

In describing the good life, Rogers adds that it is characterized by "an increasing tendency to live fully in each moment." He explains that this requires childlike openness and freedom from defensiveness. That sounds a lot like Enlightenment. It's the heart of Integral Psychotherapy and it is the essence of **Psychology in the Light of the East**.

Michael Gelb
Author of *How to Think Like Leonardo da Vinci*

Introduction

One of my earliest memories is from when I was three years old. In that hazy, washed-out feeling that those earliest of memories have in my mind's eye, I see a young version of my father. He said his back was hurting. I reached up toward him and intuitively knew where it hurt. I not only "perceived" the physical pain but sensed his emotional state as well. Think about your earliest memory. What was it? Why do you think it's there? There is a good reason this memory is chiseled into your mind, a reason that it persisted even after millions of neuropathways sprang up around it—like a small cottage owner who refuses to sell and soon finds himself overshadowed by a sea of skyscrapers. For me, I choose to believe that this memory was the start of my inner conviction that there is more to life than what we see. We are here in this life to evolve, to find our inner truth, which is simply love. I feel compassion for other people's suffering.

Apart from growing up in the hippie era with its embracing social ideals of freedom and peace, a handful of personal experiences left a deep impact on me. When I was twelve, my mother and I attended yoga classes. The silence, deliberate flow of the movements and the sense of energy made me feel more alive and on track. When he wasn't teaching yoga, our teacher released captive eagles back into the wild. Seeing those powerful and elegant birds train and take off on their final flight to their original home awoke a deep sense of meaning and purpose that, at that point, did not have a name or form. When I was fifteen, reading the *Autobiography of a Yogi*, those same early inklings were reignited in me. Like countless others who have read it, I was deeply moved and inspired. I prayed with all my heart to someday have the guidance of such a wise and loving spiritual teacher.

At nineteen, I grew restless with my international business studies. They felt distinctly mismatched with my inner calling. I knew inside that my calling was to help people. I dropped out of university and went to Europe for the summer—my waffle-stomper boots and Grateful Dead t-shirt were my constant companions. France took me in, and I found myself enrolled at the American University of Paris to finish my degree. My creative and rebellious streak was reduced to a hot pink and lime green zebra-striped bicycle which I rode down La Rue Des Ecoles, past Les Invalides, and to class every day. This kept my free spirit alive in those dreary, rainy, and textbook-filled years.

My first trip back to the States was two years later during summer break. Basking in the Arizona sun in the sublime Saguaro Desert just outside Tucson, Lee, a friend of the friend I was staying with dropped by for a visit. As we were introduced, he looked at me contemplatively and asked, "Why did you come to the U.S.?" "For a family wedding," I blurted out. He looked at me and asked the same question again. This destabilized me for some reason. I had a sense of what he meant; leaving me nowhere to look for the answer but inside. At first, I could not find an answer. I felt his gentle and powerful presence as he patiently waited. After a few minutes, I found myself saying, "It's time to come home and reconcile with all that I ran away from when I left the States four years ago." The hour we spent together was a turning point. Lee's question awoke me from a numbness that I hadn't even realized I'd had. I realized that not only could I look inside for answers, but that doing so would make my life infinitely richer and more meaningful.

During the final summer holiday before finishing my bachelor's degree, Lee invited me to meet him in Ireland. Between the time we made our plans and the time we met, something else came up for him, and instead of spending a summer traveling together, we had only one day. Here I was again, this time in Dublin with the person who had set off my profound shift. During our day together, he continued to challenge me, inviting me to explore deep thoughts and feelings I'd never experienced before. He taught me how to sit quietly and feel energy. When he left, I found myself with time, a sense of freedom, adventure, a few Irish pounds, and an open ferry ticket back to France. The hotel staff advised me to hitchhike and even made me a cardboard sign saying "Cork," the first major town on the way back to the ferry. A BMW stopped and I found myself sitting next to a mysterious French psychic. Driving down the country lanes, he told me, appropriately, that my life was at a crossroads, and although I would not yet be able to understand what he was explaining, it would become clear very shortly. He elaborated, but, as he had predicted, I didn't really grasp what he was telling me. We reached his destination and said a roadside goodbye.

My next lift was a bit awkward—nothing traumatic, but there was an uncomfortable energy. I felt the driver's intentions weren't entirely innocent. It dawned on me that my excitement from the first lift had thrown me off-center. I was hit with a sense of how our state of mind influences or creates our experiences. I had, no doubt, always had a state of mind, but never really paid attention to it or recognized its importance. I invented a story about needing to change destinations and the driver dropped me off with no incident.

The morning's experiences began to give me a sense of the initiatory nature of this journey. I was learning to listen to and be guided by a sense stemming from deep within. A deep feeling emerges from within us telling us if something feels right or wrong. Then, there is the challenge of knowing how to interpret that feeling and the maturity to act on it. As I walked along the side of the highway, I was awestruck by mystical rolling hills and misty sea air. It felt like my soul could breathe. I took it all in, let go of expectations and desires, and relaxed into the present. My sense of safety returned and I resumed my quest for a lift along the N11. No sooner did I put up my sign than a car stopped and a middle-aged woman, Jeanne, offered me a lift. She was on her way to Arklow and agreed to drop me at the port in Rosslare. As we drove, our conversation quickly flowed into friendship and an invitation to stay with her. The trip back to Paris could wait. It was time to surrender to the adventure that was unfolding. As we passed the turnoff to the ferry, I sensed I had made the right decision, even though it seemed irrational.

Jeanne lived in an early seventeenth-century country house called Sheepwalk. Built by the Earl of Wicklow, the archbishop of Dublin had lived there in the eighteenth century. We took long walks, enjoyed cups of tea by the fireplace, and talked about her life and ideals. It was surprising in this highly conservative country to have this extraordinary meeting with yet another person living life in her own way. Jeanne was a schoolteacher and had chosen not to marry, unlike other women in her small township. After a few days, she suggested I meet her friends in Bray, a small town south of Dublin. The next morning, after a hearty breakfast and feeling grateful for her company, I headed up the coast to meet Jeanne's friends. I was both excited and apprehensive about where exactly this next detour was leading me.

Trish and Steve greeted me warmly. Over cups of tea, Trish intrigued me with her description of her work: helping people open up and discover their true selves through their breath. I accepted her offer of a session. Entering their beautiful living room with a bay window overlooking the rugged Irish coast, she directed me to lie down on my back. Trish explained a very simple breathing technique with deep and connected breath. She told me that all I had to do was breathe, let go, and let the experience unfold.

At twenty-two, despite my traveling and exploring, I had been nagged by a sense that something was missing—in a way, I felt both lost and confined. The breath took me into and *through* this sense and awakened a deep longing to connect with myself. I lost all sense of time and space and experienced profound states of awareness and realizations about myself and my life. I was left with an intense feeling of opening, going beyond the limitations of my little world and my self-image as I knew it. The session was another turning point. I realized there is both a world outside of me offering experiences and discoveries and, beyond that, a universe within. The French psychic's prediction started to become clear. I became aware of something inside, a sense of truth, meaning, and universal vastness that, from that moment on, became the center of my pursuit.

Returning to Paris to finish my degree, I also completed a one-year intensive training and certification in breathwork. The powerful course gave me increasingly deeper insights and experiences into how my early experiences had, in some cases, given me boundless courage and optimism and, yet in others, left me vulnerable and lost. My grim, teenage worldview was giving way. I devoured every book and seminar that promised answers or inner peace. I began to connect to a sense of universal energy, an underlying Oneness, a peek into the mysteries of consciousness. I knew for certain that there was a deeper, unifying cause linking all living beings. On a more concrete level, we learned to listen to and "read" the breath which reveals, in its fluctuations, the state of consciousness of the breather, including their deepest, inner relationship to themselves, along with their attitudes, unresolved issues, and, most importantly, their potential. To this day, I am just as passionate about breathwork as in those first days of discovery, and it remains my favorite therapeutic technique, bridging traditional Eastern yogic philosophy and Western psychology. The mystery and healing power of the breath has been one of the most powerful tools of my personal and professional development.

In 1988, while living in New York City, I was drawn to attend a lecture on Kriya Yoga at the New York Open Center. A sweet and simple man in orange robes explained the benefits and the scientific approach to God-realization. He asked who would be attending the initiation the next morning. As if it had a will of its own, my hand went up. Little did I realize it but this very endearing monk, Paramahamsa Hariharananda, was part of the same lineage as Paramahansa Yogananda, whose book, the *Autobiography of a Yogi,* had inspired me when I was fifteen.

The guidance of my wise and compassionate teacher and daily meditation practice were deeply enriching and gave insights into the ancient Yogic tradition of India that had inspired me so deeply when I was a teenager. In the first six months of practicing the meditation, I observed my core attitudes and understandings shifting, becoming clearer as if subtle illusions or unconstructive attitudes were gradually being stripped away. Over the years, this process of purification and evolution continues in increasingly subtle and sometimes not so subtle ways thanks to regular meditation practice.

In the late 1980s, I discovered the Findhorn Foundation and its offshoot community, Newbold House. Over the next few years, Newbold House became like a second home where I was fortunate to experience living in a spiritual community and participating in seminars and longer retreats. The tools, philosophies, and experiences with insightful people further fortified my psycho-spiritual development.

I left Newbold House in 1991 to make my first journey to India. From the moment my foot touched the tarmac of the airport in Delhi, I was struck by both a thirst and a love for the country. I felt as if I was both completely at home and in a most exotic place. India called me, drew me in, and yet scared me. It was, and still is, a threat to any status quo or rigidity that we carry in our psychic baggage. I knew inside that those three months would be the first of many trips unraveling what the place had to teach me. I spent another year traveling in Asia and Australia having countless adventures and wonderful experiences but none that touched me as deeply as the timeless and fathomless experiences of India. I eventually arrived back in the United Kingdom with the dream of setting up a healing practice.

Just as I had been happy to experience the freedom of being on the road, I was happy to build a stable work routine. I began to build a growing client base and enjoyed the wonderful feeling of helping people. After six or eight months of challenge and exhilaration, I started again to feel that familiar and painful sense of confinement, the same one I had felt years before. The breathwork attracted a small group of people pursuing new-age spirituality and personal development, but it did not give me access to mainstream society. I was limited to preaching to the converted. The approach began to seem less liberating and more like flaky pastry—touch it and it falls apart. The limitations of this approach started to stare me in the face. Much of the focus was on gaining awareness of "me and my emotions." Spiritual and emotional catharsis, while they can be exhilarating and liberating, do not build a solid foundation for a healthy and balanced life. They only lead to more emotion and strong experiences that are not necessarily balanced or transformative. The free-for-all approach to expanding our consciousness, emphasizing that we overcome all limitations and inhibitions, is dangerous. Practicing any technique without proper guidelines and structure can make us lose our balance, or worse yet, lose our way. While overcoming our limitations and expanding our consciousness are key for the unfolding of our unique human potential, the importance of respecting our nature and developing discernment became poignantly clear. Frustrated by the lack of discernment and rampant "everything goes" irresponsibility, I endeavored to work in a way that supports our evolution with a focus on our inner wisdom.

My search for answers and a desire for more credibility led me to enroll in a counseling course. I moved from Sussex to Newcastle to join a degree program in counseling. During the first day of the course, I had the sinking feeling that the material was far too basic and that the course would not teach me anything new. After class, I approached the professor to discuss my concern. He agreed with my conclusion and gave me a number to phone. The next morning, I tried ringing the number. From 9 am to 1 pm, I tried every 30 minutes or so, but the line was consistently busy. Something told me to keep trying. Finally, at 1:30 pm, a woman answered the phone. I explained my situation to her. She told me that, in fact, they had just begun a three-year Masters program and that one of the students had dropped out. The course involved practicing counseling skills in pairs and, therefore, required an even number of students. I was invited to a panel interview three days later. With five years experience working with people, but no theoretical background, the interview was daunting. Yet I was confident in my ability to understand and help people. The panel agreed and I was offered a place in the masters program in person-centered counseling (humanistic psychology). It was only later that I learned that the University of Durham is one of the top universities in the United Kingdom and that this particular course had a five-year waiting list. Synchronicity? Fate? Maybe. But whatever it happened to be, I rang at just the right moment and walked into a fabulous opportunity. The course provided a solid foundation and framework that substantiated my work with a more grounded philosophy and gave me an academically and socially recognized function and title. I went from being a new-age healer to a psychotherapist. My feet were beginning to approach the earth, but my head was still in the clouds.

Nevertheless, the next three years were challenging. I was still experiencing the familiar and uncomfortable sense of confinement. The philosophical foundations of the person-centered approach did not leave room for the countless out-of-the-ordinary experiences I had been having for years through dreams, breathwork, and meditation. These experiences had led to transformations that were beyond the scope of humanistic psychology. Nevertheless, humanistic psychology had the refreshing aspect of being expansionist: moving in the direction of human potential, and that was enough to content me for a time. The course certainly gave me a beautiful and wholesome philosophy upon which I was able to develop my own approach integrating breathwork and a range of body/mind and psycho-spiritual techniques. I was content and busy, but my soul was longing for something more. Something was still missing.[1]

In 2002, I returned to India intent on exploring the Dravidian culture and temples of Tamil Nadu in more depth. Arriving in Madras (now called Chennai), I took some time to acclimatize and assemble basic provisions for the South Indian climate and lifestyle. After visiting some of the major temples, I decided to stop in Pondicherry, a charming seaside town. My two days turned into two weeks as I got absorbed in long walks and the draw of Sri Aurobindo's Ashram and Auroville.

One morning while sitting at breakfast in the Park Guest House dining room, sipping my second cup of chai, I picked up a newsletter from the Sri Aurobindo Ashram. My eye caught the front page article on integral yoga psychology. With each line, I became increasingly intrigued. With growing excitement, I felt I had found a school of thought that reflected my thoughts, experiences, perceptions, and aspirations. Until then, each school of thought had added to my knowledge bank and personal development but did not fully accommodate my insights, experiences, and quest for truth.

The author's name and address were at the end of the article. I immediately flagged down an auto rickshaw. The remnants of monsoon season turned the drive through Pondicherry to a rural area just outside into an adventure. The author's wife greeted me. Although she did not speak English, she welcomed me and gave me a towel to clean off the mud that clung to me. I grasped that I was to wait and was served tea and a plate of sweets by their smiling daughter. A little while later, the author came in and thus began the major step that advanced my evolution as a psychotherapist and spiritual seeker: my discovery of Sri Aurobindo's integral yoga psychology. We were both excited about meeting a like-minded soul. It was as if we had always been friends and colleagues. We shared the common aspiration of spreading the vision that would uplift psychology out of its arrogant and ignorant sleep.

For nearly thirty years I have, like many others, been exploring the meeting of these two worlds, psychology and spirituality, which in the West for the past 150 years have been thought to have little in common. The current development of psycho-spiritual movements, including transpersonal and integral psychologies, is an expression of the age-old truth that psychology and spirituality are two distinct disciplines which, at the core are interconnected facets of the dance of human potential.

The force of life and evolution of consciousness, which drives us toward healing, wholeness, and our ultimate potential, is strong and resilient. It is like the force of nature that will begin to take over a corner, even of the busiest city, if it is left on its own. Integral psychology offers a foundation that allows this evolution to continue its mysterious and wonderful unfolding. Its inclusiveness of the multiple dimensions of consciousness, of tradition, modernity, and postmodernity and of both Eastern mystical and Western pragmatic worldviews, paves the way for an inclusive, multidimensional and transformational approach to psychology. It opens the way toward addressing and integrating issues at all levels of self and walking toward the lofty goal of soul-centered wholeness—the highest human aspiration.

Integral psychology gave me the mystical, philosophical, and psychological framework, room to breathe and evolve, which fit my need as a helping professional. It does not label or confine in any way, but rather creates a map which brings as much meaning to our everyday experiences, as it does to our ostensibly deepest ones, ultimately placing them all in the vision of who we are and who we can become as human beings. The persistent feelings of intellectual and spiritual confinement I felt since the beginning of my search dissolved as I delved into a meta-view that gave room to my deepest aspirations—and room to keep evolving.

I have come to believe that each person seeks psychotherapy for different reasons to address a wide range of issues. Each person has a different nature and different life track. No matter what our motivation might be, the integral approach provides a broad philosophical foundation, a wide range of techniques to address therapeutic issues and a capacity for self-education to help individuals identify and adopt attitudes and actions leading toward self-knowledge, inner peace, and self-actualization. In one session, my work looks like classic person-centered psychology, in another like shamanism, and yet, in another, like an uncharted expedition through the self into the depths of the soul.

It's been an amazing journey so far. I couldn't have imagined all of the experiences and opportunities that I've been through that have helped people rekindle their spark, find their way, and make peace with themselves. From my earliest inklings of who we really are, the inspiration of seeing eagles go back into the wild, the stillness I found through yoga, my struggles in business school, my extensive wanderings around the world, my soul searching with beloved and trusted friends, therapists, and healers that always came at just the right time, and the constant and loving guidance of my beloved Satguru and Guruji, my passion drives me ever further and deeper into the mysteries of life and consciousness.

A few years ago, a flow of ideas began to come together in my mind. I had heard about this happening to people sometimes—about being in the "zone" so much that it feels like inspiration is coming *through* you, but not from you. It just kept coming and I could not write fast enough to get it all down. I began recording—or rather, taking notation from some part of my mind—throughout the day: in the metro, walking my dog Sadie, and even in that slurry twilight between being awake and asleep. After about two months, the torrent of thoughts came to a stop, like someone had turned off a faucet. In the end, I painstakingly transcribed all of the recordings and found myself with 312 pages of insights, including some repetitions, rantings, and soapbox sermons. I took a deep breath and looked at what I wrote and realized that it wasn't the product of divinely inspired channeling—it was me. It was a Chutes and Ladders–style journey through a lifetime of experiences, observations, and inspirations along with new ideas that had never crossed my conscious mind. It was a kind of map—my map—of how my mind came to process, hold on, and let go of certain conclusions about who we are. And it *needed* to be expressed.

Over the last several years, the material has gone through a few rewrites, or I should say Willy Wonka–style candy-making machines. Apart from eliminating the repetitions, tempering my glorifying of the East and bashing Freud and other reductionist schools of the West, the bulk of my editing has been to structure my thoughts. The challenge was to find my voice while maintaining my full-time psychotherapy practice and, of course, trying to keep a balanced life at the same time. It hasn't always been easy. I wanted to capture the spirit and the passion that were there in that initial outpouring and not lose any of the spontaneity of those first connections. Finally, my work is complete and ready to present.

My goal is to present my unique view based on research, clinical practice, and my psycho-spiritual experiences and explorations. Many theoreticians have never accompanied a client into the depths of their inner world. Others have not ventured beyond the intellect into their own subtle nature. Many practitioners experience the application of theories, the flow, the sublime beauty of the healing power of presence. Theologians expound upon their theories of consciousness based on sacred scriptures and intellectual insights. Practitioners of meditation and Eastern spiritual practice gain deep psychological and spiritual insights through the opening of their hearts and minds. I aspire to bring to you the fruits of all four of these perspectives in this book which aims at being theoretical, practical, inspiring, and accessible to all those curious about human potential, Eastern philosophy, Western and Eastern psychology, yoga, and the possibility, unique to human beings, of evolving in consciousness.

In essence, my aim is to present a holistic view of the evolution of psychology for both East and West. Rather than aiming for academic validity, conveying an ethos, a higher possibility for the field of psychology is closer to my intention. I hope that this work will bring understanding and inspiration to my colleagues, the helping professionals, students of psychology, aspiring yogis, seekers of truth, and finally, those seeking healing, meaning, and evolution of consciousness.

The first five chapters of this book are research based. They are intended to give a broad overview. Chapters 1 and 2 present a compact, yet comprehensive, view of the evolution of psychology in the West—from the ancient mystical beginnings through the descent into science, and then into reclaiming a more holistic view in the newer and emerging schools. Chapter 3 begins explorations into the East, elaborating upon the implications drawn from the teachings of ancient rishis and contemporary mystics. Chapter 4 focuses on the teachings of the renowned mystic, Sri Aurobindo, whose enlightened pragmatism led to the development of integral psychology. Where Sri Aurobindo laid the groundwork for an integral psychology whose foundations were mystical, Ken Wilber, in chapter 5, presents us with an altogether more pragmatic and intellectually elaborate school which he *also* calls integral psychology.

Chapters 6–9 contain the essence of this work, the culmination of the foundations set forth by early movements in psychology. They present theoretical and applied views for an integrated and inclusive psychology model, drawing on ancient mysticism of the East, pragmatism of the West, while taking into consideration traditional, modern and postmodern, and the acute need to address human consciousness in all of its dimensions. On one hand, if we are going to help ourselves or others, should we not do so with the largest, deepest, broadest, and most complete understanding of who we are? And on the other hand, it is imperative today for us to understand that the reign of the intellect has not given us the answers we seek. It is perhaps time to venture into the farther reaches of our consciousness. I invite you, the reader, to look into your heart, to find your deep longing for truth and meaning, and to let this work inspire you, open doors for you, and ultimately help you find your own unique path back to the wild—your original home.

NOTE

1. Since those early days at Durham University I have met humanistically oriented colleagues who are clearly resistant to spirituality and yet others who, like me, embrace a spiritual worldview and integrate spiritually oriented techniques into their therapeutic approach.

Timeline of Psycho-Spiritual Belief Systems—East and West

INDIA (EAST)	YEAR	WEST
Bhimbetka Rock Shelters—first evidence of mystic belief—30,000 BCE	2.5 m.y.a–10,000 bp	Paleolithic Aurignacian Lowenmensch figurine—human/animal figure—deity Red ochre in burials—spiritual beliefs Animatism
First Sangam, Hinduism Shivan period (South India)	10,000–8000 BCE	Early Neolithic Göbekli Tepe sanctuaries (southeastern Turkey) Near Stonehenge—Pine posts erected
Bhishaja, shamanism, animism—experience-based healing modalities	8000–2300 BCE	Neolithic Communal & goddess worship—Catalhoyuk, Anatolia, Turkey Proto-Indo-Europeans—5500–4500 Polytheism, shamanism, paganism, animism, and plant based rituals*
Pre-Vedic—up 1750 Yogic philosophy—Indus & Harrapan civilization—Mother Goddess worship spiritual symbols—swastika and siva lingam Birth of Krishna—3228 Ayurveda—Experiment & analysis-based healing modalities	4000–1200 BCE	Bronze Age Mesopotamia—3500–559 Proto semitic peoples—Arabian Peninsula—3750 Sumerian Cuneiform—3000 Stonehenge—3000–2600 Ancient Eygpt—3150–150 Pyramid texts—2400 2300 　Old Kingdom—2650–2074 　Middle Kingdom—2074–1539 　New Kingdom—1539–1150 Greece—Old Kingdom—3000–2000 　Middle Kingdom—2000–1300 　Late Kingdom—1500–1070 Beginnings of Judaism—c. 1800

INDIA (EAST)	YEAR	WEST
Vedic Period Rig Veda—1750–500 Lao Tzu, Taoism—550 Vedic Golden age—1200–600	1445–1000 BCE	Iron Age Paleo-Balkan Celtic Polytheism Zarathustra founds Zoroastrianism—c. 1000
Classical Hinduism—200 BCE–1100 CE Bhagavad Gita— c. 200 BCE Besnagar— First Hindu temple	500 BCE–50 CE	The Essenes—200 BCE–100 CE Philo of Alexandria—25 BCE–50 CE Socrates 470–399, Plato 427–347, Aristotle 384–322
Kushan & Vasudeva Empire—Buddhism & Zoroastrianism— 190–230	50–230 CE	Beginnings of Christianity New Testament—First four books— 70–100
Golden Age Gupta Empire— Hindu, Buddhist, Jain— 320–550 Patanjali's Yoga Sutras—400 Adi Shankara— c. 788–820	235–900 CE	Late Antiquity Hermeticism, Gnosticism, & other mystical schools Classic Mayan Civ.—pyramids— 250–900 Prophet Mohammed—570–632
Late Classical Hinduism— 650–1100	400–1500 CE	Middle Ages Definition of psyche- mystical (Sufi, Christian, Jewish) *vs* intellectual
Islam & Hindu Sects— 1200–1700 Islamic rule—India— 1100–1750 Guru Nanak- Sikhism—1469–1539 Bhakti Movement 700–1500/1700	1200–1700 CE	Renaissance Intellectual understanding & analysis of the psyche; development of physiological and social models of psyche
Modern Hinduism— 1800 to date	1700–1800 CE	French Revolution— secularization—1792

INDIA (EAST)	YEAR	WEST
Swami Vivekananda— 1863–1902 Parliament of World Religions—1893	1800–1900 CE	Charles Darwin—*Origin of the Species*—1859 Bahá'í Faith founded— Baha'u'llah—1844 Psychology, scientific approach—W. Wundt—1879 Freudian psychoanalysis 1886 W. James—*Principles of Psychology*—1890
Sri Aurobindo 1872–1950 Jadunath Sinha— *Indian Psychology*	1900–1950 CE	Freud popularizes subconscious Predominance of behaviorism— 1910–1950 Jung ends collaboration with Freud—1913 Carl Rogers—*Person-Centered Psychology*—1942
The Mother— 1878–1973	1960–1980 CE	C. Rogers—*On Becoming a Person*—1961 A. Beck—Cognitive-behavioral therapy K. Wilber *Spectrum of Consciousness*—1973
1. Western psychiatry & behaviorism— mainstream 2. Traditional psycho-spiritual healing modalities 3. Indian psychology movement 4. Sri Aurobindo psychology movement	1950 to date**	1. *Psycho-pharmacology and physical and medical models—DSM* 2. Analytical and behavioral practices 3. Humanistic & transpersonal spectrum 4. Psycho-spiritual and new-age approaches

Note: Dates and facts vary according to source. This timeline is meant to give a general idea of the evolution of thought and a comparison between India and the West.

* These early healing and mystical practices were gradually replaced in some places but remained in practice in remote areas and until 1600s in North America.

** Until 1950 there tended to be one predominant view at a time in each East and West. Since 1950, there are four separate and coexisiting streams of thought.

Chapter One

Origins and Development of Western Psychology

As a child, I visited various places of worship in my quest for truth, but no matter where I went, the idea of a God portrayed as a separate and extrinsic being did not agree with me. In my teens, not knowing any alternatives, I rejected religion and God altogether and became a staunch atheist—with a seeking heart. That period was to be short-lived.

In my early twenties, my training in breathwork was infused with inklings of Eastern philosophy. Fascinated, I walked out of my Western foundations and floated to the East. In my experiences, I found something greater, transcendent, and ultimately mysterious. I sensed that "something," which at first I sheepishly called the Universe, was attainable and within me. Still perplexed with religion's man in the clouds, I was left with the question, "why do we, in the West, perceive God as being outside ourselves?"

My spiritual path began with an awareness of my inner longing and pondering. After a brief affair with atheism and social activism during which, in a state of disappointment, I rejected spiritual matters altogether, I finally began a long-term relationship with breathwork, and ultimately, meditation.

This chapter explores a similar trajectory, how humankind's earliest search for meaning in subtle and inner pursuits gradually shifted toward an outward-looking worldview. Each change in worldview has been a step in the direction of today's predominant approaches to psychology and psychotherapy.

ANCIENT ORIGINS

Where does psychology begin? Belief systems have existed since the earliest civilizations, attempting to explain and learn to make meaning from the

1

difficulties and mysteries that challenge humankind. Animatism is thought to be the earliest form of belief in the West. "[It] ... points to a thing, situation or state of affairs that is enlivened or animated, but not in any individual, soul-like manner."[1] Animism is the name given to early belief systems in which all life is composed of spirits and all spirits, including man, are connected. Dreams and the spirits of people, animals, and nature explained the mysteries of life, death, and life after death. Study of various animist traditions around the world revealed an evolution from "low to high, from a plurality of spirits on to a polytheist system, a hierarchy among nature spirits and ultimately some form of monotheism. ..."[2] In the middle and upper Paleolithic periods, the worship of animal spirits became predominant. Various forms of goddess worship in the Neolithic period evolved into polytheism, shamanism, and paganism. Whether the earliest matriarch (goddess) and other forms of spiritual worship were entirely based on inner experience and revelation or on human need for meaning and reassurance is not known.

In his book, *Shamanism: Archaic Techniques of Ecstasy*,[3] Mircea Eliade concluded that shamanism underlies all spiritual traditions. Contact with the spirit world through plants, the earth, and the planets provided the foundation of meaning. Shamanism was based on the ability of the shaman to enter into the subtle realms of consciousness. In their journeys, shamans gained access to mystical sources of knowledge in order to determine the causes of people's illnesses, both physical and mental. Then, through communication with the spirits, they reestablished harmony. These early worldviews were holistic approaches to well-being and healing. They took into account insights and wisdom drawn from (1) subtle and energetic perception, (2) the psychological impact of our attitudes and action on our balance and well-being, and (3) social guidelines. These three dimensions are historically common pillars of human belief systems.

Early primitive belief systems reflect the relationship between our outer selves and the mysteries within. This connection seems to have been lost somewhere along with the pursuit of inner knowledge. What is missing is the practice of cultivating knowledge based on expanded, inner states of awareness. This might explain why so many Westerners have turned to these worldviews, seeking connection between self, soul, and the universe.

I had superficially dabbled into some forms of earth and animal worship in my youth, putting what I knew of Native American practices on a pedestal. Early explorations into the unseen world, both light and dark, reflect a quest for meaning, an understanding of the themes of good and evil and a quest for power to compensate for our innate feelings of vulnerability. Over time, despite my respect for these traditions that continues to this day, my interest in delving deeper into their mysteries was more of an adolescent tinkering that did not last long.

The spiritual and political writings of Ancient Egypt represent a shift from earlier belief systems. Texts from the Unas Pyramid corresponding to the last king of the Fifth Dynasty give a good picture of the prevailing ethos. These inscriptions, found inside the Unas pyramid, contain a "combination of rituals, hymns, prayers, incantations and offering lists"[4] designed to ensure the king would achieve his purpose in the afterlife. Ancient Egyptian texts give a perspective on right living and right livelihood in respect to humankind, the gods or the unseen world, and the country's rulers. In this way, it took into consideration the material, social, and spiritual realms. Importantly, the heart was considered to be the center of both intellect and will. Texts advised going inward to speak with one's heart (ib) and consulting one's conscience (Ba) to ensure the right decisions.[5] The God Re "is hidden, omniscient, provident, responsive and just. Men are created in the likeness of God, and for whom heaven and earth were created, must worship God and provide for their fellow men. Hypocrisy is of no avail but God gave men magic to ward off what may happen."[6] These beliefs were never completely lost, and yet, as time went on, these early forms of mysticism and their corresponding worldview became more and more obscured by outward and rational approaches.

After my discovery of Hinduism and yoga philosophy, my almost nonexistent knowledge of Western thought was collecting dust in a deep corner of my mind. Then, one day, in awe of Robert Svoboda's mastery of Vedic knowledge I picked up his book, *The Greatness of Saturn.*[7] What I found was a complete surprise. I sensed I had struck upon the answer to my question about the Western extrinsic perception of God, in ancient Greece.

Let me start from the beginning. The Greeks were evolving their own social, psychological, and spiritual worldviews at the same time as the Egyptians:

> When the Greeks came into contact with the older advanced civilizations of the East ... the rational intelligence of the Greeks was fired and fused with the religious and philosophical experience of the Eastern mind. Contacts with Persian, Indian, Egyptian, Hellenic and Judaic cultures laid the foundations from which Christendom and Islam would later develop. The impact of this interaction stimulated not only an intellectual approach to cosmology, but psychology, as the Greeks began to extract from their own myths a rationale for the structure and dynamics of the macrocosm and microcosm, the Universe and mankind.[8]

The early Greeks, by taking into account both the outer and inner aspects of life and consciousness, provided a holistic worldview addressing psychological, social, intellectual, and mystical hierarchies.

Zeroing in on the Psyche

The concept of the psyche dates back thousands of years and was drawn from both direct perception and realization. It was then conceptualized into thoughts that could be written, conveyed, and debated. Its origin was not cognitive, but ethereal. In ancient Greece, Socrates,[9] Plato,[10] and Aristotle[11] each referred to the psyche in their philosophical writings. Socrates distinguished between body and soul, conveying a sense that when the body no longer exists, the soul carries on. He believed in the transmigration of the psyche toward better lives in future incarnations.

Like Socrates, Plato also equated the psyche with the mystical, immortal, and transcendent soul, the source of true knowledge, which was separate from the body. Plato's primary interest was the role between the psyche and morality. There is a distinctive shift in the thinking between Plato and Aristotle whose interest was the psyche's role in human behavior.

Aristotle is considered by many to be the father of psychology. In his view, both psychology and physiology, which he also explored, needed to be validated empirically. He believed that knowledge was first gathered by the senses and, from there, it entered into the psyche. This marks a traceable philosophical shift from the inner, mystical view of the psyche to an extrinsic, worldview:

> [The spiritual worldview] ... went out of fashion in ... the west ... when the Greek philosophers of old openly declared that they no longer knew how to interpret their most ancient writings, rites, and symbols. Instead of turning inward to find those fleeing significations, these savants turned their minds outwards ... and decided to accept as real only that part of the nature that we can hear, touch, see, taste and smell. ... They reject[ed live mythology] as illogical and conclude[d] that all gods are simply inflated memories of illustrious men and women.[12]

Upon reading this, I jumped up and picked up the *Encyclopedia of Religion* that I had inherited from Jim, my college philosophy professor–turned friend. I attentively scoured articles on Socrates, Plato, and Aristotle. I confirmed that while Socrates and Plato had implicitly spiritual worldviews, the shift toward a more intellectual and materialistic paradigm appears to have occurred with Aristotle, who began to equate psyche with mind. Excited by my discovery, I kept reading, rang knowledgeable friends, and became increasingly excited that I had found an answer to the question that had perplexed me for so long.

The gradual shift in focus from the Socratic and Platonic worlds of ideal forms to their expression in outer physical nature emphasized by Aristotle was further externalized by the early Greek physicians. They became interested in phenomena, including the relationship between behavior and the brain.

Hippocrates,[13] considered the father of Western medicine, proposed that the brain was the seat of sensations, the five sense organs, and the intellect. His hypothesis was partially determined by accumulated knowledge acquired from dissections and battlefield injuries. Galen[14] also combined what he learned from animal dissections and from treating the injuries of gladiators to form his views on brain function, building on Hippocrates' analysis. He identified the functions of some areas of the brain and proposed that it controlled the movements and sensations of the body through the nerves. His views were dominant for about 1500 years until revised through more modern methods of medical experimentation.

EMERGENCE OF SEMITIC RELIGIONS

At the time that the Middle Kingdom of Ancient Greece[15] was bringing its thought and reason to the forefront in Europe, Judaism,[16] the first of the Semitic religions, was emerging to the East, introducing the concept of worshipping one God versus many Gods. Religion addresses the human predicament, providing guidelines for existence in the world and the unseen realms. Philosophy ponders the mystery and meaning of our existence while questioning rather than being based on any type of theism. Religion "brings together many individuals in a spiritual unity that transfigures life. ... Philosophical analyses and visions are the products of solitary thinkers ... whose schools of thought are primarily focal points of understanding and a place for the meeting of minds."[17] While it is beyond the purview of this book to trace the evolution and development of religion, a brief notion will give important insights into the development of Western psychological and spiritual views.

Judaism became an established, community-based religion where men sought to be at one with their twelve tribes and God. At the same time, mystical sects emerged reflecting an intention to keep beliefs and practices more inwardly focused and truer to what they felt were the roots of Judaism. Being inwardly focused, these movements emphasized the link between our outer, psychological self, experiences in the world and the innermost core of our being. The Essenes,[18] the Therapeutae, and the Gnostics[19] carried forward these mystical threads of thought at various points in history. Some of these mystical schools reflect early beliefs and practices from the Indian subcontinent.[20] The Therapeutae, led by Philo Judaeus or Philo of Alexandria,[21] were an example of the holistic vision, in both theory and practice, that existed in ancient civilizations. The Therapeutae aspired to align their thoughts, words, and actions to be congruent with the inner self. Theirs was a path of transformation and not mere intellectual speculation. Their lifestyle incorporated taking care of

the entire being, body, psyche, and spirituality. In so doing, they enumer-
ated the ills of the soul, where they came from and how to care for them, a
profound statement on the disturbances of the being. The soul or the inner
self is perceived as the center of our being, not the outer self or ego. Philo
Judaeus expounded upon the divine and described various ways of worship. Based on observations of his own psycho-spiritual ascent, he gave
profound psychological insights on the comings and goings from ego to
soul, the trajectory to higher levels of integration and states of consciousness. He conveyed insights, from his personal experiences, on the weaknesses that can lead to a fall from grace.

THE BIRTH OF PSYCHOLOGY

Following the Greek movement toward reason, the mystical aspects of life
began to disappear from modern Western thought. Study, categorization, and
addressing life from a matter-based view became the predominant means of
identifying worldviews. This paradigm contributed to the development of the
fields of medicine, science, and technology. However, it left behind the spirit
and entrenched a unidimensional understanding of reality.

Western civilization continued its trajectory into the Renaissance and,
eventually, the Industrial Revolution. Roger Bacon, Leonardo da Vinci, and
Galileo ushered the West into the dawn of the physical sciences. Scientific
method spurred economic development and Western nations emerged as
superpowers in the new world. Da Vinci's "Principles for the Development
of a Complete Mind [were]: Study the science of art. Study the art of science.
Develop your senses—especially learn how to see. Realize that everything
connects to everything else."[22] These developments also spurred mutations in
the realm of psychology.

The term "psychology" was coined in the mid-1600s to describe the study
of the soul. *Psyche* refers to breath, spirit, and soul, and *logia* means "the
study of." In the mid-1700s the meaning of psyche became ever more closely
synonymous with mind, leaving the breath gasping!

Religion too was edged out of mainstream Western psychology. While
psychology filed for divorce from religion, religion did not dismiss psychology. Christianity developed pastoral and biblical counseling in response to
psychology's secularity. Judaism, Islam, and especially Sufism have also
remained open to psychology, personal development, modern self-help
approaches, and the idea of cultivating self-knowledge. It is here that we
definitively part ways with religion and take leave from spirituality. Do not
despair; our break with spirituality will be relatively short-lived. We will
rejoin it again in the not-too-distant future in chapter 2.

I cannot help but notice the similar pattern between how I left off my own spirituality in my earlier rebellious phases and then came back to it later on. Perhaps, such a trajectory is not uncommon. Just as individuals have to find, identify, and become established in a healthy ego before they can evolve in post-egoic directions addressed by mystical schools of philosophy and psychology, perhaps the larger society reflects similar growth patterns, veering away from spirituality, to come back to it later on with a healthy ego built, and feet on the ground. If this is the case, then, just as we, as individuals, run the risk of getting distracted in outer phenomenon and losing sight of the higher possibilities of human and societal consciousness, what is to stop the collective from doing the same?

Early Medical Models of Psychiatric Disorder and Assessment

The early medical model of psychiatry was dedicated to the study of brain function. In contrast to ancient animism in which all living beings were linked to spirit, the medical model for mental health that emerged was structured on the belief that all living organisms have energy that they are motivated to conserve. Therefore, abnormal behavior was seen as a physiological problem. Early on, medicines were used to treat severe illnesses, such as depression and schizophrenia. In 1938, electroshock treatment was introduced.

Wilhelm Wundt,[23] often called the father of experimental psychology, based his work on observations of physiological responses in his subjects. This reinforced the trend in modern psychology for a view of human functioning and consciousness based on external observation. With the onset of the scientific and industrial developments, early psychologists such as Wundt turned their focus to the quantification, systematization, and categorization of outer aspects of human behavior, especially pathologies. This outside-in approach gives an image of man as a metaphorical "paper doll" paying no heed to the possibilities of perspective, causation, depth, and breadth.

With the onset of World War I, the American Psychological Association asked R.S. Woodworth[24] to assist in trying to prevent shell shock. The personality test he developed attempted to measure emotional stability by determining a soldier's susceptibility to mental breakdown during combat. Subsequently, many personality tests were developed by others to measure both normal and pathological personality characteristics. These tests continue to be used in research on the causes and correlates of psychological disorders as well as on experimental treatments. The contrast between this direction in psychology, in comparison with the perspectives of our "elders," is stark.

Since time immemorial, mystical worldviews have been giving us a mind-over-matter perspective, implicating our responsibility for our states of mind as well as acknowledging the many environmental and subtle factors at play.

And then science began telling us that we are simply mechanisms falling prey to our brain chemistry. Implicit in the earlier, holistic schools of thought was our responsibility for that part of our being, mind, and life over which we have the power to influence. We have, more or less, the ability to control or shape our environment depending on the situation. The ultimate responsibility for our attitude and mindset is in our hands. With the dawning of the age of science, we lose that which is most sacred to us: our power and responsibility to evolve. This shift in responsibility has personal, societal, and spiritual implications.

FREUD'S PSYCHOANALYSIS

Sigmund Freud[25] began his career with the study of the physiological manifestations of disorders. He went on to explore the inner depths of the mind through free association, dream analysis, and hypnosis. The goal of psychoanalysis or "talking cure" was to locate and release powerful emotional energy suppressed and imprisoned in the unconscious. He believed this repression impeded the normal functioning of the psyche and could even cause physical retardation. His renowned work with dreams stemmed from his belief that they carry and help us process emotionally charged aspects of our subconscious.

Freud's theory of personality revolved around the id, the conscious and unconscious impulses and desires that seek pleasure and instant gratification. The id is the only element of our personality at birth and it drives our motivation in early life. The ego develops in childhood and acts as a filter, taking reality and social context into awareness and helping us adapt our behavior. The superego is the last element of our personality to develop and causes us to further channel our behavior between ego ideal (good) and conscience (bad) acts. Mental health, in this context, depends on the balance between the id, the ego, and the superego. The ideal is to have an ego that is strong enough to keep our impulses in check, but not so strong as to make us rigid and explosive when the levee breaks.

Central to Freud's work was his theory of the libido, the entire range of psychic or instinctual energies and desires stemming from the id. Freud believed that, right from the early stages of childhood, nearly all human tendencies could be attributed to the sexual urge and that repression or expression of the libido, for social conformity or other reasons, was the cause of most mental problems. The libido has different natural expressions at different stages of our development. If it gets blocked or "fixated" at one of these stages, it results in corresponding pathological personality traits. This could be resolved by bringing these drives out from behind any built defense and into the forefront thereby liberating the fixation. This helps develop a "constructive sublimation" or the libido naturally settling into a healthier balance.

Psychoanalysis put psychology on the map by introducing key ideas that are still in use. Integral psychologist Brant Cortright,[26] points out that psychoanalysis explained psychosis, narcissism, and neurosis in very sophisticated ways. He observed that we can no longer isolate psychoanalysis to treat psychopathologies and humanistic psychology to address potential and growth. Some patients need to deal with their past first and resolve issues before they can embark on a path of growth whereas others may still need to address unresolved issues from the past even while already on the path of holistic development.

See Annex I for an in-depth case on Freudian psychoanalysis.

POST-FREUDIAN PSYCHOANALYTIC
THOUGHT—JUNG, ADLER, RANK, AND HORNEY

Carl Gustav Jung[27] started out as a student, and then a contemporary of Freud. When Jung began to differ with Freud's view that natural science was the only means to understand the human psyche, this led to conflict in their friendship and collaboration. While Jung agreed with Freud that we have an animal nature, he felt that we undeniably have the potential to have different and higher capacities.

Jung strongly disagreed with Freud's belief that man's deepest drive is the libido. Instead, he defined it in a broader, more expansive sense as psychic energy. His concept was validated and further developed when he ventured into Eastern thought.[28] Freud reduced the "universality of religion ... to the universality of incestuous desires. ... [whereas] for Jung, the projections of religion can be traced back to a natural predisposition of the psyche for wholeness."[29] These fundamental differences of opinion led Jung to become the first of a stream of Freud's contemporaries to break out of the straitjacket of a purely ego-centered psychology. His newfound freedom left him free to develop his school of analytical psychology.

In addition to a personal unconscious resulting from the repression of certain types of conscious experiences, Jung believed there was also a collective unconscious that contained psychic patterns or archetypes common to all human beings. As evidence for this collective unconscious, Jung cited the existence of common images and themes from many cultures. He included as empirical evidence the world of dream myth and folklore to understand man's deeper nature.

The predominant goal of Jungian psychology is individuation, the psychological process of attaining healthy integration of the conscious and unconscious parts of the psyche. The unconscious is discovered through dreams, myth, art, religion, folklore, and the symbolic dramas we enact in our relationships and life pursuits. Jung defined "self" as the "archetype of wholeness and the regulating center of the psyche." This involves merging the individual's consciousness with this broader collective through symbolic language.

Neurosis results from a disharmony between the individual's unconsciousness and his higher self. The psyche is a self-regulating, adaptive system. If the life-energy naturally flowing in humans gets blocked, the psyche gets stuck or sick. Jung proposed that if adaptation is thwarted, the psychic energy will stop flowing and regress due to maladaptation to one's external or internal reality. In Jung's view, the aim of psychoanalysis was to assist the individual in reestablishing a healthy relationship to the unconscious. They should neither be flooded by it resulting in characteristics of psychosis such as schizophrenia nor be out of balance with it leading to neurosis which results in depression, anxiety, personality disorders, or a life devoid of deeper meaning.

Jung was the first modern psychiatrist to view the human psyche as naturally spiritual. Spiritual and religious experience and symbols were core themes in his work and research. Much of his life's work was spent exploring tangential areas such as Eastern and Western philosophy, alchemy, astrology, and sociology, as well as literature and the arts. In this respect psychology began its reunification with the soul that it had left behind in ancient Greece. In chapter 2 we'll revisit Jungian thought in its more expansive aspects.

Alfred Adler[30] is considered, along with Freud and Jung, to be one of the three founding figures of depth psychology, emphasizing the unconscious and psychodynamics occurring within the various parts of the mind. Adler later broke away from Freud to develop his school of individual psychology which had an enormous influence on the disciplines of counseling and psychotherapy as they developed over the course of the twentieth century. Adler believed that humans were an indivisible whole, an *individuum*, in interaction with the surrounding world and seeking to find an integrated place within it.

Adler's most famous concept, the inferiority complex, addressed the problem of low self-esteem and its effects on human health. He espoused the development of social interest and democratic family structures for raising children and emphasized that being treated equally was important in preventing various forms of mental illness. While his emphasis on power dynamics was rooted in Nietzsche's philosophy, Adler framed his theory on "will to power" in a positive light, believing it to be driven by the individual's creative power to change for the better. He was an early supporter of feminism, making the case that power dynamics between the sexes and gender associations are fundamental keys to understanding human psychology. He believed feelings of superiority and inferiority were often gender-based and expressed differently by men and women.

Otto Rank[31] was Freud's right-hand man for almost twenty years and a strong defender of the mainstream psychoanalytic straitjacket as disputes with Adler and then Jung arose. He was a prolific author whose work increased the scope of psychoanalytic theory taking into consideration certain creative and cultural phenomenon.

Eventually, Rank too, had a falling out with Freud. In *Das Trauma der Geburt*[32] (*The Trauma of Birth*), he suggested that the Oedipus complex might not be the supreme causal factor of psychopathologies and suffering. Rank felt that psychoanalysis put too much emphasis on the past, on transference, and on seeking an Oedipal complex in every patient. Rank's post-Freudian work focused on clinical practice rather than theory. He coined the term "psychotherapy" to describe his work which *rehumanized* classical psychoanalysis by focusing on

1) the present as opposed to the past, 2) the conscious expression of the ego rather than expression of the unconscious and its repressed contents, 3) will and creativity as opposed to unconscious wishes and instincts, 4) experience and the expression of emotion in place of intellectual understanding; intimacy in the actual therapeutic relationship in place of detached interpretation of the transference, 5) the role of the fear of life in neurosis in place of the role of the fear of death and 6) the development of individuality as opposed to regaining a generalized "normalcy."[33]

The changes he introduced are reflected in most modern approaches to psychotherapy.

Karen Horney[34] also differed with some of Freud's notions, including Oedipal complex and penis envy. She reformulated Freudian thought into a more holistic, humanistic approach emphasizing cultural and social differences and introduced a feminine perspective. She argued that societies worldwide encouraged women to be dependent on men for their love, prestige, wealth, care, and protection, interfering with their pursuit of self-actualization.[35] Horney believed that neurotic people become blocked by clinging to core needs not met earlier in life. This dynamic plays a key role in the way they relate to others.

Neurotic people experience conflict between their real self, which includes the potential for growth and deficiencies, and their ideal self, who they strive to be. They become fixed and cannot progress to their ideal self because their goals are not realistic. She understood that this cycle of false identification with "the tyranny of the should" vs "the search for glory" must be broken so individuals can actualize their true potential.

LIMITATIONS OF PSYCHOANALYSIS

The positive contribution of Freud's work is indisputable and so are the criticisms of many of his theories. Today many of his ideas are considered obsolete due to shortcomings, exaggerations, and serious omissions, giving them the label pseudo-science. His theorizing was highly speculative and, in general, based on case studies of a few individuals with significant psychological disturbances.

By reducing the foundation of our personality to the id, Freud placed a "Danger, Do Not Enter" sign on looking within ourselves. This is ironic because for millennia, looking within was the key to health, balance, wisdom, and a meaningful and wholesome existence. This does not mean that we should just dive into the id willy-nilly. In fact, placing the id as the foundation of our personality is, in itself, what makes it dangerous. If the id with its comrades, the ego and the superego, are all we've got, then the world is flat! On the other hand, putting it into the larger perspective of the whole self-balances it and helps identify the source of many of our troubles.

The same can be said about the libido. From the spiritual worldviews we will be visiting later on, while it is true that each individual's libido is more or less dominant, ancient spiritual traditions tell us that it is not the only driving force. Many spiritual traditions teach us that it is possible to sublimate or rise above the drives defined by the libido and allow the soul or spiritual self to come forth and become our driving force. And yet, Freud stated that "[r]eligion is comparable to a childhood neurosis."[36] He believed religion was an illusion and religious inclination in humans reflected a deep underlying distress stemming from unresolved family issues. He also viewed religion as a social phenomenon aimed at repressing and containing man's antisocial impulses.

Freud's work focused on unconscious instincts and other behavior patterns developed early in childhood and diminished the higher psychological faculties. The prime focus in psychoanalytic treatment is almost exclusively delving into the past. A personal development blunder furthers my conviction that the sole quest of delving into one's past, and in the case of psychoanalysis—our childhood—is not necessarily fruitful.

Many years ago, in a fit of evolutionary fervor, I began praying to God to show me my shadow so I could eliminate it. The concept of shadow refers to the parts of ourselves that are unacknowledged, resisted, or repressed. It can contain both positive and negative characteristics and memories. I won't go into detail here, but suffice it to say that I went through a very dark period meeting my demons face to face and holding court with them. Don't get me wrong. This was not due to resistance to meeting and owning my shadow, since I readily dive in when necessary and have quasi-mastered the ability to swim with the sharks. Repeated experience has shown me that there is nothing to fear and only to gain in terms of liberating oneself from the holds of our shadow and deeper and deeper states of integration of the self. One day, after nine months of living in hell, it occurred to me that delving into my own shadow was not having the desired effect but instead was causing endless suffering. I began praying for upliftment, strength, and clarity and went on about my merry way.

If we want to find darkness, it is always there. If we focus on darkness, we will be in darkness. Psychoanalysis, rather than putting us together, can make us narcissistic and neurotic. If we simply focus on the present, the past will come up when it needs to be addressed and integrated. It should not be our primary focus.

When I studied humanistic psychology in the United Kingdom, Freud's theories were barely mentioned. My primary experience with psychoanalysis is from clients who worked with me after or during psychoanalysis. These clients presented with particularly rigid and compartmentalized personalities rather than fluid and integrated ones. Letting go, getting out of the mind and into feeling experience was nearly impossible. The inner self seemed to have been imprisoned deep within, behind a solid, outer suit of functional armor.

Vignette—Fragmented Personality

Gracie was in her early 40s when she consulted me for help with social phobia. The problem began when she was 12. In keeping with a long-time family tradition, Gracie's parents sent her from their home in London to a Swiss boarding school. It did not occur to them to tell their daughter why she was being sent away. Gracie took the decision to heart. She felt misunderstood and abandoned. In an effort to come to terms with it she began a painful and fruitless process of speculating and ruminating. Gracie tried to speak to her parents about her suffering, but the words would not come out of her mouth. As her inner turmoil turned into guilt, self-recrimination, and self-doubt, she began experiencing distress in social situations. She ended up isolating herself.

After years of suffering, Gracie went into psychoanalysis for nine years. It had helped her in some ways, but had not alleviated her social phobia. She heard about mind/body approaches to therapy and decided to try working with me. After an initial dialogue about her chronological history and the reason for her visit, she decided to try a breathwork session.[37]

The breath reveals the state of our psyche through sometimes pronounced and other times subtle variations and patterns. Gracie's breath indicated that her psyche was fragmented and even dissociated. I detected three distinct and equally inaccessible "pockets": subconscious, life force, and mind. Her breathing patterns revealed a profound inner conflict; a mix of wounded self-image, conditioning, fear, and existential sadness of the inner child who cannot find her place or voice. Her breath would start out with one rhythm, never letting go of control, but heading in one direction and then, just before reaching a crucial edge that would mean opening up, her breathing would shift, escaping into one of the other pockets. Her psyche was in a state of defensiveness and fragmentation.

With each session, she would touch upon and release pockets of pain. With each release, her breathing became more fluid, less marked by defensive "jumping." She began to open up to the healthy essence that was beneath the wounds.

It is uncanny how psychoanalysis seems to fragment and dissociate us. The mind, which is the key focus of psychoanalysis, is only the surface of our being. Jung noted that nature of the mind, in isolation, is rigid, not fluid. Working at the level of mind can help us shift its contents and therefore, in some cases, lead more adapted lives. It addresses subconscious issues but does not access their roots which lay at deeper, more subtle levels of our being not normally accessible from ordinary states of consciousness. Part of this limitation is the same as with any therapy limited only to dialogue, but part of it is also due to the reductive worldview which does not leave room for deeper integration and healing.

Vignette—The Ego as a Suit of Armor

Gina consulted me because she felt unhappy and unfulfilled. She had undergone 29 years of psychoanalysis. We met regularly and she was committed and perseverant. Yet, her personality structure was so rigid that it took a long time before she could get through her suit of armor and get in touch with her core wounds and emotions. Her psychoanalysis had built up a suit of armor rather than a fluid and integrated psyche. It was difficult to get her out of her rigid mind and in touch with her feelings. The sessions were painstaking, like playing chess. Over time, as she was able to let go, she began to open up and flourish.

Integral psychologist A.S. Dalal observed that the shortcomings of Freud's work led to two developments important for the growth of psychology. First, it gave way to the birth of depth psychology—the study of the human being's unconscious motives, impulses, and attitudes, which revolutionized the fields of psychiatry and psychology. Second, the patently lopsided view of psychoanalysis gave rise to several schools of thought, most notably analytical psychology and individual psychology. These later formulations of psychoanalytic theory overcame many of its worst tendencies and opened up a more positive and wholesome view of the human being and human potential. Despite post-Freudian developments being as strongly evolutionary as Freud's work was revolutionary, we can nevertheless classify them as reductionist insofar as they reduce their definition of being human to the physiological, mechanistic, and scientifically quantifiable. Furthermore, they place varying definitions of what we will later understand to be the outer self at the center of our being.

STEPPING STONES TOWARD AN INTEGRAL PSYCHOLOGY—PSYCHOANALYSIS

The integral approach to psychology that we aspire to in this work is built of stepping stones. We can start by acknowledging the aspects of each school that, set in a larger context, contribute to holistic theory and techniques. We are going to be walking, step by step, West and East, examining the discoveries, strengths, and weaknesses of our forebears, building foundations for an approach that enables us to progress, evolve, and achieve our purpose as human beings. With that goal in mind, what elements, from this early and reductive period, can we take forward with us?

Psychoanalysis, with its insights and innovations, set off a revolutionary shift in Western society. Its roots are inextricably embedded into many subsequent schools of psychology. Freud's seminal writings on the effects of the unconscious parts of the psyche on behavior, his basic approach of talking with clients as a method to uncover and work through these unconscious influences, and his definition of defense mechanisms and transference are widely used by therapists to gain insight into their clients' unconscious processes and are still implicit elements in our current understanding of psychology.

Adler, and some of his post-Freudian contemporaries, began to move past Freud's confining ideas. They shifted their focus toward human potential, building the foundations for later schools of humanistic and transpersonal psychology. Rank emphasized greater intimacy and expression of emotion rather than just intellectualization. Horney called our attention to the power dynamics between men and women, awareness of feminist concerns, and our tendency to move between states of being open and closed or, in some cases, to be in a fixed state of closed. Jung, in particular, opened Western psychiatry to Eastern thought and practices, His work provided a foundation for further investigations and developments into the relationship between Eastern and Western psychological thought.

DEVELOPMENTAL PSYCHOLOGY—PIAGET, AND VYGOTSKY

Developmental psychology scientifically studies the phases of human development from early childhood to the end of life. Jean Piaget's[38] developmental psychology and Lev Vygotsky's[39] social development theory addressed sensorimotor, psychological, and social development. While until recently, it has primarily been applied in the area of learning and education, in chapter 5 we will see how the school of integral psychology has adapted it into a model that addresses a larger psycho-spiritual spectrum of development.

BEHAVIORISM—PAVLOV, WATSON, AND SKINNER

Behaviorism developed partly as a reaction to psychoanalysis' tendency to focus on speculations about subjective intrapsychic processes. Behaviorism sought to develop a more scientific and objective approach. Pavlov,[40] Watson,[41] and Skinner[42] argued that behavior is conditioned by natural responses to our environment. Early behavioral theories were based on the supposition that it was possible to understand, predict, and control human behavior by studying relationships between environmental stimuli and behavior and by manipulation of the environment.

Behavioral techniques such as counter-conditioning, operant conditioning, and systematic desensitization are still in use. Behaviorism aims to help clients change abnormal or unwanted behaviors to new, desirable behaviors. It is effective for addressing specific, definable problems such as severe psychotic disorders and some neurotic conditions such as phobias, but is less successful in treating depression. Similarly, care is taken to not give excessive attention or sympathetic responses to dysfunctional behaviors and attitudes to avoid reinforcing them. Treatment may involve identifying people in the client's family or close associates who may be reinforcing the client's unwanted behaviors or attitudes, or discouraging or failing to support the client in the development of healthy change. The client develops better insight into interpersonal dynamics and implements countermeasures suggested by the therapist. Key people from a client's entourage may also be brought into the psychotherapeutic process in the form of systemic or family therapy.

COGNITIVE-BEHAVIORAL THERAPIES— BANDURA, ELLIS, AND BECK

During a period dominated by behaviorism, Albert Bandura[43] believed that the external rewards and punishments of Skinner's operant conditioning were an inadequate framework to explain human behavior.[44] His early research led him to the conclusion that children learned aggressive behaviors by observing others, the basis for his influential social learning theory.[45] This theory helped shift the focus in academic psychology from pure behaviorism to cognitive psychology, thereby making him a transitional influence between the two schools.

Bandura developed a social cognitive theory which delved into inner drives by conceptualizing individuals as self-organizing, proactive, self-reflecting and self-regulating, in opposition to the orthodox conception of humans as governed by external forces.[46] This led to further research on the importance of a person's beliefs about their self-efficacy.

Albert Ellis's[47] rational emotive behavior therapy was based on the idea that, "humans, in most cases, do not get upset merely by unfortunate adversities, but also by how they construct their views of reality."[48] Ellis' A-B-C model redefined the way we construct our views of reality based on a combination of philosophical meanings derived from inner constructs, learned ideas, the way we give meanings and place assumptions on events, and our personal preferences and desires. This process is evaluative and involves cognitive, emotional, and behavioral dimensions. Events that trigger reactions may be dealt with in two ways. Evaluating an event through rigid, absolutistic, and dysfunctional beliefs about events leads to self-defeating and destructive emotions and behaviors. Alternatively, employing flexible and constructive beliefs leads to self-helping and functional thoughts and behaviors. Through gaining perspective on the underlying beliefs behind the ways they evaluate events, people gain the possibility to reevaluate them along more positive and constructive lines.

Aaron T. Beck,[49] inspired by Albert Ellis, developed cognitive-behavioral therapy (CBT) to help patients identify and change dysfunctional thinking, behavior, and emotional responses.

CBT is often used in conjunction with medication to treat conditions like bipolar disorder and schizophrenia. One of the main aspects of CBT is identifying the dysfunctional cognitive-affective-behavioral habit or process, in the form of a thought or attitude, wreaking havoc in patients. The next step is to help the patient examine the habit or process so that its incoherency becomes apparent. It can then be replaced by a more rational, positive, and constructive construct. The client–therapist relationship requires transparency and openness in order for the therapist to be able to identify issues and develop strategies for modifying the client's behavior, attitudes, and work toward improving their lives. This may take considerable effort and time.

LIMITATIONS OF BEHAVIORISM
AND COGNITIVE BEHAVIORISM

The phenomenon of human conditioning exists. Yet, reducing the whole of human experience into this mechanistic theory is limiting and has the potential to be damaging. Our human tendency toward the comfortable arrogance of absolutism—"my way is the only way"—distances possibilities toward achieving a greater vision and potential that can free us, rather than enclose us. Neither should we react to this by falling into the "either-or" trap: "Behaviorism has some ideas I cannot relate to therefore, I am going to systematically reject it in all shapes and forms." No school is 100 percent wrong, and no school is 100 percent right. While neither of these two limiting attitudes are exclusive to behaviorism, they seem to go hand in hand with early behaviorist views.

Behavior only reflects the surface of who we are and not actually who we are. Behavioral approaches are useful to treat symptoms. Likewise, the problem-focused nature of cognitive-behavioral approaches can be effective and powerful for addressing identifiable issues and problem areas. In this context, the surface fixes help us become more functional and adapted human beings. The assumption that our mental scripts and beliefs are the fundamental cause of psychological disorders carries some weight, yet does not merit stopping there.

Behavioral and cognitive-behavioral approaches do not take into consideration or seek to treat the deep, underlying causes or aspects of the client that are not perceptible through external observation. They do not explicitly help us attain the greater potential of wholeness, nor do they open the individual to their higher psychological or spiritual ranges of development. While addressing behavioral issues may clear away enough clouds for our self-actualizing drives to wake up and take off, mind, body, and soul connection are not a part of its purview. In his book *The Psychology of Man's Possible Evolution*, P.D. Ouspensky, a Russian philosopher and mystic, sums up his observations of Western psychology in 1950:

> To begin with I must say that practically never in history has psychology stood at so low a level as at the present time. It has lost all touch with its origin and its meaning so that now it is even difficult to define the term "psychology": that is, to say what psychology is and what it studies. And this is so despite the fact that never in history have there been so many psychological theories and so many psychological writings.[50]

Since the nonquantifiable and nonobservable phenomena such as the soul were not acknowledged, they were largely eliminated from the field of psychology, at least for a time. As psychology identified more with the material plane and its laws, unscientific notions such as God were gradually exiled. All that would be left for us to chew on is the outer, observable, and quantifiable aspects of human experience. In contrast, Sri Aurobindo, whose works we will introduce in chapter 4, placed the mind into a different perspective altogether:

> The utmost mission of the Mind is to train our obscure consciousness which has emerged out of the dark prison of Matter, to enlighten its blind instincts, random intuitions, vague perceptions till it shall become capable of this greater light and this higher ascension. Mind is a passage, not a culmination.[51]

Self-analysis may be useful in helping us navigate in our experiences and convey them. However, it is ill-equipped to get us to the roots of our issues, release blocked emotions, and heal a wounded sense of self.

Vignette—Contacting and Healing the Core Wound

Véronique was a chronic overachiever, a super student, then career woman, athlete, and mother. Like most people, she felt good when she achieved a goal, got recognition, or had a productive day, but that good feeling was short-lived. The minute something was less than she expected of herself, she free fell into self-pummeling, anxiety, and depression. Véronique, like many French clients I have worked with, had done a great job of analyzing the cause of her suffering. She knew with perfect clarity that low self-image was the root cause of her suffering. She also knew that it was her mother's standoffishness in childhood that had caused her to backfire on herself by developing the low self-image.

Without wanting to stereotype Véronique, what was also typically French about her was that in spite of her detailed understanding of the causes of her suffering, she had been completely unable to change anything and put an end to her pain. Through working together, beginning to delve inward, and feel the core emotions, rather than think through the sequences of events and patterns, she began to get in touch with the root of the pain. As it arose, little by little, she started to feel herself shift. She did not have to make an effort to raise her self-esteem, but only to go within and bring out the core wound and its surrounding "matter." When the pressure this caused started to be released, Véronique's face opened, the tension left, and her eyes began to shine. In the weeks that followed, Véronique began spiraling upward.

BEHAVIORAL AND COGNITIVE-BEHAVIORAL STEPPING STONES TOWARD AN INTEGRAL PSYCHOLOGY

Early approaches such as behaviorism are macrocosmic, exploring the outer self, our relationship to the world and others in terms of behavior, adaptation, and functionality. Modifying behavior and developing functional social skills, while not the be-all-and-end-all of human potential, are valid and effective therapeutic tools. Looking at our struggles in terms of behaviorism adds an objective understanding to our inner process thereby inciting self-reflection and empowering us to change. Its emphasis on the impact of environmental factors on the formation of our behavior and attitudes contribute to our self-understanding and personal growth. Entering into the cognitive world of the individual uncovers an important layer of her being. Social learning theory and CBT represent a significant development moving from the purely external focus and approaches of behaviorism toward the inner life of the individual's thoughts and perceptions and their role in psychological problems. Advocates of behaviorism and cognitive behaviorism can further their contribution and become an important stepping stone by letting go of their absolutist stands and acknowledging and integrating the contribution of holistic approaches. Behaviorism then becomes one valid viewpoint that is part of a larger, holistic perspective.

CURRENT MEDICAL MODELS

Psychology, like consciousness, has developed in two distinct directions. The predominant scientific paradigm reduces the definition of human experience, functioning, and development to that which is scientifically verifiable and quantifiable. At the same time, there is a small but persistent wave moving in the direction of expanding and reintegrating aspects of human experience and potential and moving toward a holistic and multidimensional conception. Until now, we have covered schools more or less chronologically, but we have arrived at a fork in the road—the divide between the expansionist and reductionist schools. Before we move on to expansionist schools, we owe a visit to the predominant medical trends of psychology.

The classification of psychological disorders that began in the 1800s has gone through various phases of development leading to publication of the first *Diagnostic and Statistical Manual of Mental Disorders* (*DSM*) in 1952 with subsequent revisions in 1968, 1980, 1994, 2000, and 2013. In spite of controversy over the most recent version, the *DSM* has attempted to classify families of symptoms useful for filling out assessments, applying for research funding, and publishing articles and health care insurance claims. Today, the field of psychopharmacology in conjunction with drug companies has developed a wide variety of drugs designed to treat psychiatric disorders defined in the diagnostic manual.

The medical model, by and large, attributes abnormalities in attitude and behavior to physiological causes. Undeniably, providing diagnosis and medication gives hope and improvement to many people. Addressing the physiological aspect of mental disorders creates the possibility of treating them with pharmaceutical medicines. Medicines may help in the management of symptoms of depression, anxiety, schizophrenia, and other psychotic spectrum disorders. While not providing a cure, in many cases, medication allows some people to regain a level of normality, with greater autonomy and life satisfaction. In cases where psychotherapy is not enough to stabilize a patient, medicine picks up the slack. Medication may bring patients onto a more solid ground from which psychotherapy helps address the underlying causes. In this case, medication becomes a short or mid-range tool as part of a multidimensional or multispectrum approach.

According to the staunchest advocates of the medical model, psychotherapy cannot be truly effective because the real cause of the mentally ill individual's problems is physiological. However, in most current psychiatric practice, psychological, social, and physiological factors are all seen as contributing to mental illness. While drug therapies are usually the focus, other types of therapy may be used to address the psychological and social factors, often with the help of social workers and psychotherapists.

Vignette—Antidepressants

Melissa was referred to me by a general practitioner because she was distressed and highly emotional. During our first three sessions, Melissa sobbed most of the time. After determining that she was in no imminent danger, I suggested she hold off on the antidepressants she had been prescribed to see if we could stabilize her without them. I tried through dialogue to help her gain a cognitive sense of what was going on so that we could walk her to solid ground. After the third session, I could see that she was drowning in a sea of tears. There simply was no solid ground within reach. In my observation with Melissa and other clients over the years, there seems to be a tipping point in the level of emotionality beyond which we are taken over by emotion and no longer have recourse to solid ground. In the case of a clear, identifiable cause, such as grief, I believe it is good just to let the grief run its course. But, if the state becomes too lengthy or intense it may take the client "off the map." Medication may then be very helpful in reestablishing a stable base from which psychotherapy becomes possible.

Seeing that Melissa clearly did not have recourse to her own will to bring herself to solid ground, she started a six-month course of antidepressants. She quickly stabilized and we were able to start examining her life and her state of mind. As things began to fall into perspective, she began digesting the childhood wounds that were wreaking havoc in her life. She started to feel able to make decisions regarding her life direction. After four months, Sarah was more clear-headed and felt back in control of her life. She talked about wanting to come off the antidepressants. By the time she got to the six-month point, she had pretty much weaned herself off the medication and was on her way to being autonomous. She made leaps and bounds toward establishing greater balance and fulfillment in her life. The short course of antidepressants made Melissa's treatment easier and helped her get back on her feet in a short timespan.

LIMITATIONS OF THE MEDICAL MODEL

Science has remained an anti-intellectual movement based on naive faith.

Alfred North Whitehead

Western psychology is characterized by the scientific study and quantitative measurement of thought and behavior. For example, theoretical constructs pertaining to psychological disorders such as depression, bipolar disorder, anxiety, schizophrenia, obsessive-compulsive disorder, and attention deficit hyperactivity disorder (ADHD) have been developed, measured, and studied to ascertain causes, consequences, and remedial interventions. These theoretical constructs are often conceptualized as if they were distinct entities with which the individual is "afflicted" and which can be cured, alleviated, or managed with distinct interventions, whether medicines or other means. Certainly, some physiological disorders may account for our mental imbalances, such as in the cases of thyroid disorders, brain tumors, or Alzheimer's disease. Yet, can our psychological kinks be entirely attributed to physiology without taking into account lifestyle and psychological wounding? If this school of thought was right and our disorders were purely physiological then wouldn't treatment be systematically effective? Why do psychotropic medications only work while they are being taken, rather than providing a lasting cure? Conceptualization of psychological problems as discrete diseases, while administratively convenient for health care providers, insurers, and pharmaceutical companies is reductive and questionable, especially given the wide variability in the type and severity of symptoms and disorders and their causes.

The practice of labeling people with disorders may itself be harmful and even reinforce the unwanted tendencies of distress or acting out. Moreover, individuals so labeled may be penalized, discriminated against, or stigmatized by society. Dividing issues into normal and abnormal leaves out possibilities for understanding, making meaning from, and working with the difficulties and challenges of life encountered by most human beings. According to Chogyam Trungpa, "[f]rom the Buddhist point of view, there is a problem with any attempt to pinpoint, categorize, and pigeonhole mind and its contents very neatly. This method could be called psychological materialism. The problem with this approach is that it does not leave enough room for spontaneity or openness. It overlooks basic healthiness."[52]

Science has indeed proven that there are chemical aspects related to our states of mind. And yet they too quickly assume that all illness, both mental and physical, begins and ends in the physiology. An integral view tells us that disturbances begin in the subtle bodies. "To whatever cause an illness may be due, material or mental, external or internal, it must, before it can affect the physical body, touch another layer of the being that surrounds and protects it."[53] If they are not addressed, they gradually densify until they create visible disturbances and imbalances in our mental and physical health.

There are secondary effects caused by taking psychotropic drugs such as weight gain, sluggishness, impaired organ function, and in the case of antidepressants, an increase in suicide. Many fringe and holistic approaches consider medication to be a chemical straitjacket with no contribution to mental health. Others consider it only part of the solution. They advocate instead either avoiding medication altogether or prescribing medication along with psychotherapy for many pathologies. For example, the symptoms of post-traumatic stress disorder (PTSD) respond to treatment by antidepressants, anxiolytics, and other classes of medication depending on the nature of the trauma and how it affected the individual. However, once the patient stops the medication, the symptoms return. Therapies such as EMDR have been proven to cure PTSD.[54]

Finally, a word must be said about the authoritarian methods of many of those who subscribe to the medical models. Taking medication should be the choice of an informed individual, not influenced or imposed by politics or pharmaceutical lobbies. The predominant medicalized view attempts to monopolize the field of mental health, marginalizing, disinforming the public, and even making laws against complementary views and treatments. The medical approach understates the potential and importance of the individual's personal evolution in favor of masking the symptoms through chemical modification or surface adaptive change.

I believe the physical body is to a great extent a mirror of the mindset or consciousness of the individual. I do not believe the Western, medical, and disempowering view that we are victims to our physiology and neurobiology. Medicating our psychological symptoms may deprive the individual of the opportunity to learn, grow, and overcome. And yet, this is a sensitive issue. Professionals and patients alike have differing opinions. In the therapeutic setting, I navigate around this gingerly, by informing the client about the choice and implications of taking medications so they can decide for themselves. My role is to support them in their decision, not bring them over to my camp. Another reason the decision to medicate is not to be taken lightly is that the effects are not just physiological and psychological. The term chemical straitjacket is not just imagery. When meeting clients, I can intuitively perceive when they are on medication even before they tell me because I sense a barrier or fog between their mind and their psyche. Medication may make our suffering more manageable, but to what extent do they cut us off from ourselves.

This raises yet more questions: What of extraordinary or transformational phenomenon such as near-death experiences, out-of-body experiences, and various forms of spontaneous awakenings experienced by a surprisingly high percentage of people? How does the field of mental health explain the occurrence of such experiences and their universal commonalities? Is it enough just to chalk it up to neurons? Is it possible for the field of mental health to open up to the full spectrum of human experience? In the face of so many possibilities, can the field of mental health justify turning away from nonordinary experiences or higher potentials?

In the interest of taking on the challenge of personal growth, medication should be a last resort, not a first. The fact is that neither medical science nor any other school has the complete solution to psychological disorders. Therefore, neither medical science nor any school should hold an intellectual or clinical monopoly. By working together, in a mutually respectful and pluri-disciplinary fashion, each with our perceptions, experiences, scientific proofs, and intuitions, we are more likely to come up with a comprehensive understanding and treatment modality for mental illness.

MEDICAL MODEL—STEPPING STONES TOWARD AN INTEGRAL PSYCHOLOGY

Experimental and quantitative approaches to psychology may be useful in managing symptoms thereby creating a possibility for stability that will facilitate and help the outcome of psychotherapy. While dysfunctions of the brain or nerves may be factors in psychological distress, other factors may also be involved and may indeed lead to physiological dysfunctions. An integral approach is needed which looks at all the different levels of the human being—physiological, emotional, mental, spiritual—in an integrated way.

CONCLUSION

It is interesting to observe how over a relatively short period, the predominant worldview of the West went from primitive, mystical belief systems and practices to a much narrower, albeit, scientifically verifiable worldview. What does this signify? What are the personal and societal implications of leaving behind consideration of subtle realities in our worldview and treatment modalities? Our current definitions of "normal" and "healthy" mostly signify lack of pathology and do not leave much growing room. Without the inner references, that we turned our back on, we are left with only the outer phenomenon as a point of reference. Is the scientific paradigm enough to explain our existence, address our suffering and angst, and to give our lives meaning, purpose, and a sustainable worldview?

Just as Western religion with its anthropomorphized concept of a Creator sitting in the clouds did not fulfill my quest for a holistic perspective and sense of universal truth, neither did the reductionist schools of psychology. The élan that drove the development of reductionist practices was to understand, systematize, and categorize observable human behavior somehow trying to make it fit into the laws of the material sciences. This reflects one of the two directions on the spectrum of consciousness, the impulse to contract and control reality. If we don't contract it into boxes and categories, we cannot pretend to control it. In spite of their limitations, reductionist schools if taken with a both-and approach, rather than the current "either-or" or "us-and-them" dichotomy, will provide useful elements for building a holistic approach to psychology.

Although the gap between science and consciousness is being bridged through dialogue and research, the medical view still remains largely reductionist and exclusivist in practice. Reductionist worldviews, although they have much competition from the later movements we will be exploring in the upcoming chapters, are still the predominant paradigm. Let us move forward into the next wave of approaches and take a refreshing turn in the direction of expansion.

ANNEX I: IN-DEPTH CASE STUDY ON PSYCHOANALYSIS

Reason for Therapy

Claudine was in her early 20s when she began seeking a psychoanalyst. She had recently left a stable job and relationship due to strong feelings of dissatisfaction.

Background

An acquaintance of Claudine's encouraged her to begin therapy. A few weeks later she went to an osteopath for back pain. He did not find anything physically wrong and felt her problem was emotional. He advised her to try psychoanalysis. She interviewed several psychoanalysts, who she chose not to work with because they lacked the warmth and reassurance she sought. She wanted to work with a foreigner to escape the French mentality that had felt suffocating to her in her childhood. The foreign male psychoanalyst she wanted to work with felt she wasn't ready and referred her to a female colleague. Claudine underwent psychoanalysis with this analyst for one and half years and then was referred back to the original psychoanalyst. She worked lying on the couch for the first three years. She liked the fact that he engaged in dialogue instead of just passively listening. Then, because he felt she was ready and it was important for her to "sit upright" and start to face life from the standpoint of an adult, they worked sitting face to face for another year and a half. Her psychoanalysis was primarily focused on transference; what the patient projects onto the analyst that reflects unresolved relationship issues from childhood. Psychoanalysis, in this sense, mainly addresses the relationship of the individual to others based on learned dynamics.

What Happened During Her Psychoanalysis?

During our work together, I asked Claudine if I could interview her about her experience in psychoanalysis for my research. She enthusiastically agreed.

During the six years of her psychoanalysis, Claudine revisited the main themes of her life. She began with a lengthy period focused on the death of her father when she was a child. Claudine had been excluded from all the events around her father's hospitalization, death, and funeral. No one spoke with her about it. She felt utterly unimportant, betrayed, abandoned, and unable to properly grieve the loss of her father, the family member with whom she felt the strongest connection. She experienced painful feelings of not belonging to her family. Her mother quickly met someone new and was clearly happy, but outwardly played the grieving widow. These mixed messages and hypocrisy broke down Claudine's ability to trust and open up to people.

Her analyst encouraged her to build her impulses, drives, desires, and ego needs by seeking out and giving herself permission to have pleasure at all costs. He felt that her shame was caused by having an oversized superego. His antidote was for her to replace her superego with instinct. He placed a lot of importance on talking about sex and overcoming taboos and inhibitions. He encouraged her to ignore her conscience and engage in sexual activity that did not feel good and wholesome to her and sometimes left her feeling dirty. While she felt this helped her to grasp the life force that is inherent in sexuality and give herself permission to express herself sexually, for her, he took it too far. She sometimes was left with the odd feeling of having a body and a head with distinctly different and dissociated needs, wants, and desires. The pressure he put on her made her feel out of harmony with herself. Her analyst insisted on her identifying incestuous aspects of her relationships with her father and brother and jealousy of her mother although she could not relate to this at all. Claudine struggled with this and other aspects of her psychoanalysis as it went against her inner feeling that some desires are healthy for her and yet others did not feel right to her. Her analyst brushed this off. This left her feeling lost about how to understand what was good for her and what was not good.

Claudine described her psychoanalyst as a macho, Latin, pipe-smoker, meat-eater, carnal, hot-blooded, incarnated but not embodied, and as some-one who gave himself full permission to live out his physical desires. She felt he was on a power trip and did not like his ways. She wished to pursue a healthier life more focused on light. Psychoanalysis clearly did not have room for that part of her, and yet, it is perhaps partly through this experience which is so opposite to her sensitive and fragile nature, that she was able to start identifying who she is, what is good for her, and how she would like to envisage her therapeutic process.

Claudine's experience was a mix of positive and negative. She stated that she often felt good and valued in the therapeutic relationship. She was moti-vated to please her therapist. On the other hand, in her moments of panic, her therapist lacked empathy and acknowledgment. This made her angry and frustrated with him and enlarged the gaps in her self-structure.

Observations

The way Claudine's psychoanalyst was the one holding the power throughout the relationship—making the decisions as to how and when he would work with her—is alien to someone from my humanistic background.

Claudine said she felt utterly lost. She was left with the impression that psychoanalysis is about destruction of many aspects of the self that may be inhibiting but just like antibiotics; it kills the good bacteria along with the bad. His approach places the ego at the center of our being, encouraging her to disregard her inner truth and common sense. Claudine shared her impres-sion that Freud held the belief that we are animals. According to his view, we can exercise the ego and superego to channel our animal drives. There is no concept of higher nature and even a belief that spiritual and religious aspirations are pathological.

I believe that devaluing her essence made her more fragile, made her doubt herself and ignore the deeper senses that emerged in her moments of strength and clarity. This resulted in a relatively meaningless and empty life behind the suit of armor that is built by strengthening and justifying the ego; hence the feeling of being "utterly lost."

Focusing on the ego to the exclusion of the soul in therapy is an oxymoron insofar as the ego by its very nature is fragmented and fragmenting and, there-fore, cannot lead to the harmony that will allow us to function optimally. So, that which is at the core of integral philosophy, many religions, and wisdom tra-ditions, that which gives meaning and creates harmony between the disparate

parts of the ego (body, mind, and emotions) is brushed off by psychoanalysis. Psychotherapy has the potential to lead us to higher qualities such as
wholeness, harmony, healing, meaning, oneness, sense of belonging, and
responsibility. In Claudine's case, classical Freudian psychoanalysis did
the opposite, leaving her alienated from the very source of meaning of her
existence.

The End of Her Psychoanalysis

One day as she was leaving yoga class, Claudine started crying. Her yoga
teacher, a colleague of mine, gave her my card. She came to see me for an
initial consultation and we began our therapeutic relationship while she was
still in psychoanalysis. In accordance with the code of ethics of a psychotherapist, I maintained a neutral attitude toward this dual relationship and
tried to work with her in ways that would compliment her psychoanalysis.
And yet, in our first weeks together, she began to feel a sense of rebellion
against the analyst. She had talked over and sometimes cried over all the
major themes of her life and yet she felt she was not evolving, her problems
were not improving, and she was going around in circles. She told him she
was frustrated at not moving forward, revisiting the same issues without
resolution.

Finally, in session one day, he told her that their work could go no further and that this would be their last session. He wished her well as they
said goodbye. Claudine experienced the end of her psychoanalysis as a
liberation.

Our Work

When I began working with her, Claudine was morose, glum, and tearful.
Our sessions were rich in content as she brought up emotionally charged
life events both in story form but also in metaphors. The loss of her father
came up regularly. She needed to express her grief, loss, unfulfilled needs,
dreams, and wishes in respect to her father through emotional release. We
were able to work with this content in a cathartic way through the humanistic
techniques of gestalt and inner dialogue with parts of herself, her past, and
members of her family to help her liberate blocked emotions, resolve inner
conflict, and complete unresolved issues. Gestalt dialogue with her father and
family allowed her to get in touch with her grief, and behind that, her anger.
Therapeutic breathwork was used to access and heal the deep-seated emotional wounds, liberating the blocked energy that had not been released by
psychoanalysis. Behind anger is often an effort to reclaim our power or sense
of self. As Claudine released her negative emotions and accessed her anger

and the inherent power in it, there were moments when she had a light in her eyes, a sense of knowing the part of herself that is good and whole. As she continued to empty the contents that were under pressure inside, it left more and more space for her real self to emerge. Sometimes, however, she was still very fragile, subject to depression, and completely dominated by fear, anxiety, self-doubt, and chronic self-pummeling.

When fragility rose we addressed it through creating a safe space based on Carl Rogers' three main principles: (1) Congruence—authenticity, genuineness and honesty with the client; (2) Empathy—walking alongside the client, in their world and; (3) Respect—acceptance and unconditional positive regard toward the client. The warm and safe environment helped her to start to create this type of inner environment for herself; making it safe for her to be herself and to remain present with herself, through her highs and lows. I encouraged her to begin a daily mindfulness meditation practice; simply watching what "is" without judgment. I asked her to do some journaling exercises aimed at starting to recognize her needs and take care of herself rather than to judge herself and react when weaknesses arose. When we can be kind, nonjudgmental, and gentle with ourselves in moments of distress, we have less tendency to escalate into strong emotional states. Our emotional states have corresponding brain waves, neurons, and receptors in the brain. Going too far into negative states and staying for too long changes our brain functioning and it becomes more difficult to control and pull ourselves out of it. This can turn a tendency toward depression or any other negative state into something quite stubborn. Over time, esoteric beliefs are that this even creates subtle formations in the aura that take on a life of their own and become very stubborn houseguests.

Most people practice self-observation, but their observation is filled with harsh self-judgment, criticism, and even self-hatred, self-punishment, and psychological self-harm. This can be blatant, but it can also be imperceptible. This uses a lot of energy and is the most common cause of us feeling bad. The mindfulness practice helped Claudine learn to watch over herself with lovingkindness. This created inner spaciousness, objectivity, and a potential for self-mastery.

Every thought, word, and action is driven either by our positive or negative drives. Mindfulness helps us develop the objectivity to avoid acting on impulses driven by fear and other weaknesses. When we let our weaknesses be the decision makers it lowers our self-image and can lower others' image of us; we go into a downward spiral.

We worked with mindfulness to help her create space for her ups and downs rather than get into a vicious circle where she judges and beats herself up mentally and as a result, escalates and spirals into states of strong emotional distress.

Cognitive work provided mental structure to help Claudine understand where she was and how to relate to her experiences, emotions, and her deeper instincts. I tried to paint a map to help her better orient herself in the face of her unstable mind and emotions. I helped her understand where these difficult and dark parts of ourselves lay in the scheme of the whole self and how to call upon our inner qualities and strengths to help us smooth out the ride. I think this "map-making" of consciousness and functioning helped her to understand herself.

In humanistic and attachment theories, fulfilling the client's unfulfilled need for nurturing and safety fills the void that was left from childhood and wakes up the client's drive toward autonomy. Since my client was very fragile in the beginning, I followed my intuition and allowed her to ring as needed. Later when I sensed that this phase was over and that far from making her feel safe and supported, as it had in the beginning, it was turning into a crutch eating away at her self-confidence. Coincidently we both came to the conclusion that it was time for her to start trusting her instincts and ability to navigate in her emotions simultaneously. Together, we decided that she would cease to ring me between sessions.

Evolution

Claudine talked about her spiritual longing and an inner sense of spirituality that emerged from time to time. And yet, Claudine's psychoanalyst systematically shunned this topic. She was attracted to my spiritual worldview and techniques and attended regular yoga classes and intensives. Despite her Catholic origins, she did not attend church or observe Catholic practices. She experienced her spirituality in nature.

After the first few months of wading through some very dense emotions from childhood experiences and also her tormented relationship to herself, Claudine began having moments of feeling connected spiritually. In one of our last sessions, Claudine had a breakthrough during her breathwork session. She said, "I realized I'm like a primary number. No matter how many facets I have, I can only be divided by One. One is constantly there, inside of me, behind all of the other facets."

I acknowledged this experience and the meaning it held for her to understand this imagery of the "One behind the many." I encouraged a brief dialogue exploring how it might be useful to keep an awareness of this realization, keep contact with the "One behind the many" facets, voices, and experiences throughout the inner and outer ups and downs of daily life. She was inspired and strengthened by the experience and our development of this imagery and the sense of purity it evoked for her.

Our work together ended when Claudine moved to another town. She continued to go through some very difficult patches. Today, she continues her work in psychotherapy and has taken up mindfulness-based stress reduction. She is exploring compassion, openness, and transformation on, what she says, is a very enriching path. Claudine is dedicated to working on herself and to developing more balance, autonomy, and peace with herself. I am certain she is on her way.

NOTES

1. Kees W. Bolle, *"Animism and Animatism,"* in M. Eliade, ed., *The Encyclopedia of Religion* (1987, New York: Macmillan), Vol. 1, p. 296.

2. Bolle, 1987, p. 298.

3. Mircea Eliade, *Shamanism: Archaic Techniques of Ecstasy* (NJ: Princeton Press, 1951).

4. Leonard H. Lesko, *"Egyptian Religion: An Overview,"* in M. Eliade, ed., *The Encyclopedia of Religion* (1987 New York: Macmillan), Vol. 5, p. 42.

5. Lesko, 1987, p. 42.

6. Lesko, 1987, p. 42.

7. Robert E. Svoboda. *The Greatness of Saturn: A Therapeutic Myth.* (1997, Wisconsin: Lotus Press), p. 9.

8. Z'Ev Ben Shimon Halevi, *Psychology and Kabbalah* (1992, New York: Samuel Weiser), p. 1.

9. 470–399 BCE.

10. 427–347 BCE.

11. 384–322 BCE.

12. Svoboda, 1997, p. 9.

13. c. 460 BCE to c. 370 BCE.

14. 129–217 CE.

15. Middle Kingdom, 2000–1300 BCE.

16. Judaism, c. 1800 BCE.

17. John E. Smith, *"Philosophy and Religion,"* in M. Eliade, ed., *The Encyclopedia of Religion* (1987, New York: Macmillan), Vol. 11, p. 296.

18. 150 BCE to 74 CE.

19. The term is derived from the Greek word *gnosis* which means "knowledge" (235–285 CE).

20. Romila Thapar, *The Penguin Early History of India: From the Origins to AD 1300* (2002, Kindle edition, Penguin), p. 254.

21. 20 BCE to 50 CE.

22. Bulent Atalay and Keith Wamsley, *Leonardo's Universe: The Renaissance World of Leonardo da Vinci* (2008, Washington: National Geographic), p. 96 (from da Vinci's handwritten notebooks).

23. 1832–1920.

24. 1869–1962.

25. 1856–1939.

26. Brant Cortright, *Psychotherapy and Spirit: Theory and Practice in Transpersonal Psychotherapy* (2008, New York: SUNY Press), p. 34.

27. 1875–1961.

28. Carl G. Jung, "Jung and Eastern Thought," p. 32, in C.G. Jung, "The Concept of Libido," in *Symbols of Transformation*, CW 5 (1948, NJ: Princeton University Press, 2nd edition), p. 131.

29. J. Heisig, "Psychology of Religion," in M. Eliade, *Encyclopedia of Religion* (1987, New York: Macmillan), Vol. 12, p. 63.

30. 1870–1937.

31. 1884–1939.

32. 1924.

33. http://www.ottorank.com/essays/the-evolution-of-psychotherapy-since-freud.

34. 1885–1952.

35. Karen Horney, *"The Problem of Feminine Masochism,"* *Psychoanalytic Review*, Vol. xxii (July 1935), p. 241.

36. Sigmund Freud, *The Future of an Illusion* (1927c) (2011, Create Space Independent Publishing Platform), p. 78.

37. Breathwork, introduced here, in the context of this vignette, will be extensively covered in chapter 9.

38. 1896–1980.

39. 1896–1934.

40. 1849–1936.

41. 1878–1958.

42. 1904–1990.

43. 1925–.

44. Jose A. Fadul, Gen. Ed., *Encyclopedia of Theory and Practice in Psychotherapy and Counseling* (2015, London: Lulu Press), p. 99.

45. Fadul, 2015, p. 99.

46. IBID, p. 100.

47. 1913–2007.

48. Albert Ellis, *Overcoming Destructive Beliefs, Feelings and Behaviors: New Directions for Rational Emotive Therapy* (2001, Amherst: Prometheus Books).

49. 1921–.

50. P.D. Ouspensky, *The Psychology of Man's Possible Evolution* (1950, NY: Hedgehog Press), p. xx.

51. Sri Aurobindo, *"The Life Divine,"* *The Complete Works of Sri Aurobindo*, Vol. 21 and 22 (2005, Pondicherry: Sri Aurobindo Ashram Trust), p. 136.

52. Trungpa Chogyam, *The Sanity We Are Born With: A Buddhist Approach to Psychology* (2005, Boston: Shambhala), pp. 137–138.

53. The Mother, *Collected Works of the Mother* (1997, Pondicherry; Sri Aurobindo Ashram), Vol. 3, pp. 85–91.

54. See chapter 9.

Chapter Two

History of Modern Western Psychology

The expansionist schools of humanistic and transpersonal psychology, covered in this chapter, stretch beyond the limits of material science. Humanistic psychology began by enlarging the definition of what it is to be human, reclaiming our right to be fully human. Transpersonal psychology continues the evolutionary movement toward a holistic worldview by considering the more subtle aspects of being human. Within the expansionist category, there are countless schools, institutes, and healing modalities emerging that also reflect our human and spiritual potential. Rather than attempting to cover the entire range, examining the most established schools that address our higher potentials will suffice insofar as they represent the general movements and evolutions of psychology in the West. These movements reflect an expansionist mindset, the promise of moving in the direction of our higher potential.

HUMANISTIC PSYCHOLOGY—MASLOW, MAY, AND ROGERS

Humanistic psychology originated in the late 1950s and 1960s reflecting an emerging interest in higher drives, values, and potentials. It aimed to reestablish the qualitative dimensions in psychology and to explore human potential and aspects of psychology that are not scientifically quantifiable, such as phenomenology and experiential development. This movement marked a new era in psychology by moving beyond the constraints of the mechanistic and deterministic views of psychoanalysis and behaviorism.

The pioneers and principle figures of the humanistic vision were Abraham Maslow, Rollo May, and Carl Rogers. They developed a common vision of humanity as having an inherent drive toward healing and wholeness, enabling them to become liberated from negative propensities and reach their highest ideals. Today there are many contributors to the continually evolving humanistic theory and many therapeutic techniques that fit into the humanistic worldview. Reading their works, and many others during my masters program, filled me with a sense of warmth, well-being, and possibilities.

Abraham Maslow

Maslow[1] began his explorations into psychology with Alfred Adler. Although he did not completely reject Adler's theories, after World War II, Maslow began exploring the idea that we are not merely a product of outside influences and forces, but that we also have internal forces constantly driving us toward wholeness. He focused on enlarging the scope of psychology beyond abnormal functioning, instinctual, and early developmental stages. Maslow felt that to create a psychology leading to well-being and realization of human potential, it was necessary to study optimally functioning, healthy, or what he called, self-actualizing individuals. Self-actualization develops through peak experiences or moments of heightened awareness, profound perception, deep insights into our lives, and other phenomenon reflecting the higher spectrum of human possibilities.

In his theory of the hierarchy of needs, Maslow examined the forces that motivate us to act. He recognized two types of needs: "subsistence or deficiency" and "fulfillment." As our basic needs are met, higher ones evolve and reflect our potential until the drive for self-actualization is reached, which is in itself a continual process. Where earlier in our development many different motivations come into play, self-actualizing people no longer seeking fulfillment of basic needs are driven by meta-motivation.

Vignette—Integrating Levels of Functioning

Simone consulted me to address a relationship issue. She described herself as a spiritual person and said that she had chosen to work with me because of my spiritual orientation. In our first session, it was obvious that any reference to views more spacious or universal than her personal self-esteem and survival issues visibly brought up tension and resistance. Simone's perception and worldview instinctively contracted to a basic "lowest common denominator" level. She projected this contracted picture of herself onto those around her, including me. What was the message in Simone's knee-jerk reaction? What this impulse to contract and control said to me is that Simone had a need to address a survival issue. In spite of her spiritual persona, something in her psyche was holding on to a basic blockage, causing her perception and action to revolve around it. I turned the dialogue to the places which might be the origin of Simone's blockage. Simone's body language and dialogue indicated immediate relief as core survival and self-identity issues—around which her personality had inadvertently become "imprisoned"—came to the forefront. Identifying the anguish, the fears, and the disappointments of the core lack of stability and predictability that she grew up in seemed to release the pressure around these wounds. Over the weeks, it was wonderful watching her personality structure broaden and become more fluid. Once her core tensions had been addressed to some extent, I felt ready to bring my observations of her trajectory to her attention. Together we began building a roadmap of her experience and therapeutic process in the context of a larger and more whole perception of reality. After a few months of our working together, Simone began to spontaneously integrate the spiritual aspects that somehow, at the beginning of our work together, she had idealized but had not felt safe enough to integrate.

No matter at which level of Maslow's pyramid the client functions, they have elements of all the levels. These levels may be disorganized, dormant, or resisted. At other times, they are an implicit part of the client's structure. Likewise, issues, wounds, and blockages can occur at any level of our being. Making these aspects explicit through gentle, nondirective, nonconfrontational statements helps the client gain a deeper sense of self and perspective on their life and issues. This, in itself, is empowering. The client comes to realize that not only is it safe to address their issues, in a gentle way, but it is also a way of loving themselves. Sometimes this occurs naturally and, at other times, I'm not opposed to a gentle invitation. Some clients, like Simone, may repel such interventions. Yet others will grab onto them and feel that a lifelong thirst is being quenched. Working with each client in respect to their worldview, level of functioning, and perception naturally and gradually opens the doors, giving them space to venture out and to breathe.

For most of his career, Maslow placed self-actualization at the top of his pyramid of needs. His dedicated efforts in exploring human potential through introspection and observation led Maslow, toward the end of his career, to identify self-transcendence as the highest need. Peak experiences open up what Maslow termed being-cognition, which drives us toward b-values (being-values). In contrast, d-cognition (deficiency-cognition) motivates us at the lower levels of the pyramid. I find that being-values come from within when we are in open and fluid states of being. Today we know that this involves activating the frontal lobes of the brain. On the contrary, when we are in survival mode, defensive or resistant states, d-cognition and values come to the forefront. This reflects activity of the limbic brain. Although Maslow called his work positive psychology, that term has only recently been brought to the forefront and was developed into a school of psychology in the late 1990s. Maslow defined therapy as a search for value. His openminded, expansionistic, and intuitive thinking opened the doors to a greater psychology.

Rollo May

Rollo May,[2] an existentialist psychologist, explored the human condition in ways that offered understanding and helped individuals to derive meaning from their experiences. Existentialists typically view the human condition as characterized by a sense of confusion and disorientation in regards to a world that seems meaningless or absurd. Existential philosophers such as Kierkegaard and Nietzsche emphasized that exercising our free will to make choices based on core values and beliefs plays a key role in modifying an individual's nature and identity.

In *The Meaning of Anxiety*, inspired by Kierkegaard's writings, May defined anxiety as "the apprehension cued off by a threat to some value which the individual holds essential to his existence as a self . . . [and] anxiety is the dizziness of freedom."[3] A common cause of normal anxiety is our vulnerability to the powers of nature, sickness, fatigue, and eventual death. Another cause is the loss of psychological or spiritual meaning. A third cause is associated with living in a social world defined in part by interpersonal relationships that inevitably dissolve or are broken, often as a corollary of personal growth.

Normal anxiety is proportionate to the objective threat. It does not involve repression or other forms of intrapsychic conflict. Neurotic defense mechanisms are not required for its management and it can be confronted constructively on the level of conscious awareness. May argued that anxiety cannot be avoided, but it can be managed by "reducing [it] to normal levels, and then to use this normal anxiety as stimulation to increase one's awareness, vigilance, zest for living."[4]

To some extent, we must accept various threats as an inevitable and normal part of the human condition, live with them, and treat them as a learning experience. These threats can stimulate us to channel our anxiety in productive ways, such as art, science, and other forms of culture. However, in cases of neurotic anxiety, ultimately the person must confront the source of their anxiety consciously. The therapist's role is to provide a basic context of security in which this can be done without overwhelming the person's sense of self.

In *Love and Will*,[5] May suggested combining the interdependent forces of love and will for dealing with the anxiety of life, as well as the apathy he identified as a rampant problem in American society. He explained that love without will tends to degenerate into sentimentalism or experimentation, and that will without love tends to degenerate into manipulation of others for one's own ends. Through their integration, we can reach out to others and positively influence them, remaining open to them and their positive influences upon us. Through loving relationships and their mutual support and influence, we can successfully and productively confront the anxieties of life as well as find meaning and social engagement.

May felt that the 1960s' sexual revolution reflected an increasingly inverse relation to love and will. He argued that it led to a growing detachment from love and commitment which represented a distraction from or repression of the fear of death.

Vignette—Love and Will

Claire was a successful international model who had moved from New York to London as part of her work. After settling in London, she began suffering from bulimia and complained of anxiety around her relationships with multiple men.

On one hand, she did not know what to do with her overabundance of money, time, and freedom. On the other hand, her only sense of purpose was remaining slim enough to continue her work as a model. Having nowhere to turn in order to address or resolve her anxiety, she turned it against herself. Both her bulimia and her promiscuity were an expression of this anxiety which came out in the form of self-sabotage. In addition to exploring self-image and body-image issues, I sensed that Claire was lacking a sense of purpose. She had made a few references to her concern for the environment. I suggested she might like to look into joining the local chapter of Friends of the Earth. Claire took to this new direction with a passion and sense of purpose that surprised both of us. Her bulimia completely disappeared as did her promiscuity.

Claire's issues stemmed from classic existential angst. When that anxiety had nowhere to go, she turned it against herself. Her adopted behaviors, while providing short-lived respite, ultimately increased her spiral into anxiety. Claire's concern for the environment was channeled into meaningful action and eliminated her troubles. This reflects May's examination of various forms of existential anxiety which led him to the conclusion that both learning to live with anxiety and channeling it into a sense of purpose were means to a more wholesome existence.

Carl Rogers

Person-centered psychology, pioneered by Carl Rogers,[6] forms the foundation of clinical psychological practice today. Fostered as a reaction to the reductive and problem-focused approach of psychoanalysis and behaviorism, person-centered psychology is a wholesome, positive, and potential-based approach.

According to Rogers,[7] to understand another person, it is necessary to understand their frame of reference, perceptual field, sense of self, and values. Seeing and understanding from the client's perspective forms the basis of Roger's person-centered psychotherapy.

The therapist creates a comfortable, nonjudgmental environment with congruence, empathy, and unconditional positive regard toward their client.

Nondirective dialogue invites the client to gain deeper insight into their ideas and unresolved emotional and mental tensions, enabling resolution. Creating a safe space enables clients to walk through current and past difficult situations, and bring to awareness and release disharmonious beliefs, attitudes, and behaviors. As the client is able to bring out delicate issues, it releases the pressure and stigma attached to them. The client will experience an increasing sense of comfort and freedom to be themselves. Finally, self-disclosure in this safe environment wakes up the client's innate drive to self-actualization, finding their own sense of self and solutions to their problems. The person-centered approach empowers clients to take responsibility and proactively engage in their therapeutic process. They develop a more healthy, flexible, and realistic sense of themselves and the world, as well as a willingness to grow toward the fulfillment of their higher potential.

Vignette—Person-Centered Presence

At the beginning of our therapeutic relationship, Janie was a jumpy, nervous, and underweight young woman. Her speech was hesitant as if she had to weigh each word for fear of retribution. Janie explained that during her childhood her parents constantly shouted and occasionally ended up throwing and breaking dishes and other items. Janie cowered in the sidelines, eventually taking refuge in her bedroom and her love of reading. Her relationships with others were inhibited by her fear of their potential volatility. I felt her pain and her fear and sensed how important it was for me to provide a steady and comforting presence for Janie. Over the weeks, Janie's hesitant speech turned into a torrent, unleashing anger, frustration, and sadness in its wake. I sat steady, listening, sharing her pain, validating her experiences, ensuring a safe and holding space. In the fourth month of our work together, Janie's language began reflecting an awareness of her emotions and nervous mannerisms. Alongside this awareness came moments of expansion and fluidity. Her torrent of raw stories and emotions gave way to occasional moments of excitement, a sense of a new life opening up before her. I shifted with her, reflecting back to her not only the change in content but also in her tone and body language. She was able to see that as her unexpressed emotions and core wounds came to light, more wholesome feelings were emerging. As the process continued, rather than being in a continual state of distress, she had started to go back and forth between difficult areas and what I would call an emerging life force and ability to open into the present.

Person-centered dialogue, simply through providing skilled listening in the context of a safe environment, invites us to unveil the root causes of our suffering. From there we can start to digest and come to terms with them. We can gradually leave behind the mechanisms that, in an effort to make them bearable, imprison us and stop us from evolving toward wholeness.

The person-centered approach introduced me, as a young and budding therapist, to the core idea of skilled presence: being with the client in their world, at their pace and in their language. Before that, my work had a different structure and tone. It is not entirely comfortable to remember the directive and goal-oriented way I worked with clients believing that they had to get somewhere in relationship to my high-flying worldview. Working from a person-centered approach has helped eliminate the bombastic enthusiasm of my early days as a therapist. Having full faith in clients' tendency toward self-actualization and resilience makes these early memories more comfortable. To this day, in spite of my strong resonance with the person-centered approach, I have to admit that the purely nondirective style does not fully suit my nature or worldview. I try to find a balance between being driven by my intuition and philosophical inclinations while fully respecting the client's worldview.

LIMITATIONS OF HUMANISTIC AND PERSON-CENTERED APPROACHES

The humanistic approach focuses on human potential rather than on pathology. The foremost criticism of these approaches is a lack of ability to diagnose and treat serious pathologies. Certainly, while we, as humanistic therapists, do not want to give our clients labels or put them in boxes, a semester or two of training in psychopathology is very useful. In so doing, we are not confined to the mainstream psychiatric approach. It might be appropriate to find a course that not only covers the *DSM* categories but also explores psychopathology from other angles. Alternative views exist from the esoteric explanations of Rudolph Steiner to the comprehensive, multidimensional model of Ken Wilber. Finding a course in psychopathology with a broader orientation provided me with the basics but also with a perspective that was sufficiently holistic so as to satisfy me. This has been very useful on many occasions in my clinical practice.

Although the person-centered approach has proven to be effective and the concept of being person-centered, been widely adopted as a core way of being with clients, no matter what the orientation of the therapist, the behaviorists criticize it for being too unstructured. In some ways, while I subscribe, by and large, to working in a person-centered way, sometimes I feel it is useful to be direct or directive. While being too directive can prevent clients from finding and engaging in their own process, my experience with Jared demonstrates that being too nondirective can lead to turning around in the hamster wheel.

Vignette—A Directive Kick in the Behind

Jared consulted me when I was working as a student counselor at a university in northeast England. His fears were paralyzing him and narrowing his perspective on who he was and what he wanted to do with his life. Over the weeks, gaining perspective on his fears brought him visible relief. He started to experiment with changing dress styles and developed a sense of humor about the ways he had been trapped in his fears in our early sessions. Toward the end of his final year at the university, Jared brought up a fresh view on his fear of his girlfriend. He cowered around her anticipating judgment and retribution. He walked on egg-shells rather than being himself. We explored this in a sometimes deep and soul-ful way, and yet at other times, he saw it in a humorous light. On the day of his last session, I felt both a bit rebellious and like joining in with his humor. Those were the days when we used to wear steel-tipped Doc Marten boots with long skirts. As we said goodbye, I wished him well, encouraged him to get out and achieve his potential, not letting his fears get the better of him. Then, I playfully added, "If you catch yourself falling prey to your fears, give me a call. I'll come over there and give you a kick on the bum with my steel-tipped boots!" We had a light-hearted laugh and said goodbye. I guess I was showing him that he could keep his fears in perspective and in check with a light-hearted view of them.

Sometimes person-centered is misinterpreted as self-centered. Becoming aware of our emotions and building a healthy, balanced way of working with them when they arise is an essential part of *hygiène de vie,* or life hygiene. I do not believe that our experiences should start and stop with awareness of our emotions. And yet, in the person-centered milieu, although not the only ones who fall into it, therapists sometimes misinterpret the approach, mistaking the way for the means. The self-awareness we develop by learning to pay attention to what we are feeling inside, unless it is kept in context, can turn into bellybuttonism, a trap that leads us to swim directionlessly in a world based on awareness of ourselves and our emotions. My rule of thumb: Be centered, not self-centered.

While humanistic psychology acknowledges the potential for a human being to evolve toward his higher potential and take full advantage of his life, it does not specifically address spirituality or step into that zone which attempts to partner the ego with the soul. This was the biggest challenge of my studies and associations with colleagues. When attending meetings and conferences, I find that about half of my colleagues have a real aversion to spiritual matters while the other half have deeply involved spiritual lives which they integrate into their clinical practice much as I do.

While doing my masters program, I spent my six-week summer break with my Indian guru in our Austrian retreat center. I enjoyed the simple and austere lifestyle, 4 a.m. meditations, light vegetarian meals, quiet time in the gardens, and inspiring lectures by my guru and other disciples. I have been on many retreats over the years. I usually arrive for my retreats in vary-ing states of mental activity and sometimes agitation. I have found that if I spend three days and three nights in silence, avoiding all mental stimulation,

I can reach a state where the mind is completely silent. Once I have established that silence, I can resume simple activities, like helping around the ashram while easily mastering my thoughts and states of mind. From there, the meditations can get very deep with insights into myself, experiences of oneness, love, and peace to which words can do no justice. These powerful experiences and insights have, on countless occasions, resulted in permanent foundational shifts in my personality. On that challenging and blissful retreat, I enjoyed a constant sense of inner peace. At the end of summer, I headed back to Durham to resume my course. Part of each class was spent listening to lectures, but most of the time was spent practicing psychotherapy with each other in pairs. On our first meeting after summer break, after a brief sharing about our summer breaks and intentions for the semester, we were asked to pair up with a classmate for clinical practice. I chose the person whom I felt was the most inclined to understand and appreciate my postretreat glow. When it was my turn to be the client, I shared some of what I had experienced during my retreat, of course, expressing my deep feelings of bliss and inner peace. My classmate attempted to paraphrase my words in a characteristic person-centered way aimed at making me, the client, feel deeply heard. I broke out laughing as my words came back to me, nothing like in the way I'd expressed them: "I am hearing that you found a subpersonality you would call inner peace." In my experience, inner peace stems from the higher self; it is beyond personality but can stream in and light up our personality when we simply let go and let it come in.

CONCLUSION

The emergence of humanistic psychology, reflecting a conscious effort to explore the further reaches of human potential, is an indicator that psychology is evolving in consciousness. The Association for Humanistic Psychology is composed of various schools and techniques striving in this direction. It is now closely associated with the Association for Transpersonal Psychology reflecting its evolution toward our higher possibilities. Humanistic conferences afford a mix of deep, rich, and purely humanistic workshops and speakers and yet others who are deeply and overtly spiritual.

TRANSPERSONAL PSYCHOLOGY—JAMES, JUNG, ASSAGIOLI, GROF, AND VAUGHAN

As psychology evolves, it reintegrates more aspects of the spectrum of human experience and potential. Transpersonal psychology took the comprehensive, expansionist outlook of humanistic psychology to the next step by reintegrating the notion, potential, and experiences of spirituality into the scope of psychology. Sometimes it is also referred to as "spiritual psychology." Sri Aurobindo and other mystical schools explain that there is a pull toward evolving in consciousness, toward our highest state of being. Each human being experiences and expresses that pull in their own unique way. This is essentially a spiritualized view of Maslow's theory of self-actualization. This pull inevitably draws us through the experiences we need to eventually achieve our full potential. Upon discovering transpersonal psychology, I began to feel I had more room to breathe. The mystical worldview that I had been single-mindedly focused on since my discovery of meditation could finally start to grow pillars and foundations, the very beginnings of a bridge between spirit and matter.

Brant Cortright[8] says transpersonal psychology can be understood as the melding of the wisdom of the world's spiritual traditions with the learning of modern psychology. The term transpersonal refers to that which is inherently spiritual or beyond the ordinary, limited perception of consciousness. It sheds light on nonordinary states of consciousness and encourages their widespread acknowledgment and understanding so these experiences may contribute to healthy growth and development of individuals. Roberto Assagioli argued that,

> Scientifically speaking [transpersonal] is a better word [than spiritual]; it is more precise and, in a certain sense, neutral in that it points to that which is beyond or above ordinary personality. Furthermore it avoids confusion with many things which are now called spiritual but which are actually pseudo-spiritual or para-psychological.[9]

A wide variety of phenomena are studied under the name of transpersonal psychology, but the common factors are: nonordinary states of consciousness, transcendence, man's spiritual potential, and spirituality. The underlying principle is to understand the full range of transpersonal experiences, the factors leading to their onset, and their contribution and meaning to our experience as human beings with respect to our spiritual potential. Due to its holistic, inclusive characteristic, transpersonal psychology departs from its predecessors in its outlook towards other schools of psychology. Cortright sums it up succinctly, "the idea in transpersonal psychology is to integrate the three previous forces in psychology with the perennial wisdom of the ages. None of these models were seen as wrong from a transpersonal perspective, just limited."[10]

Transpersonal states are experiences and perceptions that transcend our ordinary waking consciousness such as: intuition, conversion, shamanistic openings, premonitions, premonitory dreams, and other nonordinary states of consciousness. These experiences have always occurred and are widespread throughout history and cultures. While their interpretation is historically and culturally centric, a universality becomes apparent when they are studied in depth. Far from being pathological, they have been proven to contribute to human development—greater understanding, compassion, and sense of meaning. They actively lead to individual and collective change and transformation. Transpersonal psychology brings significant therapeutic benefits through acknowledging and exploring spiritual experiences, beliefs, and aspirations.

The predominant scientific model of psychology does not acknowledge nonordinary states and experiences. Their meaning and relationship to our psychological and spiritual development are lost. This means that in a therapeutic setting they can be judged, or worse yet, diagnosed as pathologies rather than heard, understood, and addressed.

The way a transpersonal experience contributes to a person's process of evolution depends both on the individual having the experience and on the understanding and skill of the helping professional. Due to the nonordinary nature of transpersonal experiences and the general lack of understanding about them, some individuals seek help in managing or understanding these experiences. Working with a therapist who is nonjudgmental and well-versed in transpersonal states can help the individual to optimize the potential of these experiences for stimulating psychological growth. It is unfortunate that the medical profession, modern psychiatry and psychology, limited by the scientific paradigm does not have the ability or motivation to understand and guide individuals who experience nonordinary states. This may lead to tragic results since a genuine opportunity for breakthrough can instead be labeled and treated as a mental illness, turning it into a psychological breakdown.

In cultures based on ancient tradition, nonordinary states of consciousness are an integral part of life. Healers, shamans, or other individuals with wisdom and insight might be called upon to accompany people experiencing such states, as necessary. In the West, however, transpersonal experiences are often overlooked and misunderstood. In so doing, we pass up the profound opportunities they provide us with for self-understanding and connecting to a sense of deeper, universal meaning. A balanced and fluid ego structure enables us to accommodate and learn from subtle experiences and integrate the insights and healing they provide into our daily lives.

Transpersonal psychology adds new dimensions to the scientific understanding of human experience. A transpersonal therapist takes into consideration imbalances and disturbances that can occur on all levels of our being, from the densest physical level to the subtlest spiritual planes. Many imbalances can stem from subtle levels of consciousness, so it is necessary to understand them in reference to the levels of consciousness from which they originate. This allows us to develop appropriate modalities for treatment. This multidimensional view helps to avoid pooling all subtle experiences together and labeling them as psychosis. Through learning to distinguish between spiritual opening and psychosis, mental health professionals can avoid pathologizing all subtle realm experiences and can assess and treat better those who require spiritual or psychiatric assistance.

Transpersonal psychology also addresses the therapeutic use of mind-altering substances. Maslow[11] did a study in which he used LSD to induce "peak experiences" in patients suffering from alcoholism. He discovered that patients who had a peak experience had a much higher recovery rate and less relapse due to the perspective engendered by transcendent visions and peak experiences. Scientific exploration of nonordinary states of consciousness would help make it a recognized aspect of the field of mental health. Furthermore, it would add another piece to the puzzle of consciousness and make a step toward a more complete vision of human life.

We can credit the development of the transpersonal psychology movement to the early thinkers who acknowledged man's transcendent possibilities. Among the early psychologists who preceded the formal establishment of the field, but who contributed greatly to its thought and impetus, two theorists stand out: William James and Carl Jung.

William James

William James[12] was the first professor of psychology at Harvard University and in the United States. At a time when psychoanalysis was in full development, Mircea Eliade concluded that William James did not adhere to the "fallacy of reducing states of mind to organic states or dispositions" and instead argued that, "man's religion is the deepest and wisest thing in his life."[13] He was one of the earliest psychologists to apply scientific thought to psychology, including the psychology of religion and mystical experience and, on a more practical level, the psychological effects of Eastern spiritual practices. Although his research was scientific, he did not limit his theories to materialistic science.

In his two-volume *Principles of Psychology* published in 1890, James based his approach to psychology on pragmatism and the introspective exploration of his own consciousness. He argued that "introspective observation is what we have to rely on first and foremost and always."[14] He believed the value of any truth was utterly dependent upon its use to the person who held it. As a radical empiricist, he viewed the world as a mosaic of diverse experiences that can never be halted for an entirely objective analysis. The mind of the observer and the simple act of observation will affect the outcome of any empirical approach to truth. James deduced that consciousness consists of many levels, not just the conscious and subconscious. While waking consciousness allows us to navigate our way through ordinary life, our perception of it is altered through external factors and the internal resonances or reactions they engender.

James explored many aspects of human consciousness, from physiological processes of the senses to memory and judgment, psychic perception, and higher states of consciousness. James' classic work, *The Varieties of Religious Experience*,[15] covers his philosophy of religion, interpreting religious and mystical experiences according to his pragmatic leanings. He asserted that mystical experiences are a natural occurrence for man and a perfectly normal part of man's potential. He concluded that mystic revelations are subjective and only hold meaning for those to whom they are revealed. James explored his own mystical experiences, sometimes aided with such substances as nitrous oxide and peyote which led him to the belief that consciousness is flexible and has a functional nature. Extraordinary experiences allow individuals to observe, analyze, and adjust their beliefs and behavior in a different light. Unlike many of his contemporaries, James recognized humanity's inner or spiritual intelligence and drive toward wholeness. The importance of a multidimensional perception of reality and experience was fundamental to James' conception of psychology. He felt that no theory could be truly scientific if it did not address metaphysical realities.

Carl Jung: Transpersonal Aspects

Chapter 1 covered Jung's beginnings in psychoanalysis. Jung could not remain within the confines of Freud's views. He was driven by the desire to "free [himself] from all unconscious and therefore uncriticized assumptions as to the world in general."[16] Jung attempted to develop his understanding of human experience through decoding his phenomenological exploration beyond ordinary states of consciousness. Like James, Carl Jung's explorations into psychology ventured into man's relationship to himself and the inner, intuitive realms, acknowledging subtle and mysterious aspects of human experience and potential.

Jung's work reflects his strong desire for addressing higher consciousness and a perception of reality which is increasingly profound and free of illusion. He was realistic in recognizing that we cannot know when we have achieved freedom from conditioning, but he felt that in order to become truly ourselves, it was nevertheless important to try. This approach is also basic to the philosophy of yoga and is, perhaps, what led Jung to explore Eastern thought and yogic philosophy.

Jung believed that the ultimate quest in therapy, and in life, is the process of individuation or achieving ultimate wholeness. This process involves exploring and integrating elements from our conscious and unconscious mind and establishing balance between our faculties of sensing, intuition, thinking, and feeling. He observed that in the later years of life, the individuation process involves a greater need to find inner meaning. I have found this true in my work with older clients. Perhaps the meaning we seek as we get older gives us a sense of purpose and fulfillment that helps us feel more at peace with such things as the ups and downs of life and the inevitability of death. Jung explored the theories of alchemy in great detail, a journey of learning to listen and align to the voice of the inner self. He described his theory of individuation as a psychological approach to alchemy.

Jung's explorations into synchronicity touch on a body of wisdom found in ancient mystical traditions involving the multidimensionality of consciousness. Synchronicity refers to the phenomenon of the coming together in space and time of two independent but related processes of thought or activity. For example, we may be thinking of wanting to meet with someone, and suddenly that person coincidentally appears before us. Two people may simultaneously come upon similar unusual or creative ideas. Several seemingly unrelated circumstances may arrange themselves in such a way that they lead us to a certain outcome we had been unsuccessfully trying to achieve. When consciousness is perceived as multidimensional, going beyond the material and conceptual (intellectual) levels and into more subtle levels of consciousness, one can perceive the unity of consciousness. Jung's theory of synchronicity touches on this universal truth.

Eastern thought began to intrigue Jung as it responded to his quest for knowledge in a way that Western psychology would not allow at that time. When Jadunath Sinha, a twentieth century philosopher and spiritual seeker, was writing his works on Indian psychology, Jung began delving into the mysteries of yoga. He worked with Richard Wilhelm, the famous Sinologist, and then traveled to India in the early 1930s. In his essay *Yoga and the West*, Jung observed that Western civilization had developed a separation between intellect and intuition. He felt that balance between these two was essential and that due to the gap created by the West's retreat from a spiritual worldview in favor of a scientific one, there was an imbalance and a lack of meaning for many people. This gap began to be filled by Indian spirituality and yoga due to its potential to address and reunite intellect and intuition, science and soul.

Jung interpreted the psychological aspects of kundalini yoga, an ancient technique for awakening the inherent but dormant spiritual energy that opens our consciousness, bringing with it the possibility to realize our higher potential. In 1932 Jung gave a seminar in Switzerland and the lectures were published in *Psychology of Kundalini Yoga*.[17] While he was unable to penetrate to the very depths of the mysteries of kundalini yoga, he was able to grasp aspects of Eastern thought that were accessible to him, especially those pertaining to Western psychology. In Indian terms, this concerns the psychological processes related to the first five chakras, the subtle centers of psychic energy arranged along the vertebrae from the sex center to the highest center at the top of the head. He did not feel that the sixth and seventh chakras, which relate to the inner subtle and higher consciousness, were accessible to Westerners and steered away from them. In fact, Jung did not feel that yoga was suitable for Westerners: "There are many different kinds of yoga and Europeans often become hypnotized by it, but it is essentially Eastern, no European has the necessary patience and it is not right for him."[18] Nevertheless, many of Jung's perceptions provided inspiration to modern psychology in the West. Jung was one of the first Western psychologists to show interest in the East and to delve deeply into its meaning and relevance to the field of human psychology, consciousness, and potential.

Jung has been criticized by some transpersonal psychologists for his view that yoga is not suitable for Westerners. Although it is true that many Westerners face the obstacles of an analytical mindset, such as unwillingness to surrender to a guru and a strong individualistic will, these are mere obstacles just as Indian sadhaks (aspirants) face obstacles of a different nature. In the ascent to soul consciousness, obstacles can and will be overcome.

While Jung did not fully do justice to yogic philosophy, he was fundamental in acknowledging and exploring it in the West and laying the groundwork for the schools that would follow him. Jung's contribution to psychology opened doors to a deeper, more complete understanding of man and consciousness. The depth of his perceptions gained through introspection and inner observation, rather than just analysis, emphasize the importance of phenomenology, or self-experience, in building self-understanding. His consistent seeking into and beyond the limitations of the thought of his contemporaries, along with his sense of scientific inquiry, rigor, and introspection, set a precedent for a vision of psychology that moves past the limitations of the scientific paradigm and in the direction of expansion and evolution of consciousness. Jung went beyond the limits of both ordinary human consciousness and the scientific approach to psychology and was a pioneer in the effort to move toward a more complete vision of man and consciousness.

Roberto Assagioli

Dr. Roberto Assagioli,[19] an Italian psychologist, developed the school of psychosynthesis. He began his career as a psychoanalyst and member of the Zurich Freud Society along with Carl Jung. Like Jung, Assagioli's striving for wholeness and achievement of humanity's higher potentials led him to venture beyond the scope of classical psychoanalytic theory early in his career. He felt intuitively drawn to develop theories and a therapeutic approach that address a broad spectrum of consciousness. One can easily assume that Assagioli's detailed and clear description of the functioning of the subtle aspects of consciousness, which appeared to be the foundation of his work, stem from his connections with esoteric movements. His quest for exploring human potential, rather than the more limited focus on pathology, and his descriptions of transpersonal realms of consciousness classify him as part of the movement of transpersonal psychology.

Assagioli expanded Jung's notion of the unconscious by distinguishing between the lower, middle, and higher unconscious or superconscious (figure 2.1). The collective unconscious as defined in his theory was wider and more inclusive than individual levels of consciousness. "Assagioli wanted to distinguish between the archaic and primitive contents of the collective unconscious and the superconscious contents of the same."[20] Corresponding with his division of the subconscious, he defined two types of archetypes. Archaic archetypes are referred to as prepersonal, coming from a level of consciousness that has not yet been differentiated through the individuation process. Superconscious archetypes are transpersonal and come from the higher unconscious. Assagioli further differentiated between the higher states of consciousness in the superconscious and the Spirit or Self. His theory, illustrated in his egg diagram, demonstrates three main levels of consciousness and their interrelationship, adding precision and depth to our understanding of multidimensionality:

1. The Lower Unconscious.
2. The Middle Unconscious.
3. The Higher Unconscious or Superconscious.
4. The Area of Consciousness.
5. The Conscious 'I'.
6. The Higher 'I' or Self.
7. The Collective Unconscious.

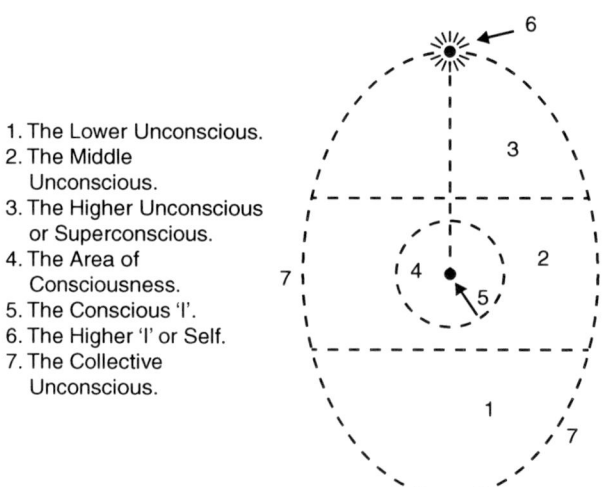

FIGURE 2.1 Assagioli's Egg Diagram. *Source:* www.psychosynthesisonline.com.

The Lower Unconscious (1) relates to the denser aspects of our consciousness such as the physical drives we require for functioning and the parts of the self that are repressed. It relates to "Freud's unconscious arena of fundamental drives and elementary activities."[21] The Middle Unconscious (2) is the part of our awareness currently not being used but that which gives us ready access for our daily functioning. The Higher Unconscious or Superconscious (3) is where our higher qualities, nature, and perceptions reside as well as our evolutionary drive. The Area of Consciousness (4) consists of the immediate activities occurring in the mind at each moment. The Conscious "I" (5) includes aspects of our "self" of which we are aware. The Transpersonal Self (6) represents the higher spiritual Self. And finally, the Collective Unconscious (7) relates to the unconscious reservoir of the collectivity of beings.[22] From a multidimensional perspective, our perception of ourselves as separate beings is in the material plane, the plane of consciousness in which we function on a normal basis. Intuition, instinct, and premonitions come from subtle levels of consciousness such as collective unconscious or transpersonal levels which reach our normal, waking awareness.

Personal and spiritual development make our outer waking awareness (ego) more permeable so that it does not dominate the field of consciousness. We gain access to deeper, more subtle parts of ourselves and the various levels of the unconscious, collective unconscious, and superconscious. Note that in Assagioli's diagram, the lines between the different parts of consciousness are dotted. This is because it is possible to move freely between the different realms of consciousness—from the waking consciousness to the subtle or unconscious parts of the self. The more open and fluid our consciousness is, the more easily we can flow between the different levels. Psychotherapy, deep relaxation, breathing exercises, and other practices open up the flow. In contrast, mental rigidity, fight or flight, and other defensive states turn the dotted lines into solid lines as we close ourselves into the normal waking conscious (4). Assagioli sought not only to understand and theorize about human consciousness but also to help individuals develop. This led to the creation of his therapeutic system of psychosynthesis.

Psychosynthesis unites psychology with universal wisdom traditions in a therapeutic approach that aims to create harmony and congruence between the different parts of the person through harnessing our innate drive to healing and wholeness. In psychosynthesis, the spiritual self plays the important role of bringing higher qualities and deeper meaning to our lives. We center around the new identity that emerges through the process of our therapeutic work. The process begins with constructing, purifying, and then surrendering our sense of self (ego) in order to realize and center our consciousness around our core spiritual nature. In order to facilitate harmony between all the parts of the self and realize our higher potentials, psychosynthesis seeks an integration of the higher and lower aspects of the consciousness and self.

A wide variety of techniques and methods may be used, including dialogue, dreamwork, guided imagery, affirmations, meditation, art therapy, journaling, drama therapy, bodywork, and various cognitive-behavioral techniques.

Stanislav Grof

Stanislav Grof[23] was trained in Czechoslovakia as a psychiatrist and Freudian psychoanalyst. He later emigrated to the United States and became one of the foremost figures of transpersonal psychology. His pioneering work explored possibilities for healing, growing, and understanding the human psyche through the use of nonordinary states of consciousness.

He is known for his early studies of LSD and its effects on the psyche—the field of psychedelic psychotherapy. Following the illegalization of LSD in the late 1960s, Grof began exploring and developing means of inducing nonordinary states without drugs. His technique of holotropic breathwork involves inducing nonordinary states through deep breathing and sensory stimulus in a supportive environment.

Holotropic breathwork opens up the barriers of consciousness, giving access to the various aspects of subconscious: personal unconscious, family unconscious, ancestral unconscious, cultural unconscious, and other forms of collective unconscious. Giving access to these "places" enabled him to identify and elaborate on the development of the perinatal matrices, the experiences, perceptions, and impressions we receive from conception to birth, and the role they play in our self-definition and subsequent behavior. This work is a valuable contribution to our understanding of the developmental spectrum.

Grof distinguishes between hylotropic and holotropic consciousness. Hylotropic states refer to the "normal, everyday experience of consensus reality." Holotropic means the mystical, meditative, or drug-induced psychedelic experiences that are "oriented toward wholeness." Holotropic theory places theoretical and therapeutic importance on experiences not accessible in ordinary states of awareness such as the perinatal matrix. In Grof's terms, the hylotropic relates to the Hindu concept of namarupa (name and matter), the separate, individual, illusory self and the holotropic to Atman-Brahman, the universal, absolute, supreme soul and self-soul. He explains that experiencing holotropic states can lead to profound changes in perception, emotion, and thought processes.

Grof believes that the holotropic mode has been uniquely de-emphasized in the modern West. He writes:

All the cultures in human history except the Western industrial civilization have held holotropic states of consciousness in great esteem. They induced them whenever they wanted to connect to their deities, other dimensions of reality, and with the forces of nature. They also used them for diagnosing and healing, cultivation of extrasensory perception, and artistic inspiration. They spent much time and energy to develop safe and effective ways of inducing them.[24]

In contrast, he argues that in contemporary Western psychiatry, holotropic states are often categorized as psychotic.

Holotropic breathwork comprises five elements: group process, intensified breathing (hyperventilation) accompanied by powerful sense stimuli (auditory, touch) and finally drawing or painting images from the experience. It amplifies psychic processes, facilitating the psyche's natural capacity for healing. Although individual sessions are possible, it is typically done with groups arranged in pairs who rotate roles as "breather" and "sitter," the latter who is simply available to assist the breather but not interfere in the process. Each breather lies on a mat with the eyes closed. The combination of breath and loud, primal music evokes nonordinary states of consciousness. The breath expands the state of awareness. It brings about a healing journey through the breather's psyche. The journey is facilitated by the sitter but guided by the breather's own conscience.

Spiritual Emergency

Stanislav and Christina Grof have done groundbreaking work on the topic of spiritual emergency. Spiritual emergencies are overpowering experiences or episodes of transpersonal states of consciousness resulting from an evolutionary crisis rather than mental illness. If a spiritual experience is too strong and the person experiencing it is too fragile, ungrounded, or unstructured, they can be thrown off balance and get lost in chaotic and troublesome experiences.

Grof explains that such experiences may occur spontaneously, or they may be triggered by emotional stress, disease, accident, psychedelic drugs, or various types of meditative and other spiritual practices. Others have observed that spiritual experiences can be set off by any activity involving singular concentration, such as running or giving birth. In some cases they may arise in the context of existing mental illness, complicating their differentiation and treatment. Grof distinguished various types of spiritual emergencies, but he explains that all of them represent "dynamic exteriorizations of deep unconscious and superconscious realms of the human psyche, which form one indivisible, multidimensional continuum without any clear boundaries."[25] Traditional psychiatric and psychological therapists may not distinguish between spiritual emergency and mental illness if they do not acknowledge and understand the reality of transpersonal experiences.

Research into the phenomena of spiritual emergency and other transpersonal experiences has potential to enrich the field of mental health in important ways. If they are understood and treated as difficult stages in a natural developmental process, they can result in positive emotional and psychological healing and growth, personality transformation, and evolution of consciousness. Through making sense of nonordinary experience/crises, distinguishing them from psychosis and learning to work with our clients who are experiencing them, the benefits to individuals and society are evident. After much negotiation, some types of spiritual crisis have been included in the *DSM-V* published in 2013.

The Grofs contributed valuable observations in the area of addiction by drawing attention to the idea that addictions to drugs, alcohol, as well as other substances or activities may represent a misplaced search for transpersonal wholeness. Personal crises, commonly referred to as "hitting bottom," sometimes lead to a spiritual rebirth.

Frances Vaughan

Frances Vaughan is a founding member of the Institute of Transpersonal Psychology and a past president of the Association for Transpersonal Psychology. While closely aligned with the school of transpersonal psychology, her views are largely influenced by Ken Wilber's integral psychology, which we will examine in chapter 5. Vaughan's writings on transpersonal psychotherapy perhaps best represent the state of the art in this field.

Vaughan views transpersonal psychotherapy as aiming "at the integration of physical, emotional, mental, and spiritual aspects of well-being."[26] Like traditional therapies, it aims at normal healthy functioning, while recognizing the healing potential of transpersonal experiences. This multidimensional approach allows her to explore spiritual issues from a psychological perspective. The client may be encouraged to explore the inner psyche when this is likely to lead to the discovery of inner resources and capacities for self-healing. When the client is specifically seeking to understand their own transpersonal experiences, the transpersonal therapist affirms the potential for healing and growth that may come from such experiences and does not pathologize or otherwise invalidate them. At the same time, Vaughan recognizes that an important task of psychotherapy is to help the client stabilize such experiences by integrating them into everyday behaviors, values, attitudes, subjective experience, and interpersonal relationships.

Vaughan's approach to psychotherapy draws from a variety of methods in order to address its broad aims which include physical, emotional, cognitive, and spiritual well-being. Her work employs techniques both from traditional psychotherapies and spiritual disciplines. Diet and exercise, bioenergetics, hatha yoga, tai chi, and movement therapies may be used to increase awareness of subtle physical sensations and increase mind–body integration. The release of emotional blocks for healing wounds of the past and freeing the person to live fully in the present may be facilitated through breathwork, guided imagery, and dreamwork.

On a more cognitive level, mind training helps clients to think differently about their painful experiences, so they may begin to see difficulties as learning experiences and learn to look at both themselves and others with greater compassion. Clients may be encouraged to confront existential questions of value and meaning in their life, especially when circumstances, life, or the proximity of death presses for this type of inner exploration. Imagery and dreamwork, including dream analysis, active imagination, and gestalt dialogue techniques, are useful for building ego strength, initiating new ego development, or exploring transpersonal dimensions of the psyche. Meditation is used to increase self-awareness, and concentration techniques help focus and calm the mind. Insight practice can be useful for uncovering repressed memories and unconscious tendencies that need to be cleared in order to open the way for a more harmonious life and personal evolution. Concentration techniques can also be used to disidentify with the contents of the consciousness and experience pure awareness or consciousness directly.

Through providing a safe place where the dark regions of the psyche may be freely discussed and explored, a confessional role may be taken to facilitate the acceptance and reintegration of rejected or repressed aspects of the self. Various techniques may be used, when deemed appropriate, to induce altered states of consciousness—such as music, fasting, chanting, shamanic drumming, or holotropic breathwork to induce their accompanying therapeutic effects.

Vaughan emphasizes the development and characteristics of the transpersonal psychotherapist. Therapists who have personally explored the transpersonal domain, experientially as well as intellectually, will be better able to help others in this endeavor. The therapist should be attending to his or her own inner work and spiritual practice. Vaughan also stresses that the therapist should be a model of authenticity, in touch with his or her own deeper self and soul, and be genuinely caring for the soul of the client.

LIMITATIONS OF TRANSPERSONAL PSYCHOLOGY

Transpersonal psychology addresses a larger spectrum of consciousness, human experience, and potential than its predecessor, humanistic psychology. It, too, is a step on the way to the larger, more encompassing school of integral psychology.

Transpersonal psychology has been criticized for its tendency to be focused on altered states of consciousness, mystical or spiritual experiences to the exclusion of ordinary states of consciousness, developmental stages, and other basics of human experience. On the opposite or highest end of the spectrum, transpersonal psychology tends to forget the capstone, or highest potential of man: transformation of consciousness and spiritual realization.

> There's a lot of things in yoga psychology that are very well defined, based on thousands of years of experience, that transpersonal psychology does not know about. . . . Transpersonal psychology is still confused. You need Sri Aurobindo [see chapter 4] in order to understand it, but not the other way round. You need him to clarify some of the fuzzy issues of transpersonal psychology, because they don't know what the difference is between the psychic being and the self, and the psychic being and the pranic being.[27]

Transpersonal psychology has something to gain by acknowledging the tried and tested ancient traditions descended from realized, spiritual masters and their corresponding disciplines. Stanislav Grof explains that his three main approaches to self-exploration—use of LSD in psychotherapy, spiritual crisis, and holotropic breathwork—"do not require the same degree of commitment and personal sacrifice as the ancient spiritual practices. They are more accessible and practical for westerners who are trapped in the complexity of modern life."[28] Grof seems to confuse peak and nonordinary experiences with the maturation process that comes with time and sincere, long-standing effort. The trials and tribulations of personal and spiritual growth are a necessary process for the development of the qualities, strengths, clarity, and understanding we need to ultimately realize our highest potential. While nonordinary experiences are often part of our evolution and development, the highest goal of human life is psycho-spiritual development leading to the realization of our greatest potential and not nonordinary experiences.

Traditional yogic methods for our spiritual development are slow, steady, and lead us gradually along the path of our psycho-spiritual development toward our highest potential. They provide us with insights and the strength and balance we need for our continued growth. Some approaches to yogic philosophy warn students to avoid focusing on nonordinary states as it is too easy to get spellbound and lose focus on the higher potential of spiritual realization.

In regards to the general psychological community, transpersonal psychology's overemphasis on nonordinary states of consciousness has resulted in the marginalization of their valid and pertinent contributions and sometimes led to its association with the new age. The result is that the field does not get the recognition and accreditation that could be mutually beneficial to transpersonal psychology and the larger mental health and medical communities.

STEPPING STONES—HUMANISTIC AND TRANSPERSONAL PSYCHOLOGIES

As the definition of psychology expands through humanistic and transpersonal psychologies, the schools become stepping-stones in themselves. Humanistic psychology aims to explore self-actualizing individuals and, in a sense, to reclaim the human element by moving beyond a mechanistic and theoretical approach and jumping into a more human way of working with individuals. And yet, humanistic psychology only borders on spiritual issues, and proponents of these schools range from being "allergic to spirituality" to being profoundly spiritual. Many of the major proponents of humanistic psychology in their later writings began to feel that humanistic psychology was only a step on the way toward a more holistic approach.

Transpersonal psychology, in some senses, takes over where humanistic psychology leaves off. Addressing nonordinary, subtle, and transcendent states of consciousness that have been excluded from the previous models of psychology opens up widespread possibilities for contributing to man's understanding of spiritual dimensions and their contribution to our overall development. Transpersonal psychology has thus made a unique and vital contribution to clinical psychology by providing a context for understanding and helping those suffering from spiritual disorders and disorders with spiritual dimensions. Nonordinary states of consciousness are a fact of life for the majority of people; therefore, including them in our psychological theories and approaches makes a lot of sense. So, while we start out with a largely materialistic and mechanistic worldview, we reclaim our right to be human, and not just a by-product of our DNA, neurons, and past experience. We finally grasp that there may be something deeper and more transcendent that makes each one of us unique and yet part of the whole of humanity and the universe.

CONCLUSION

Psychology began with the Greeks whose philosophy included study of the soul, breath, and spirit. Over time, however, the outer physical dimensions of psychology took precedence, with an emphasis on physiology. Despite the developments of a few isolated pioneers, the early period of modern psychology enclosed its view and corresponding practices into the box of reductionism, stressing the physical, the environment and objective measurement. Humanistic and transpersonal psychologies emerged as an answer to the reductive nature of psychoanalysis and behaviorism. They moved away from a pathology and problem-oriented focus to a positive, potential-oriented approach.

There are two major directions in psychology, each one reflecting, in varying degrees, the polarities of contract and control, the drive behind our tendency toward reductionism, and integration and evolution which result in expansion. The first axis, as mentioned in chapter 1, is a reflection of the ego or the outer nature of man. It is driven by fear. To compensate for that fear, we are compelled into outer world identifications and achievements. This leads to fragmentation of our being and mistaking the finite outer and material realms for the whole of reality. Western culture's tendency to be driven by exteriority, quantitative reasoning, and the masculine, "doing" aspect of consciousness, foregoing the qualitative inner, feminine "being" qualities, has led to a mainstream worldview which works on an ego level and seeks to define life in purely scientific terms.

The second axis is the evolutionary pull toward wholeness and universality. When we allow this force to shine through and lift us up, our lives and the world we create become more wholesome and meaningful. Both forces exist and have their proper place in the larger picture. We seem to require this contrast in order to identify that which is ultimately right for us. When we contract into the smaller world of the ego out of fear and ignorance, it eventually feels confining and wakes up our impetus toward expansion and evolution, and we begin to move toward the opposite axis of universality. When we embrace a psychology that transcends the ego and is a quest for soul, we cultivate and align to a deeper understanding of our higher purpose and nature that fuels a desire to cultivate and bring higher qualities both in our lives and in our society. We expand our awareness and worldview in respect to the greater mystery of consciousness. Consciousness and, let's face the facts, human life are an unfathomable, uncomfortable, and inconvenient enigma that cannot entirely be explained by science. Within that unknown lies the refreshing question of personal and spiritual potential and aspirations.

Despite the effort, which began around one hundred and fifty years ago, to make psychology into a scientific discipline, there has been a steady, and now increasing, stream of thinkers and psychologists who uphold a more holistic view of man and psychology. We can see here that psychology and spirituality are opposite axes on the same continuum and that both are integral and essential parts of our experience as human beings. On one end, we have the mind, body, and emotions that we can learn to heal and consciously navigate. Exploring ways to integrate the full spectrum of human consciousness into our psychological approaches gives way to true healing and wholeness. It allows us to transcend our fragmented nature and develop a sense of purpose beyond ego motivation, and ultimately moves us toward greater congruence, harmony, and fulfillment. It appears that history is coming full circle and once again turning toward becoming a true science of the soul.

We've explored the evolution of contemporary psychology in the West from the early schools of psychoanalysis and behaviorism and saw a gradual shift towards encompassing a larger spectrum of consciousness. However, the intellect, our primary tool for conceiving of our notions of psychology in the West, is limited in itself. It is for this reason that we are now going to shift east. The East does not traditionally have a school of psychology because it has always maintained the understanding that psychology—purifying and understanding the functioning of the psyche and its role in our life and evolution—is an inherent part of a spiritual path. In the next chapter, we will explore some Eastern ideologies and their views on psychology.

NOTES

1. 1908–1970.
2. 1909–1994.
3. Rollo May, *The Meaning of Anxiety* (1967, New York: Norton), p. 72.
4. May, 1967, p. 364.
5. 1969.
6. 1902–1987.
7. Carl R. Rogers, *On Becoming a Person: A Psychotherapist's View of Psychotherapy* (1961, New York: Houghton Mifflin).
8. Brant Cortright, *Psychotherapy and Spirit: Theory and Practice in Transpersonal Psychotherapy* (1997, New York: SUNY Press).
9. Roberto Assagioli, *Transpersonal Development* (2007, Forres: Inner Way Productions), p. 12.
10. Cortright, 1997, p. 39.
11. Abraham Maslow, *The Farther Reaches of Human Nature* (1971, USA: Esalen/ Viking).
12. 1842–1910.
13. Eliade, 1987, Vol. 12, p. 60.
14. William James, 1890/1950, "Principles of Psychology," in *The Oxford Handbook of Religion and Science*, Philip Clayton and Zachary Simpson, eds (2006, Oxford Handbooks in Religion and Theology, USA: Oxford University Press), p. 31.
15. William James, *Varieties of Religious Experience* (1982, USA: Penguin).
16. Jung, 1933, p. 119.
17. Carl G. Jung. *The Psychology of Kundalini Yoga, Notes of the Seminar Given in 1932 by C.G. Jung*, Sonu Shamdasani, ed. (1996, New Jersey: Bollingen Series, Princeton University Press).
18. Jung, 1996, p. 30.

19. 1888–1974.

20. John Rowan, *The Transpersonal: Psychotherapy and Counselling* (1993, London: Routledge), p. 40.

21. Brown, Molly Young, *Unfolding Self: The Practice of Psychosynthesis* (2004, New York: Allworth Press), p. 19.

22. Brown, 2004, pp. 19–20.

23. 1931–.

24. Stanislav Grof, *The Cosmic Game: Explorations of the Frontiers of Human Consciousness* (1998, Albany, New York: SUNY), p. 254.

25. Christina and Stanislav Grof, *Forms of Spiritual Emergency in Spiritual Emergency Network Newsletter* (1985).

26. Frances Vaughan, "Healing and Wholeness: Transpersonal Psychotherapy," in Roger Walsh and Frances Vaughan (Ed.), *Paths Beyond Ego* (1993, New York: Tarcher/Putnam), p. 158.

27. Natalie Tobert, *Spiritual Psychiatries* (2014, Kindle edition), loc. 4044.

28. Stanislav Grof, *The Cosmic Game: Explorations of the Frontiers of Human Consciousness* (1998, New York: SUNY), p. 4.

Chapter Three

Eastern Psychology

I regard the spiritual history of mankind and especially of India as a constant development of a divine purpose, not a book that is closed, the lines of which have to be constantly repeated.[1]

Sri Aurobindo

As a practicing psychotherapist born in the West and deeply inspired by the teachings of the East, I feel a unique sense of excitement as I contemplate the profound and fathomless ocean of Eastern philosophy. Even after discovering Hinduism and, more specifically, yogic philosophy in my teens through reading Paramahamsa Yogananda's *Autobiography of a Yogi,* and since that time avidly exploring it through reading, lectures, and meditation retreats, I feel as if I have only touched the surface of its unfathomable mysteries. I am by no means an expert on the topic. My intention here is to share the insights and the way Eastern thought and, mainly, yogic philosophy has enriched my life and—in later chapters—how I integrate some of its practices and principles into my clinical practice.

As we saw in chapter 1, in ancient Western traditions, psychology and spirituality were two sides of the same coin which over time morphed into distinct disciplines. The psyche, the inner essence that originally was synonymous with the soul, became excluded from Western psychology. What emerged was an effort to develop purely objective sciences of human neurobiology and behavior reflecting only the outer self. The spiritual side withdrew into the shadows of academia and, where admitted, remains on the fringe in the still nascent school of transpersonal psychology.

In India, spirituality and psychology are inseparable and an implicit part of the culture and way of life. This is not the case, as we will see, in psychology clinics and academic institutions dominated by Western approaches whose suitability for the Indian psyche are questionable. Yet, in times of distress, the majority of Hindus, both educated and illiterate, turn to their loved ones, ritual, prayer, devotion, study of the scriptures, and guidance from astrologers and spiritual masters rather than Western psychology.

At the same time, in the West, Eastern ideologies are increasingly being studied and adapted into Western models, as in the case of mindfulness and yoga therapy. Integral psychology, examined in later chapters, integrates Eastern techniques and approaches to psychology and aims toward a synthesis of East and West.

Mysticism and religion are the living foundations of Eastern thought and lifestyle. Psychology is an implicit part of these foundations. It interprets the mystical teachings rendering them more accessible and providing the meaning and means for human and spiritual evolution. Eastern psychology can be deconstructed into two main areas: India and Southeast Asia. India, the birthplace of so many religions and philosophies, is undeniably the cradle of Eastern philosophy.

Countries or regions colonized for a protracted period invariably absorb the culture of the ruling class. Conversely, the imperial class also adapts to the way of life, local customs, and philosophies of their colony. Mogul rule has left its mark on India, Pakistan, and Bangladesh in the form of Islam and Sufism, whereas China, Japan, and Tibet have influenced the southeastern countries through the spread of their branches of Buddhism, Taoism, and Zen.

Let's begin by delving into the mystical origins of Indian thought elucidating the psychological dimensions of these traditional Eastern schools.

HINDUISM

Vasudhaiva Kutumbakam—The world is one family.

Sanskrit saying

My relationship with Hinduism can be summed up by a conversation I had with a dear friend from a village in Gujarat, India, 100 km away from Gandhi's birthplace. Sitting at a café in Paris, I asked him, "What do you dislike the most about India?"

"The chaos."

"And what do you love the most about India?"

"The chaos."

So, what do I love about Hinduism, which, I need not mention poses a large part of the foundation of the Indian mindset? The chaos. Unlike Buddhism with its orderly theories and guidelines, worldly and monastic life, Hinduism is simply unfathomable, especially from the predominantly intellectual Western perspective.

Whether an ordinary task such as an errand, a visit to a temple, or a pilgrimage to a maha kumbha mela, the largest (and certainly most chaotic) gathering of human beings in the history of our civilization, there is nothing logical or linear about Hinduism. What do I love about that? Well, our only viable option is to let go of control, wants, desires, and attachments and take a leap of faith! Of course, there is also the option of blowing a gasket but that's not very appealing is it? Yet, the occurrence of westerners blowing a gasket in India is not uncommon, as conveyed in Régis Airault's *Les Fous de l'Inde*.[2] My experience is that India will mirror back to us anything in us that is rigid and not in the flow. Mother India gives us the exquisite choice of letting go or getting a slap in the face lesson. During my months and years spent traveling, living and working in India, this has mostly come in the form of strange and transformational illnesses and assorted mishaps.

The challenge of dis-identifying with the sheer intensity and chaos of India and coming to roost in the inherent, much more nourishing but still unfathomable spiritual foundations is, in itself, enough to bring anyone to the edge of a breakdown or enlightenment, depending on the way we face its mysterious, warm, and messy chaos. Of course, this does not stop both Western and Indian theologians from elaborating theories and guidelines. Even then, like God, Hinduism is still mystifying. We can either try to get it to fit into the confines of some reductionist theory or content ourselves by accurately describing one dimension of one aspect of one branch. Either way, we miss the point because Hinduism is essentially a living, breathing experience and I don't believe we can do it justice by trying to see it any other way.

> The flexibility and catholicity of Hindu civilization enables her "at once to renew herself in terms of her own essential nature and to change herself so as to bring herself in harmony with the form of age in which we live. In plain terms, the ancient Indian spirit takes on a new form without ceasing to be itself. India's religions have all been natural religions. They have grown and prospered naturally. They were not self-aware because they were expressions of cosmic reality. They did not define themselves. But when the Christian challenge arose, they had to define themselves. They did. Lokamanya's, Gandhiji's and Aurobindo's commentaries on the Gita were part of that effort at self-definition. ... This intellectualization of the life of the Spirit, if we may so describe this phenomenon, has deprived it of some of its natural flow but has also given a strength which is valuable in our days."[3]

Hinduism has its roots in ancient yogic philosophy. Early records date back to the Harappan Civilization that resided in the Indus Valley, which covered the whole of present day Southern Pakistan and northwestern regions of India.

Although the early script of the Indus Valley Civilization remains undecipherable, images of a man sitting in the holy posture of *padmasana*, the lotus posture, depicted from this civilization indicate that spiritual disciplines and development were practiced. Further evidence from excavations is the swastika symbol,[4] an ancient, esoteric representation of goodness and well-being. This suggests that awareness of spiritual powers, understanding of consciousness, and mastery over the lower aspects of human nature were cultivated. Psychological development is implicit to spiritual development as it requires a profound and detailed understanding of the forces that animate us from within and those that influence us from outside. Ancient yogis had profound knowledge of the workings of the mind, the more subtle realms of consciousness, and the vibrational influences of physical symbols such as the swastika. Languages, too, can have vibrational significance. Living examples can be found in the Tamil, Sanskrit, Latin, and Hebrew languages. These ancient languages were developed not only with their uses for the physical, practical world, but each letter has a particular vibrational quality and meaning. Each syllable has a vibrational resonance and can be used for healing, such as in the form of prayers and mantras.

Sanatan dharma (eternal law), commonly known as Hinduism, is the foundation of Indian philosophy and religions. Stemming from visions of the enlightened rishis over five thousand years ago, it is inherently mystical, philosophical, and psychological. It covers the entire spectrum of human experience from birth and early development to the realization of our divine nature. The theories of Indian psychology explore and elaborate upon the entire scope of human consciousness and are not limited to behavior and cognition. The essence of human psychology is conveyed, by the ancient texts, in a descending sense. The highest universal truths are the guidelines, foundations, and ultimate aspirations. Whereas, the West tends to be more outward-looking, learning, and searching for meaning based on life experience without the same "transcendent capstone" that seems to be the strongest point of reference in India.

The spiritual texts of India are revered by each practicing Hindu and form the basis of their worldview. The Vedas, Upanishads, Bhagavad Gita, and the Yoga Sutras of Patanjali, to name a few, are the beacons of Hindu psychology.

Insights into our psychological nature and functioning found in these sacred texts, provide us with the keys to our spiritual development and realization. The hallmark of Indian psychology is that it provides three primary paths to self-realization. Bhakti yoga, the path of devotion, touches the hearts of those who are devotional in nature. Those who are more intellectually inclined will feel more drawn to jnana yoga, the path of knowledge. Karma yoga, the path of selfless action and service, appeals to those who are action oriented.

Hinduism is made up of a vast, complex, and fluid web of sects and subsects. There are no dogmas. Believers may pick up any thread that appeals to their sentiment and carve out their path. This sprawling and inclusive structure descended from the great rishis (mystical seers) inspired various spiritual adepts to promote distinctive belief systems which branched off into religions such as Jainism, Sikhism, and Buddhism. The common beliefs found in the family of Hindu sects are karma, dharma, reincarnation, the existence of an all-pervasive divinity, and many deities representing different facets of the one divine force. In addition, the practices of worship in temples and at personal or family altars and sacraments, yoga and the guru-disciple tradition are a commonality. The Vedas as the primary scriptures, along with the concepts of samsāra (the cycle of birth, life, death, and rebirth), the more psychological notion of samskāra (cognitive impressions remaining from every experience we have in our lifetimes), and the common belief in pratibha (yogic intuition) are almost universal to these schools.

The Indian tradition is holistic. It is a lifestyle or philosophy rather than a religion. Its central focus is on the ultimate goal of self-realization. According to the ancient masters, human development and consciousness are inseparable. Hinduism fully appreciates the need for the overall development and well-being of the individual as part of the path toward the supreme goal. It views the physical body not as a means to fulfill desires, but as a vehicle needed to the reach the ultimate goal of spiritual realization. Hence, it is important to keep the body strong and robust. Likewise, it views the mind and the life force as needing to be purified and mastered in order to avoid pitfalls and facilitate the quest for spiritual realization.

This mission is not foreign to the present-day practitioners of Hinduism, but there is an increasing tendency to leave behind the lofty goals of the ancient *rishis* who originally grasped these universal truths of human potential. The laws of karma, birth and rebirth, nonviolence, yogic practices, and meditation are in their DNA. But for many, the goals of materialism have superseded the goals of spirituality. Hence, it seems that a growing trend of the Indian populace is to embrace these teachings and practices with the intent of fulfilling worldly goals in a quirky and colorful form of spiritual materialism replete with rituals, symbols, superstitions, and amulets. In addition, as a reflection of the over-riding influence of certain interpretations of Western thought in India, there is a visible tendency to harden ritualistic practices into beliefs and dogmas that do not necessarily reflect the spiritual fluidity of the Vedic Dharma.

The Vedas

It is said that all spiritual knowledge, however it is approached, has been elucidated in the Vedas, the first written spiritual texts of India. Although we can find the first traces of spiritual and yogic disciplines in hieroglyphs and cave markings dating back to 3000 BCE, these teachings were probably passed on orally for a long period before being put into written form around 1500 BCE.

The four principal Vedas are the Rig Veda, Sama Veda, Yajur Veda, and Atharva Veda. The Rig Veda is considered the most important because it represents the first recorded exploration of the mind and spirit as a path to realization of the ultimate truth. A single verse from the Rig Veda demonstrates the spiritual advancement of this early civilization:

> This is the omniscient who knows the law of our being and is sufficient to his works; let us build the song of his truth by our thought and make it as if a chariot on which he shall mount. When he dwells with us, then a happy wisdom becomes ours. With him for friend we cannot come to harm.[5]

The sheer age of the Vedas, and the fact that they were written in an ancient form of Sanskrit, makes their interpretation difficult. Like any spiritual scripture, each translation differs according to the nature and state of inner development of the interpreter. It is traditional for those considered to have reached the great spiritual heights, to each render their own interpretation of the great texts.

Max Muller, a German whose translation became popular in the 1800s, depicted the Vedas to be a mix of spiritual brilliance and superstitious nonsense. He lacked the requisite cultural sensitivity and spiritual development to grasp their deeper significances. But the mysteries of the Vedas have not been fully grasped. Even Sayana's classic Indian translation from the 1300s, on which Max Muller depended, could not fully enter into the spirit of these earliest human accounts of balanced lifestyle, right thinking, and spiritual ascent.

One of Sri Aurobindo's greatest contributions to Indian spiritual thought was his translation and interpretation of the Rig Veda in his book *The Secret of the Veda*. His translation of many of its verses was published in *Hymns to the Mystic Fire*. He emphasized the double sense of the Vedic hymns. One aimed to convey religious rituals to the common people and another, deeper esoteric sense was intended to impart psychological and spiritual meaning to mystical initiates. He argued that the early Sanskrit language was well-suited to this double significance, because the meanings of words were not so intellectually precise and fixed as they became in later languages. Even the modern version of Sanskrit holds multiple levels of meanings, not just in each word, but for each syllable. Sri Aurobindo summarizes the central ideas in the Veda:

> I had already seen that the central idea of the Vedic Rishis was the transition of the human soul from a state of death to a state of immortality by the exchange of the Falsehood for the Truth, of divided and limited being for integrality and

infinity. Death is the mortal state of Matter with Mind and Life involved in it; Immortality is a state of infinite being, consciousness and bliss. Man rises beyond the two firmaments, *rodasi*, Heaven and Earth, mind and body, to the infinity of the Truth, Mahas, and so to the divine Bliss. This is the "great passage" discovered by the Ancestors, the ancient Rishis.[6]

Sri Aurobindo described the psychological dimension of the gods and demons and each of the elements in the ritual fire sacrifice, the offerings made, and the boons requested and received. He details the psychological qualities and powers of the Gods such as Agni's power of the will, Indra's power of the divine mind, Surya, master of the supreme truths, and other primary deities who represent qualities that are essential for our ascent. There are numerous other gods and goddesses, other key symbols of the sacrifice each with their own psychological significances, but these are perhaps sufficient to give a sense of the esoteric meaning of the Veda and its complex and sophisticated teachings of spiritual development.

Sri Aurobindo argues and defends his interpretation in *The Secret of the Veda* with evidence from the hymns themselves, showing how the significances he attributes to the terms fit naturally and consistently throughout the text and reveal a lucid and spiritual meaning to the verses. In contrast, he shows how the significances of the expressions attributed by various earlier scholars were often inconsistent, giving one meaning in one place and a different meaning in another, often seeming forced and leading to banal and sometimes nonsensical meanings. The deeply mystical and spiritual vision implicit in his translations and interpretations overcomes the conundrum faced by scholars of how these archaic texts (according to earlier interpretations) could be so revered by later Indian mystics and sages, and form the historical basis for the profound philosophical treatises of the Upanishads.

The Upanishads

Although there is disagreement about the age of the Upanishads, it is estimated that the first twelve treatises, referred to as the principal or *Mukhya* Upanishads, were composed between about 600 BCE and 200 CE. Later Upanishads continued to be composed in the medieval and even the modern period totaling over two hundred treatises. The principal Upanishads lay down the fundamental principles of the Vedanta philosophy and the theoretical framework for myriad forms of the Hindu religion.

The Vedas provide the theoretical framework for the Hindu religion and the Upanishads, considered to be an esoteric annex to the Vedas, were written in response to a need for a means to attain the supreme knowledge of the self in the Vedas. The composers of these treatises were not merely philosophers speculating on the nature of existence, but yogis who practiced a rigorous spiritual discipline and attained their knowledge through direct revelation. As such, like the Vedas before them, they are considered by Hindus to be revealed scripture.

Adi Shankara, who lived in the eighth or ninth century BCE, wrote an elaborate commentary on the ten most important Upanishads. His work largely shaped later interpretations stating that the phenomenal world we experience is *maya* and that the only reality is the transcendent Brahman.

> Māyā (nescience, ignorance, illusion) is responsible for the one appearing as the many and so it is the principle of objectivity. It is also known as avidyā, and Śaṅkara uses these terms synonymously. The nondual Brahman which is unmanifest becomes manifest in association with māyā. In the process, Brahman, which is nirguṇa, becomes saguṇa. Māyā is defined as the power (Śakti) of Īśvara as it brings about the manifestation of the universe. Māyā has two aspects: the power of concealment (āvaraṇa) and the power of projection (vikṣepa) with which it brings about the appearance of the universe.[7]

Sri Aurobindo wrote a new translation and interpretation of a substantial selection of the principal Upanishads, which argues that many of the Upanishads proclaim the reality of the phenomenal world and the imminence of Brahman in it while also affirming the existence of a transcendent reality beyond. In describing the principal ideas of the Upanishads, we again turn to Sri Aurobindo's interpretation of three realizations:

> They realized first as a fact the existence under the flux and multitudinousness of things of that supreme Unity and immutable Stability ... that It is the one reality and all phenomena merely its seemings and appearances, that It is the true Self of all things and phenomena are merely its clothes and trappings. They learned that It is absolute and transcendent and ... therefore eternal, immutable, imminuable and indivisible.[8]

This then was the first realization through Yoga, *nityonityanam*, the One Eternal in many transient.

> At the same time they realized one truth more,—a surprising truth; they found that the transcendent absolute Self of things was also the Self of living beings, the Self too of man, that highest of the beings living in the material plane on earth.[9]

This then was the second realization through Yoga, *cetanascetananam*, the One Consciousness in many consciousnesses.

> Finally at the base of these two realizations was a third, the most important of all to our race,—that the Transcendent Self in individual man is as complete

because identically the same as the Transcendent Self in the Universe; for the Transcendent is indivisible and the sense of separate individuality is only one of the fundamental seemings on which the manifestation of phenomenal existence perpetually depends. In this way the Absolute which would otherwise be beyond knowledge, becomes knowable; and the man who knows his whole Self knows the whole Universe. This stupendous truth is enshrined to us in the two famous formulae of Vedanta, *so 'ham*, He am I, and *aham brahma asmi*, I am Brahman, the Eternal.[10]

The Vedantic philosophy described in the Upanishads provides a universal and comprehensive model for understanding the human psyche. It is one of the earliest treatises on the functioning of the mind. It recognizes three primary levels of consciousness. The ego or ordinary surface consciousness is based on the sense of being a distinct individual separate from others and the world around. Next, there is the subconscious buried beneath the surface awareness and retains the impressions received through our physical, emotional, and mental faculties and with them influences the surface consciousness. The third level is the superconscious or spiritual awareness.

Vedanta also distinguishes between *chitta* (the sense mind, the mind-stuff, the repository of past accumulated impressions or experiences, *manas* (the sense mind, the mind's ability to deliberate and make associations), *buddhi* (cognition and discriminative intellect), *ahamkara* (ego, the sense of individuality), and *Atman* (Self). The Atman is the real knower whereas mind is enmeshed with the object of knowledge. This is what gives us the ability to observe our own mind! The substance of the mind retains all of the *samskaras* (impressions) experienced through the physical senses, thoughts, and actions. Vedanta holds that life development is based on development of the mind. It is only through the development and proper nourishment of the mind that we can cultivate the physical, moral, aesthetic, and intellectual faculties that can lead us to the realization of the self.

Vedanta not only gives us understanding of the functioning of the mind, but it also provides recommendations for our personal development, a path of overcoming the lower nature, gaining self-mastery, and reaching our spiritual potential. Through keeping good company and positive thoughts, people, and surroundings, we can slowly build strength to overcome the *samskaras* (impressions) accumulated from our past experiences. This leads to gradual purification and mastery over the mind. This path gives us the means to and requires us to be constantly aware. The minute our guard is down, our weaknesses are waiting for an opportunity to take over. Constant mindfulness along with awareness of our strengths and weaknesses helps us to consciously navigate, build our strengths and overcome our negative tendencies. We are also to cultivate self-discipline to align our emotional life with our rational life and direct all our energies towards realizing our Ideal. Meditation on the real self is the greatest contributor to personal and spiritual evolution. It helps us to make the transition from domination by our lower nature to self-mastery and aligning our life with divine will. This occurs through cultivating objective understanding of the workings of the mind. Meditation helps build concentration and mastery over the mind so that it becomes a sharp tool that can be used with precision to attain to realization of the spiritual self. Rama Coomaraswamy pointed out, "One cannot fight the enemy when the chariot (the mind) is out of control."

The spiritual self is unchanging. Spiritual development means purifying and balancing our outer being and cultivating our awareness of the inner light of the self so it can shine through with greater and greater intensity and bring light to the otherwise lost and disparate elements of the outer self. Finally, we come back to the fact that the Upanishads help us to understand how the mind can be our best friend on this path of evolution, or it can be our worst enemy. Vedanta is pure psychology; its aim is our spiritual evolution and realization.

The Bhagavad Gita

The Bhagavad Gita is one of the most widely revered, read, and analyzed spiritual books. A segment of the great Indian epic Mahabharata and its spiritual core, its storyline concerns a dialogue between Arjuna, the great warrior, and Lord Krishna, his charioteer, at the center of the battlefield just as the great war of Kurukshetra is about to begin. The two armies face each other in a civil war, in which family members are pitted against each other. Arjuna, about to lead the charge of the righteous warriors against the evil betrayers, is suddenly overcome by the moral dilemma and horrible prospect of fighting against his friends and relatives whom it has been his duty to defend. Confused, despondent, and unable to act, he turns to Krishna, who counsels him and reveals to him great spiritual truths that enable Arjuna to see and understand a higher principle on which to stand and fight.

The scripture, says Sri Aurobindo, is one of the great integrations of ancient spiritual thought, especially in revealing the harmonized relations and higher possibilities between karma yoga, bhakti yoga, and jnana yoga that had previously represented distinct and competing paths. The Gita conveys the goal of realization of the impersonal transcendent Brahman through meditation and inner discrimination between the pure impersonal self and the ceaseless activity of nature—on the one hand—and the cult of devotion to Krishna, the Avatar of the Supreme Lord, on the other. There was the gospel of sacrifice and performance of one's duty, and the injunction to transcend duty, and to renounce life and worldly action on the other. The Gita synthesizes these contradictory teachings.

Again, Sri Aurobindo brilliantly sums up The Bhagavad Gita's essential spiritual method and message:

> To break out of ego and personal mind and see everything in the wideness of the self and spirit, to know God and adore him in his integral truth and in all his aspects, to surrender all oneself to the transcendent Soul of nature and existence, to possess and be possessed by the divine consciousness, to be one with the One in universality of love and delight and will and knowledge, one in him with all beings, to do works as an adoration and a sacrifice on the divine foundation of a world in which all is God. ... It is a transition from the apparent to the supreme spiritual and real truth of our being, and one enters into it by putting off the many limitations of the separative consciousness and the mind's attachment to the passion and unrest and ignorance, the lesser light and knowledge, the sin and virtue, the dual law and standard of the lower nature.[11]

Sri Aurobindo brings to the forefront the profoundly psychological nature of the Gita and at the same time uses its psychological disciplines as a path to spiritual realization.

The Yoga Philosophy of Maharishi Patanjali

Believed to have been written around the second century BCE Patanjali compiled and commented the Yoga Sutras around 400 CE. He created a systematic elaboration of ashtanga yoga (eight-limbed yoga) and kriya yoga (action yoga), spiritual disciplines aimed at the realization of the transcendent reality. Scholars[12] and spiritual teachers[13] alike have written their translations and interpretations of this text. The *Yoga Sutras of Patanjali* is one of the most recognized and most important treatises on the science of Indian spirituality and psychology of India and represent the essence of the Indian psychology. It contains the means and practices for controlling the mind and for attaining the progressive states of samadhi leading to the highest state of *nirvikalpa samadhi* or enlightenment (meditative state entailing complete mastery and transcendence over the body, mind and emotions).

The book is divided into four sections. The first deals with the subject of samadhi or meditation. It begins by making the central distinction between the atman, or self, and the *buddhi*, or intellect. The Self is the sentient, conscious *purusha* (or conscious being) and the intellect is considered to be merely an extension of the insentient, inanimate *prakriti* (the nature or creative principle). According to Patanjali, the root cause of all misconception is mistaking the intellect for the true Self. This false identification with the intellect gives rise to ego and creates the false distinction between the knower and the subject to be known. The fruit of meditation is to restore the self into its original uncorrupted form of union with the Divine. In this state, the Self is distinct from all aspects of self. Only through making this distinction can the yogi establish himself in the blissful state of *samadhi.*

In the second section, Patanjali elaborates on the aspects of sadhana or spiritual practice which are the stepping stones for attaining the goal of enlightenment. He beautifully defines spiritual practice as the means of eradicating suffering. He categorically states that the only way to be rid of suffering is by establishing oneself firmly in *vivek-khyati,* pristine awareness or Reality. The third and fourth sections elaborate on mastery of the mind and other benefits and accomplishments of spiritual practice and *kaivalya,* the state of absolute unity.

Patanjali's treatise on yoga added clarity and a scientific perspective to the existing teachings. The sutras or aphorisms present yoga philosophy as a guide to spiritual attainment through yoga and meditation. It is the path of Raja Yoga, the "royal road," a psycho-physical approach to yoga. The sutras help the dedicated meditator by indicating the dangers and pitfalls encountered on the meditative path. *Avidya* (ignorance) is the cause of all of our misconceptions and blockages to spiritual development in the form of, *kleshas* (afflictions such as ignorance, ego, likes, dislikes, and the fear of death), *samskaras* (impressions), *vasana* (mental fluctuations or desires), *vritti* (mental tendencies), and *karma* (actions).

The Yoga Sutras are meant to guide us in the process of unfolding to the inner divine. Patanjali has warned us to be aware that spiritual powers (*siddhis*) acquired during the spiritual journey are mere milestones in the path and if we get too involved in them, they become obstacles in the ultimate journey. Patanjali's system has the pure vertical focus of transcendence—transcending the lower nature without necessarily transforming it.

The Yoga Sutras describe eight limbs or stages of spiritual development each one of which can be applied to all aspects of one's life, such as morality, philosophy, psychology, and spirituality. Ultimately, the Yoga Sutras are designed to guide seekers on the path to enlightenment.

The first five disciplines involve external yoga, dealing with the gross, outer nature. They are *yama, niyama, āsana, prānayama,* and *pratyāhāra.* The first stage, *yama* means restraint or adherence to moral codes. According to the teachings of Patanjali, these restraints are to be applied to such areas as *ahimsa* (nonviolence), *satya* (truthfulness), *asteya* (nonstealing), *brahmacharya* (celibacy), and *aparigraha* (renunciation, nonattachment, nonacquisition). The second stage is *niyama* which means observances for self-purification and study. This stage applies to the practice of *saucha* (purity/cleanliness), *santosha* (contentment), *tapas* (austerity or burning of impurities), *svadhyaya* (self-study), and *ishvara pranidhana* (surrender to the Supreme Lord and holding the Lord to be omnipresent without any doubt). This is similar to what is stated in the Gita:

> *Yoginaamapi sarveshaam madgateynaantaraatmanaa* |
> *Shradhhavaan bhajatey yo maam, sa may yuktatamo matah* ||
> And even among all the yogis, he who worships me with complete devotion and with his inner-self, I consider him the most accomplished.
> Bhagavad Gita[14]

The third stage, *āsana*, is the practice of postures to properly care for and orient the forces inherent in the physical body. The fourth stage is *prānayama* (controlling the vital forces through breath control) and the fifth is *pratyāhāra* (which means control or deprivation of the mind and the five sense organs).

The remaining three stages, *dhārana* (concentration), *dhyāna* (meditation), and *samādhi* (absorption or deep meditation) concern the internal workings of the mind. Practiced regularly and with sincerity, these skills engender personal integration.

The Yoga Sutras are of great value to the psychology of consciousness as well as personal growth. Patanjali's concept of *svadhyaya* (self-study) is a foundational part of my therapeutic work. It involves both gaining insight from scriptures and self-observation to build cognitive awareness. Yet, the cognitive reevaluation of our thoughts and mental functioning is not done through self-analysis, but through witnessing or mindful awareness, paying attention to our mind, and consciousness.

The primary texts illustrating the psychology of Hinduism—the Vedas, the Upanishads, the Bhagavad Gita, and the Yoga Sutras of Patanjali—prescribe a system of contemplation and self-control that eventually results in the purification of the *chitta* or mental consciousness. They lead to the eradication of psychological defects and development of self-knowledge and thereby freedom from suffering. Psychology for the Indian masters was not a discipline in itself but a rung in the spiritual ladder whose ultimate goal was union with the Infinite.

INDIAN PSYCHOLOGY

As psychology emerged as a separate discipline in the West, distinctive from its earlier mystical and philosophical roots, Indian thinkers developed their theories of sensation and perception that reflected Indian metaphysics. In 1958, Jadunath Sinha wrote his three book series, *Indian Psychology,* covering the following: *Cognition* (1958), *Emotion and Will* (1961), and *The Epistemology of Perception* (1969). These works reflect the uniquely Indian perceptions based on the ancient sacred texts. The current Indian psychology movement aims to establish a psychology and education system that takes into account the unique Indian ethos that reclaims the spiritual and cultural heritage that, according to Sri Aurobindo, if integrated have the potential to help India regain its place on the world's stage.

Indian Views and Approaches to Mental Health— Traditional and Modern

Traditional Indian worldview stems from profound and holistic mystic vision. It therefore addresses psychology in an entirely different way than traditional Western approaches. Table 3.1 gives an idea of disorders that can occur in the psyche, the level of consciousness they correspond to, and the ways in which traditional Indian healers work with them. Following the inherently spiritual and multidimensional traditional Indian worldview, the roots of disorders are explored in terms of the level of consciousness at which they exist. This multidimensional "diagnostic" leads to equally holistic possibilities for treatment. In contrast, most Western models of assessment and treatment, at best, take into consideration physical, emotional, and mental causes of disturbance neglecting or even rejecting the more subtle zones. That limits its potential.

The Challenge of Modernization

Despite its rich origins, Indian psychology in response to modernization, which it seems to equate with westernization, is too archaic and unfathomable for the common masses. The purists, spiritual adepts, and masters, steadfastly follow the traditions with an implicit belief that the singular purpose of psychology is to understand *chitta* (the inner workings of the mind) in order to transcend its bondage and to realize oneself. At the same time the teachings have been simplified for the masses to address the mundane problems of human suffering. It has become a tool to understand oneself better and derive worldly happiness through the fulfillment of desires. All along they have maintained the esoteric message of self-realization with one change—reducing the definition of self-realization to worldly happiness and success.

This transition of using advanced spiritual techniques from a supreme goal to a worldly goal is not a twenty-first century phenomenon. Even the scriptures warn of this distraction. Patanjali explicitly stated that the *siddhis* (spiritual powers) one acquires during the spiritual journey are mere milestones on the path and if one gets too involved in them, they become obstacles in the ultimate journey. Indian mythology is filled with anecdotes of great men,

Table 3.1   Level of Causation and Treatment in Traditional Indian Models

Level of Causation	Type/Root of Disorder	Treatment
Physical	Physical disorder— biological disorders, organic disorders, substance abuse	Medical treatment, homeopathy, traditional medicine
Emotional	Trauma, inherent weaknesses in emotional structure	Psychotherapy, traditional medicine (homeopathy, Ayurveda), flower remedies
Mental	Erroneous ideas, beliefs, thoughts, reasoning, and attitudes	Psychotherapy, traditional medicine (homeopathy, Ayurveda)
Generational	Ancestral karma	Inner dialogue, strengthen foundations in this incarnation
Environmental	Imbalanced family or peer environment	Behavioral, attitudinal, interventions
Planetary influences	Influences due to birth chart or solar return	Visits to specific temples, mantra, holy men, herbal medicine, gemstones
Past lives and reincarnation	Blockages and disturbances stemming from past lives	Visits to specific temples, mantra, holy men, astrologers, palm leaf oracles, traditional healers, or gurus
Subtle influences	Disharmonies in subtle bodies	Same
Spirit possession	Disembodied beings Occult forces or energies	Same

Source: Adapted from information provided in Natalie Tobert, *Spiritual Psychiatries*, (2014, kindle edition).

who performed penance for self-realization but got distracted by miraculous powers and ended up using them to fulfill their desires to attain worldly happiness and pleasures.

As a reflection of this shift toward modernization, mental health care in India today has, by-and-large, turned its back on the infinitely rich, multidimensional, and multifaceted roots in exchange for Western psychiatry and behaviorism. In her poignant book, *Spiritual Psychologies*,[15] Natalie Tobert points out the ways in which a Western approach to psychology is ill-adapted to the Indian mindset because it assumes a Western sense of individualism rather than the Indian extended social self. Furthermore, because it seems, in the West, it is assumed that all imbalances stem from postnatal experiences. It does not take into consideration the Indian belief system of the nature of our existence that inherently includes past lives, planetary, karmic, and supernatural influences.

Having seen the history, rich with mystical and humanistic meaning, what can we make of the fact that the predominant schools of psychology in India today stem from the West? True, we have a lot to offer but how can it be justifiable to throw away not only the profound mysticism but the unique makeup of the Indian psyche which is its result?

Hinduism and the West

Hinduism in the West has spread largely through the influx of the Indian diaspora and the yoga movement, although as early as the 1930s philosophers and psychologists such as Mircea Eliade and Carl Jung were heading East to begin to delve into its mysteries. Swami Vivekananda, the closest disciple of Ramakrishna Paramahamsa, was the first prominent Indian sage to spread the teachings of yoga and Vedanta in the West when he came to give his famous address to the Parliament of World Religions in 1893. Paramahansa Yogananda came to the U.S. in 1920 to address the International Congress of Religious Liberals. He spent the remainder of his life in the U.S. where he founded the Self-Realization Fellowship. His book, *Autobiography of a Yogi*, is one of the most widespread and highly acclaimed books on yoga ever to have been published. While many lifestyle tendencies related to Hinduism have been integrated in varying forms in the West, Hinduism, due to its vast labyrinth of sects and gods, has fundamentally remained impenetrable and misunderstood. While most Greek philosophers and major figures from the West are well known historical figures, the Indian masters who have produced such immense volumes of profound literature remain relatively obscure.

Many schools of yoga in the West focus almost exclusively on *āsana*, the Yoga Sutras' discipline of physical postures designed to master the forces in the body. While not a complete approach to transformation and enlightenment in itself, it has significant benefits that can greatly help in reaching these ultimate aims. Many modern relaxation techniques have been inspired by *shava asana* (the corpse pose) that has been shown to calm the mind, relieve stress, soothe mild depression, relax the body, alleviate headaches, fatigue, and insomnia and help lower blood pressure. Yoga has become a multimillion dollar industry in the West.

Meditation, another aspect of the Yoga Sutras, has also become popular in the West. Many studies have been done on the benefits of meditation for state of mind. Meditation is increasingly integrated into psychotherapy and has been shown to help people develop greater inner strength and objectivity to help them unearth and come to terms with past traumatic events that wreak havoc in the subconscious until they are addressed.

While Western religions originally had meditative traditions, the age of enlightenment brought about a shift away from such "irrational" practices. Today, movements within the Judeo-Christian traditions are reintegrating meditative practices. Experiencing the positive effects of meditation and Eastern spiritual disciplines has inspired many westerners to research into the sacred texts of India. The sheer quantity of translations of texts such as Patanjali's Yoga Sutras into Western languages demonstrates the level of interest coming from Western seekers. Eastern spiritual tradition has also been a strong influence on some schools of Western psychology, especially in the Jungian, humanistic, and transpersonal disciplines.

Although Hinduism was the earliest and is the predominant philosophy of India, over the centuries other religions and philosophies have branched out from Hinduism reflecting variations on its themes. These teachings reflect a distinctly Eastern mindset insofar as the accent is on inner development and realization and a perception of the divine as being within rather than outside. We next turn to other Eastern approaches to spirituality.

JAINISM

Jainism is believed to have begun its development during the Upanishadic period. It later developed into a philosophy or religion as a statement against the rising authority of Hindu thought with its system of sacrificial worship. Mahavira Vardhamana[16] renounced the world in pursuit of spiritual enlightenment. At forty-two, he reached his spiritual goal, established the order of the naked monks, and taught Jainism for the remaining thirty years of his life.[17] He was the twenty-fourth, last and most well-known Tirthankara[18] known for systematizing Jainism. Thereafter, it has been led by ganadharas whose role is to support the community.

Jainism's metaphysical philosophy lays the foundations for psychological thought drawn from introspection rather than empiricism or analysis. Derived from insights and observations of seers, Jain philosophy designates five types of cognition: *Mati jnana* (cognition from the five senses); *shrut jnana* (cognition of the written word); *avadhi jnana* (clairvoyance); *manahparyaya jnana* (cognition of the minds and thoughts of other living beings); and *keval jnana* (omniscience).

The Jain system teaches that the path to realization contains three aspects: right faith, right knowledge, and right conduct that consists of *satya* (truthfulness), *asteya* (nonstealing), *ahimsa* (nonviolence or harmlessness), *aparigraha* (renunciation, nonattachment, nonacquisition), and *brahmacharya* (celibacy). Like Hindus, Jains adopted a belief in the law of karma and reincarnation, originally elaborated upon in the Upanishads. This philosophy, implicit in major Eastern religions and philosophies, defines the effects of our positive and negative actions on our nature and personality. According to Jainism, life's ultimate goal is to become free of karmic bondage and liberate the soul.

BUDDHISM

Buddhism emerged in the fifth century BCE through the teachings of Siddhartha Gautama, the son of a wealthy king. His contemplation of the misery and suffering he witnessed led him to leave his home in search of enlightenment. As we all know, his journey eventually led him to achieve this goal and he came to be known as Buddha or The Enlightened. Although Buddhism is considered to be a philosophy, the rapid development and spread of a canonized system centered around the Buddha's teachings indicate that it quickly evolved into a religious order. His philosophy found captive audiences in India, China, Tibet, Sri Lanka, Thailand, Burma, Japan, and Korea and beyond. Buddhism is the most popular Eastern religion in the West due to its adaptability to the modern world and its compatibility with the Western intellectual mind-set. Many Westerners, disappointed by the lack of essence in their native religions, turn to Buddhism, which teaches us about lifestyle, psychology, and spiritual development. Buddhist philosophy is of relevance to all areas of life, from psychology to politics, inner life to outer life. The abundance of Buddhist psychologists, books, and university degree programs, attest to Buddhism's contribution to psychology.

In their comprehensive text, *Asian Psychology*, Gardner and Lois Murphy (1968) explain the main ways in which Buddhist psychology differs from Hindu psychology:

> (1) the emphasis on practical action as a source of escape; (2) the emphasis on benevolence and compassion, both for the direct appeal and for the utility in lifting one out of the cycle of rebirth; (3) the creation of a spirit of brotherhood available to both the priests and to the lay people; (4) the denial of any central and persisting soul or atman. The flux of experience goes on, but there is no abiding core of changeless selfhood.[19]

For the Buddhist, freedom from suffering lies in understanding the mind, the heart, and the will. For both Hinduism and Buddhism the primary endeavor is to break away from the identification with the ego or individuality, but in Buddhism, this endeavor has been developed into a form of inquiry that is the core of the spiritual practice. It does not subscribe to the concept of a soul that is free from death, though it accepts the concept of rebirth and continuity of life. The existence of a changeless entity like the soul is not imperative for transmigration. According to Buddhism, it is not the soul, but desires and karma (action) which result in suffering and rebirth. The law of cause and effect is enforced through the persistence of desires and the urge to fulfill them. The cycle of birth and death is broken only by nirvana—the blissful state of nothingness—when desires come to an end.

The psychological relevance of the four noble truths and eight-fold path and *sunya vada* (law of emptiness) taught by Buddhism and along with Buddhist techniques of meditation are of considerable relevance to modern psychology. Briefly stated, the four noble truths are the following:

1. Life is full of suffering;
2. The cause of suffering is desire or craving;
3. The cessation of suffering comes from the cessation of desire or craving;
4. The way to the cessation of desire or craving is the Noble Eight-fold Path consisting of right: understanding, thought, speech, action, livelihood, effort, awareness, and concentration.

Buddhism puts a primary emphasis on the cessation of desire which is cultivated by living and thinking correctly and correct focus of our consciousness. The nature of this concentration may be conceived differently, but commonly involves seeing and allowing things to be just as they are without any desire to change them. Rather than implying inaction, actions should not be motivated by a desire for an alternative state. Instead, they should be done purely, without reference to anything outside, as an inseparable part of the universal movement, just as the sun rises or the river flows with no particular aim outside itself.

The six realms of consciousness in Buddhist teaching alert us to the dangers lurking in our attitudes and actions and provide food for thought for our development. Just as they can be applied to external aspects of life such as politics or business,[20] they can also be applied to psychology and inner development. The Hellish Realm represents our states of aggression and anxiety. The Animal Realm evokes awareness of our desire for instinctual gratification and tendency toward automatic behaviors. The Realm of the Hungry Ghosts is the realm of our rage, desire, dissatisfaction, and the sense of emptiness behind them. The God Realm is the domain of our peak experiences, rapture, and sensual bliss. The Realm of the Jealous Gods represents our aggression and competitive nature. The Human Realm embodies our search for self.

Zen Buddhism

Buddhism came to China from India around the fifth century CE. Over time it began to take on the flavors of Taoism and Confucianism. Theologians started to highlight the moral values embedded in the teachings which developed into Zen Buddhism. It is a commonly accepted belief that the word Zen (*Chàn* in Chinese), is derived from the Sanskrit *dhyana* or meditation. As scholars and priests from India and China traveled the Silk Road, Zen Buddhism was established in neighboring countries.

Buddhism addresses both spiritual and practical dimensions, providing a path of wisdom through rituals and doctrine. In Zen, mind is nothing but the Buddha. The ultimate state, or True Buddha, is compared to an empty space. The psychological challenge is how to realize this Buddha. Zen de-emphasizes theoretical knowledge in favor of direct realization through meditation and practice of dharma.

Beginning with the Song Dynasty around 960 CE, the koan method became popular. Koans are paradoxical or linguistically meaningless dialogues or riddles. Answering a koan requires a student to let go of conceptual thinking and the logical way we order the world. The appropriate insight and response arises naturally and spontaneously in the mind and the truth can reveal itself unobstructed by the oppositions and differentiations of language.

Zazen (Zen sitting) is a highly valued and time-tested technique which enables practitioners to ascend in consciousness and attain enlightenment. The mind is regulated by directing the awareness towards counting, watching the breath, or by focusing on the hara (the energy center below the navel). In the Soto school of Zen, practitioners endeavor to simply hold their awareness on the stream of thoughts rather than focusing on any fixed object or thought.

Shunryu Suzuki's teachings in *Zen Mind, Beginner's Mind* expresses a clear sense of Zen practice. Regarding the posture to be taken in zazen, he says, "These forms are not the means of obtaining the right state of mind. To take this posture is itself to have the right state of mind. There is no need to obtain some special state of mind."[21] He gives insightful guidelines to help practitioners learn the importance and practice of following the breath for transcending the ego. "The air comes in and goes out like someone passing through a swinging door."[22] Concentration is key to the practice, but refers to focusing on simply observing what is and letting everything else go. In this way, "Zen practice is to open up our small mind. So concentrating is just an aid to help you realize "big mind," or the mind that is everything."[23] Obviously, when practicing meditation, thoughts will arise. In this case, he advises:

> When you are practicing zazen, do not try to stop your thinking. Let it stop by itself. If something comes into your mind, let it come in, and let it go out. It will

not stay long. When you try to stop your thinking, it means you are bothered by it. Do not be bothered by anything.[24]

Zen meditation is not restricted to periods set aside for zazen. The aim is to live in the immediacy and reality of the moment at all times. Various rituals have been elaborated to facilitate this state of pure being. Some Buddhists would prefer to label it nonbeing since the moment ends as soon as it arises. The Zen tea ceremony is performed with total awareness of harmony and beauty. Similarly, calligraphy, archery, woodworking, gardening, cooking, and other daily chores of monastery life, "chop wood, carry water," carried out with full awareness in the present moment have become part of the Zen tradition.

Mindfulness is a central aspect of Buddhist traditions. Our capacity to remain present and aware is possible in fleeting moments, but with practice, it is possible to do so on a sustained basis. Mindfulness helps us remain objective in the face of adversity. Rather than being a passive practice, it is a means to cultivate insight into the content and functioning of the mind, ultimately resulting in mastery of the mind. It is for this reason that a simplified, but not less effective, practice of mindfulness has broad applications in psychology and health care.

Vignette—Meditation

Hermione's training to become therapist required her to be in psychotherapy. We began with a general exploration of her life and issues. Her first year of training focused on personality structure and defense mechanisms. Our sessions focused on the issues that got triggered by her intensive training. We started each session with person-centered dialogue and cognitive exploration and then used breathwork to bring about deeper awareness and integration of the topics covered in the dialogue. During the first year of therapy, Hermione was able to examine many constructs or ways she habitually limited herself, such as her negative self-image and rigid personality structure replete with taboos and judgments on herself and others. During the sessions, her childhood wounds and defenses gradually came to her awareness.

Part of Hermione's training required engaging in daily meditation practice. Due to her tendency toward hyper-mentalization and disembodiment, I advised her to begin a mindfulness-based practice to develop a more positive, gentle and accepting relationship with herself. At first, she struggled with the self-discipline required for a daily practice. As a long term meditator, I could relate to this all too well. I shared insights that I developed to help myself get over that hurdle. I discovered if I finish my day with a spiritual activity, reading an inspirational book, scripture or a short meditation, I generally wake up motivated to get out of the cozy bed with my dog and meditate. This worked and Hermione developed a regular meditation practice.

*She noticed her daily practice helped her become aware that her mind func-
tioned with an automatic self-critical response to virtually every thought that
arose. We were able to explore and work on this further. Growing up in a rigid-
minded household, Hermione could do nothing more as a child than follow the
script laid out for her. As her awareness of her childhood patterns and their
impact on her grew, her self-deprecating comments were becoming less frequent. Her defenses loosened up. After a few months of meditation, Hermione's
personality was becoming more fluid, open and less rigid. The gradual change
came from within rather than from an external decision to stop being so hard
on herself.*

*It was at this point that in one of her breathwork sessions, she started to
experience spontaneous memories of sexual abuse. While she had been aware of
violence from her stepfather, this new and painful angle slowly began to surface.
In the next session, Hermione was determined to dig for more memories to put
the puzzle pieces together. When she began her breathwork, I could pick up a
sense that she was being very willful. Her will, in this case was not aligned to
her higher purpose and, therefore, was doing her more harm than good. I gently
tried to help her get back on track by explaining that the memories had arisen
spontaneously because she was ready to take them on and integrate them, not
because she had gone fishing for them. I encouraged her to let her session be
guided from within.*

*At first, I was concerned about how Hermione would deal with this phase of
our work. The memories and associated emotions that arose in the subsequent
sessions were powerful and dramatic. Yet, the understanding and objectivity
Hermione was developing through her daily mindfulness practice kept her
steady through this difficult phase. At the same time, meditation gave her the
power to witness the process and the memories objectively without engaging
in or dramatizing them. Once we stop judging, we can start to see and accept
ourselves just as we are. As Hermione's psyche became more fluid and her foundations more stable, past life memories began emerging in our work. Inspired
by the work of Brian Weiss, I was able to accompany her to journey into these
experiences.*

We will come back to Hermione's past-life recall in chapter 9.

Tibetan Buddhism

Tibetan Buddhism evolved into a much more complex and heart-centered
approach than Zen Buddhism's simple and meditative path. This difference
is apparent when comparing the austere and simple art of Zen Buddhism with
the richly ornate art of Tibetan Buddhism, with their plethora of Buddhas,
Bodhisattvas, and other beneficent and wrathful deities. Tibetan Buddhism
places a stronger emphasis on the veneration and worship of the realized
Buddhas and Bodhisattvas, who shed their grace and compassion on all

suffering creatures. There is a great emphasis on compassion both toward others and as a spiritual path towards enlightenment. In his book, *In My Own Words*, the Dalai Lama explains:

> From my own limited experience, I have found that the greatest degree of inner tranquility comes from the development of love and compassion. The more we care for the happiness of others, the greater our own sense of well-being becomes. Cultivating a close, warmhearted feeling for others automatically puts the mind at ease. This helps remove whatever fears or insecurities we may have and gives us the strength to cope with any obstacles we encounter. It is the ultimate source of success in life. ... It is because our own human existence is so dependent on the help of others that our need for love lies at the very foundation of our existence. Therefore, we need a genuine sense of responsibility and a sincere concern for the welfare of others.[25]

Tibetan Buddhism, as with all forms of Buddhism, places great importance on disciplining the mind. The mind is the source of all happiness and contentment, but also of suffering. Whatever disturbs calmness and peace of mind is considered to be a delusion. Attachment, anger, pride, doubt, and ignorance are the most common forms of delusion. The misconception that we are independent and self-existent is the greatest cause of suffering. It leads to desire and hatred. The wisdom of selflessness helps us combat the false but more accepted and facile view that we are self-existent. The path to selflessness is a hard climb involving lengthy training in discipline, morality, concentration, and wisdom laid in the rich and elaborate scriptures. In Tibetan Buddhism, enlightenment goes hand-in-hand with development of compassion for all sentient beings.

I regularly utilize the Tibetan Buddhist concept of lovingkindness in my work. When we cultivate lovingkindness toward ourselves, we naturally and authentically offer that same attitude to those around us. Many of my clients, when they begin therapy, maintain a constant inner dialogue of verbal and psychological abuse toward themselves. They constantly and unknowingly propagate an aggressive, judgmental, harsh, and conditional relationship with themselves, unaware of just how much this toxic loop tape impacts all areas of their lives. If we constantly abuse ourselves with our thoughts and attitudes, it is not surprising that we end up feeling awful. Lovingkindness toward oneself and others benefits everyone.

There are varying degrees of negative self-talk. The ways I address it depend on the level of severity. In cases where negative self-talk is simply an unconscious pattern, it may be enough to simply bring this pattern to the client's awareness. In other cases, the habit of negativity toward oneself is more insidious and takes more time to root out.

Clients with severe manifestations of negative self-relationships are their own worst enemies. When combined with victim consciousness, an investment in our own powerlessness and psychological or physical self-destruction, it brews up a particularly lethal cocktail for the soul. Impatience to get better quick is another form of self-flagellation. These extreme forms of self-negation are harder to work with, but certainly not incurable. They require more time and patience on the part of the therapist and client. The Buddhist emphasis on presence or mindfulness is particularly effective for healing the causes of negative self-talk and other forms of negativity.

THE PSYCHOLOGY OF CHINA

Until recently, from a Western perspective, India and China were thought to have much in common. The two most populous nations were primarily agricultural. They are economically and technologically forging ahead in the twenty-first century, yet their cultures have remained somewhat isolated from the rest of the world. Psychologically, they are so distinct from each other it would not be fair to either nation if we collapse them into one by using the term "Asian psychology." Indian psychology made phenomenal advancements from 1500 BCE to about 500 CE. During these periods, numerous schools of thought were prevalent, each one having psychological dimensions. Hence, it will not be worthwhile to draw parallels between India and China. Rather, let us start with a clean slate.

Archeological findings dating back to 1000 BCE make reference to beautiful pieces of art pointing to powerful dynasties, a well-developed social framework, and a sustained endeavor toward political unification and a sophisticated philosophy and culture in early China. This influence is noted by Dr. Francis Hsu's observations.[26] He maintains that contemporary Chinese thought is "situation-centric"; its psychology is less individualistic and more about social norms. Chinese novels rarely narrate the tale through the medium of the character. Romance and love are often secondary to the main storyline. The main factors influencing Chinese psychology and cultural systems are situational factors and kinships. Thus, close human relations, ancestral values, and adherence to rules, conformity to rituals such as funerals and weddings, and respect for family lineage are consolidated and strengthened.

Contrary to early Greek and Indian philosophies, Chinese thought is more humanistic and naturalistic and less mystical or transcendent in its orientation. On its more spiritual side, it focuses on the alignment of the individual with natural laws of the cosmos, as opposed to relationship with deities or a Supreme Being. Nevertheless, it was influenced by Buddhist thought which can be seen in some of its formulations. The main schools of Chinese thought are I Ching, Confucianism, Taoism (Lao Tzu), and Buddhism.

I Ching—The Book of Changes

The I Ching or Book of Changes is said to be the oldest Chinese text. Some schools claim it predates history, but modern scholarship suggests that the earliest layer of the text may date from the end of the second millennium BCE. The oldest fragments of manuscript found date back to 475 to 221 BCE.

The I Ching, an account of ancient cosmic principles, was mainly used by fortune tellers in the marketplace. This oracle offered hope and a sense of reassurance for illiterate peasants by providing an understanding of their experiences and their future. In contrast, the elite, powerful classes tended to hold a belief that their fate was determined by their virtues and actions.

The most significant events in three thousand years of Chinese cultural history bear the indelible mark of this text. Confucianism and Taoism, the two most prominent branches of Chinese philosophy, trace their roots to the I Ching. Gardner and Lois Murphy[27] explain that its pronouncements are drawn from the general principles of the universe affecting human life. Richard Wilhelm, translator of the I Ching, notes that,

> in addition to the law of change and to the images of the states of change ... another factor to be considered is the course of action. Every situation demands an action that is appropriate for it. In every situation there is a right and wrong course of action. Obviously the right course of action brings good fortune and the wrong course brings misfortune. Which, then, is the right course of action in the given case? This question was the decisive factor.[28]

Wilhelm felt that the sheer magical and oracular use of this book is only part of its potentiality:

> Of far greater significance than the use of the Book of Changes as an oracle is its other use, namely, as a book of wisdom. Lao-Tsu, the father of Taoism, knew this book, and some of his profoundest aphorisms were inspired by this book. ... Confucius too knew about the Book of Changes and devoted himself to reflect upon it. ... The Book of Changes as edited and annotated by Confucius is the version that has come down to our time.[29]

Confucianism

Confucianism is a system of moral law canonized from the teachings of the Chinese philosopher, Confucius.[30] It has a strong influence in China, Taiwan, Korea, Japan, and Vietnam. Confucianism addresses ethical, social, political, philosophical, and theological questions based on everyday human experience. It focuses on the cultivation of virtue and maintenance of morals. *Ren* states the obligation toward altruistic and humane behavior toward fellow citizens. *Yi* adds the obligation to be morally good and righteous and *li* denotes behavioral guidelines. According to Confucianism, humans can learn, improve, and attain perfection through individual and community-based effort. Confucianism exhorts all people to strive for the ideal of becoming a *junzi* (lord's child) combining the qualities of saint, scholar, and gentleman. Pettiness in mind and heart, narrow self-interest, greed, superficiality, and materialism should be avoided. The fundamental moral values of honesty and righteousness should receive the top priority, even if it means giving up one's life.

Relationships are central to Confucianism. Our relationships with parents, children, bosses, or colleagues carry specific guidelines and duties, often hierarchically determined. However, while juniors are to be reverent to their superiors, in turn, superiors are to hold an attitude of respect and benevolence toward their subordinates. These guidelines fulfill the ultimate goal of social harmony. Every individual should know and adhere to his or her place in the social order. Confucius is said to have defined government to be proper when the prince is prince, the minister is minister, the father is father, and the son is son.

The profound influence that Confucianism holds over the Chinese is observed in their psychology of bringing up children. The impact of society, environment, and surroundings on a child, even in the mother's womb, and what steps need to be taken to ensure the child is born endowed with good qualities, are still strictly adhered to in Chinese families. The Confucian influence holds morality and truthfulness to be the highest good of human nature.

Taoism

The *Tao Te Ching*[31] (The Classic of the Way and Its Power or Virtue), was purportedly written by Lao Tzu in sixth century BCE. The word Tao refers to the nature of things and the subtle omnipresent power of the Universe. Taoism had a profound influence on the culture of China and some of its neighboring countries.

It's not hard to understand why Confucius had difficulty in appreciating or acknowledging Lao Tzu. Where Confucianism is practical and pragmatic, Taoism is distinctly mystical and intuitive. Taoism's essential aim is to establish harmony with all the interrelated aspects of the Universe. It considers the intellect as a barrier and the path to enlightenment as a process of elimination rather than an accumulation of intellectual knowledge.

Taoists see humans as a microcosm of the universe reflecting the five elements: earth, wood, water, air, and fire. Taoists gain knowledge of the universe by the three jewels of compassion, moderation, and humility. Self-understanding is developed using rituals, exercises, and substances to align their physical and mental states with cosmic forces in the universe.

The concept of *yin-yang* symbolizes the way in which seemingly contrary forces are interconnected, interdependent, and cyclical in the natural world. Yin and yang are always opposite and equal qualities. When one quality reaches its peak, it will naturally begin to transform into the opposite quality. Another important concept is *Pu*, which is a symbol for a state of pure potential and perception without prejudice; seeing things just as they are.

Taoist thought is focused on the relationship between humanity and the cosmos, health and longevity, and *Wu Wei* (action through inaction). *Wu wei*, a central concept in Taoism, facilitates the goal of being in harmony with the Tao. Literally meaning "without action," it is often expressed by the paradox *wei wu wei*, meaning "action without action" or "effortless effort." Effortless effort is key to spiritual development.

The will is a funny thing. In its highest potential, we align it to the higher self. Sometimes it becomes disconnected leading us to emulate a chicken with its head cut off or a motorboat that has lost its rudder. At other times, the will is aligned to ego with its fear, doubt, confusion, and anger. We can focus our will in any direction, toward or against our soul. Taoist philosophy proposes that the universe works harmoniously according to its own ways. Taoism asserts that aligning our will with the natural universe leads to harmony with all things whereas going against it leads to disharmony.

Vignette—Realigning the Will

Mark seemed to be in permanent fight or flight syndrome as if he were facing constant danger. He complained of constant tension in his neck and shoulders and was clearly in a perpetual state of agitated rumination. When, in our first session, he described the ambiance of extreme conflict and unpredictability he experienced growing up, the origins of his distress became evident. In response, Mark had become hyper-vigilant. It was as if he suffered from an unconscious impulse to overcome an enemy and regain control. We talked about the energy he was expending to fend off a conflict that was of the past. Mark had left home but had internalized rather than left behind the dynamic.

Mark went into his breathwork session with an agenda. His breath indicated that he was fighting and under a lot of pressure inside, in addition to the pressure he put on himself to achieve something in the session. Mark habitually used his will to fight the inner turmoil. Although this seems the rational thing to do, emotional life does not follow the same rules as outside life. Fighting with our inner tensions only adds to them and leads to escalation. It's like putting a match to gunpowder.

When tendencies come to the forefront in therapy, it is because they are ready to be addressed. I gently stated my observation, "I get the sense you are fighting with something and putting pressure on yourself to get somewhere." I placed my hands on an energy lock used in Jin Shin Jyutsu that's energetic significance is "let go and let God." After a few minutes, Mark went into a deep emotional release. When the catharsis subsided, his breath became calm and rhythmic indicating he had come to a state of peace.

After the session, he was able to explain his experience to me. My cue of pointing out his use of will led him to contact the root of his feelings of powerlessness. He realized that his compensatory attempts to gain a sense of control had made a mess of his adult life. In subsequent sessions, Mark continued to gain the understanding that he no longer needed to act on this defense mechanism. He was increasingly able to let go and trust the flow of life.

Our negative or stuck patterns are thorns in our side causing our will to misalign. Integration of the realization is what counts. We come face-to-face with an old enemy—habit. Self-awareness and sincere self-observation are our allies to help us realize and then modify the habits that form around our defenses, leading to empowerment and self-mastery.

LIMITATIONS OF EASTERN PSYCHOLOGIES

Eastern societies consider tradition to be an asset, and not a phase to be overcome. Strong social ties, values, and connection to nature are part of that tradition and they have brought meaning and connection to people's lives. Despite the stable foundations it provides, it has a shadow side. Adhering to tradition or systematic rejection of modernity without a dose of wisdom can make it confining. In this case reliance on social ties becomes a form of social control. Strong community ties can give us a sense of belonging, strength, and security, but can also build a limiting wall in which the community opposes unique individual expression, creating a kind of fundamentalism. Social norms can even turn our relationship to nature into a static bond where we miss out on the potential to open our consciousness and experience our lives in new ways. We may focus so strongly on what is good in our traditions that we do not see the down sides or the possibilities for new alternatives, or for wider and higher vistas to explore. Tradition can be liberating when it provides a stable foundation from which to venture out into our unique path of evolution, but it can become binding when it closes us off to approaches that lead to our growth and transformation.

Western societies tend not to be as bound by tradition. This leaves individuals free to follow the voice of their own conscience. Western modernity adheres to a belief in freedom of thought and expression, individual emancipation, human rights, and women's rights in a way that is unprecedented. However, modernization in the West too often involves rejecting tradition, leaving us without the moral guidelines we need to make constructive choices for ourselves, society, and nature. Leaving behind tradition might feel liberating, but if it leaves us with a lack of meaning or sense of belonging that comes from healthy family and social ties, it is not freedom, but illusion. Rejection of tradition at the cost of common sense results in a mindset that justifies colonization, imperialism, and exploitation. We have created a society that has the capacity for its own self-destruction.

STEPPING STONES FOR AN INTEGRAL PSYCHOLOGY

Now that we have traversed the main tenets of Eastern psychologies, we can weave together some observations or conjectures. In both the East and West, religious and spiritual traditions lay the foundation for psychology. Indian psychology aspired toward the transcendent or cosmic consciousness. Chinese psychology was primarily focused on social norms and ethics. Its more mystical aspects aspired toward harmony with cosmic energies and laws. Neither China nor India developed a psychological system that dealt unambiguously with the specific problems of individuals. They reflect a collective and cosmic worldview. The West is rooted in individual existence and individual relationships, solving the problems of day-to-day life. The East seeks alignment within and the West seeks adaptation outside. An Eastern psychologist carries his laboratory and his apparatus within himself whereas the Western psychologist considers his environment to be his laboratory. The Eastern psychologist relaxes, contemplates, and deals with his dilemmas through yoga and meditation.

CONCLUSION

It is not easy to judge which psychology is better, Eastern or Western. Both can lead us to freedom or bondage. When followed with discernment, both Eastern and Western approaches can pave the way for our liberation. At present, these two approaches are converging. Unification brings forth the opportunity for diverse cultures to learn from each other and embrace the best of both worlds. This is possible in all disciplines, all aspects of life, including psychology in which it brings the possibility for a more universal, inclusive, and congruent way forward.

We can make our minds so like still water that beings gather about us,
that they may see, it may be, their own images,
and so live for a moment with a clearer, perhaps
even with a fiercer life because of our quiet.

William Butler Yeats

NOTES

1. Sri Aurobindo, "Letters on Yoga I," *The Complete Works of Sri Aurobindo*, Volume 28, (2013, Pondicherry, India: Sri Aurobindo Ashram Press), p. 411.

2. Régis Airault, *Les Fous de l'Inde, Délires d'Occidentaux et Sentiment Océanique* (2002, Paris: Petite Edition Payot).

3. Girilal Jain's, "Assessing India's Progress" appeared in *The Times of India* on August 15, 1986, Bombay, in M. K. Gandhi, *The Essence of Hinduism* (1987, Ahmedabad: Navajivan Publishing House), p. viii.

4. The original form of the swastika was either used alone or alongside the reverse (moon or dark) form which was unfortunately misappropriated and misused by Adolf Hitler. This has given this originally positive symbol a negative connotation in the West.

5. Sri Aurobindo, "Hymns to the Mystic Fire," *The Complete Works of Sri Aurobindo*, Vol. 16 (2013, Pondicherry, India: Sri Aurobindo Ashram Press), p. 141.

6. Sri Aurobindo, "The Secret of the Veda," *The Complete Works of Sri Aurobindo*, Vol. 15 (1998, Pondicherry, India: Sri Aurobindo Ashram Press), pp. 45–46.

7. S. Rangaswami, *The Roots of Vedanta: Selections from Sankara's Writings* (2012, India: Penguin, Kindle edition), p. 559.

8. Sri Aurobindo, "Kena and Other Upanishads," *Complete Works of Sri Aurobindo* (2001, Pondicherry, India: Sri Aurobindo Ashram Press), Vol.18, p. 356.

9. Sri Aurobindo, "Kena and Other Upanishads," *Complete Works of Sri Aurobindo*, (2001, Pondicherry, India: Sri Aurobindo Ashram Press), Vol. 18, p. 356.

10. Sri Aurobindo, *The Upanishads*, Sri Aurobindo Birth Centenary Library (SABCL) (1972, Pondicherry, India: Sri Aurobindo Ashram Press), Vol.12, pp. 6–7.

11. Sri Aurobindo, "Essays on the Gita," in *The Complete Works of Sri Aurobindo* (1997, Pondicherry, India: Sri Aurobindo Ashram Press), p. 540.

12. Georg Feuerstein, *The Yoga-Sutra of Patañjali: A New Translation and Commentary* (1989, Vermont: Inner Traditions); Edwin Bryant, *The Yoga Sutras of Patañjali: A New Edition, Translation, and Commentary* (2015, New York: North Point Press).

13. It is traditional in India for spiritual teachers to interpret scriptures. The foremost interpretations of Patanjali's Yoga Sutras have been written by: Swami Vivekananda, Swami Satchitananda, Swami Prabhavananda, and B.K.S. Iyengar.

14. Chapter VI, verse 47.

15. Natalie Tobert, *Spiritual Psychologies* (2014, Kindle edition), p. 478.

16. 600–527 BCE.

17. D.R. Sardesai, *India: The Definitive History* (2008, Boulder, CO: Westview), p. 60.

18. "Ford-Crossers, Those Who Lead Others Across the Ocean of Samsara," D.R. Sardesai, *India: The Definitive History*, (2008, US: Westview) p. 60.

19. George Murphy and Lois Murphy, *Asian Psychology* (1968, New York: Basic Books), pp. 108–109.

20. See Margot E. Borden and Prahalad S. Shekhawat, "Buddhist Practice and Principles and Their Place in Organizations," in Sharda S. Nandram and Margot E. Borden, eds., *Spirituality and Business: Exploring Possibilities for a New Management Paradigm* (2009, Heidelberg, Germany: Springer).

21. Shunryu Suzuki, *Zen Mind, Beginner's Mind* (2011, Boston: Shambhala), p. 25.

22. Suzuki, 2011, p. 29.

23. Suzuki, 2011, p. 33.

24. Suzuki, 2011, p. 34.

25. Dalai Lama, *In My Own Words* (2009, New Delhi: Hay House), pp. 2–4.

26. Dr. Francis Hsu, *Clan, Caste, and Club: A Comparative Study of Chinese, Hindu, and American Ways of Life* (1963, Princeton, NJ: Van Nostrand), pp. 163, 172, 205.

27. Murphy and Murphy, 1968.

28. Richard Wilhelm, trans., *The I Ching, or Book of Changes* (translation from Chinese to German by Richard Wilhelm, rendered into English by Cary F. Baynes, 2nd ed.), (1968, New York; Bollingen Foundation), p. liii.

29. Wilhelm, 1968, p. *liv*.

30. 551–478 BCE.

31. Lao Tzu, trans. D.C. Lau, *Tao Te Ching* (1968, New York: Penguin Books).

Chapter Four

Sri Aurobindo's Integral
Yoga Psychology

Sri Aurobindo[1] was one of India's great mystic philosophers. He combined profound spiritual realization with a detailed, in-depth, and structured understanding of human nature and potential that gave birth to a new vision for psychology.

Along with many Indians under the British rule, Aurobindo's father rejected everything Indian. Pooling together his meager resources, he sent Aurobindo, at the age of seven, to England, along with his brothers. Aurobindo became a first-class classics scholar at King's College, Cambridge. Returning to India at the age of twenty, he began exploring the roots of Indian culture and its spiritual literature while also throwing himself into revolutionary activities. He was the principal leader of the early movement for independence from British rule and his political writings were largely responsible for igniting the ideal of independence. While he was in solitary confinement awaiting trial for sedition, he began having powerful spiritual experiences which changed the course of his life. After acquittal for lack of evidence, he continued for a short time in the political field. By 1910, he left politics behind and devoted his life to his spiritual practice, writing, and teaching. In 1920, he was joined by a spiritual collaborator, Mirra Alfassa,[2] a French woman who became known as the Mother. Together they developed a new spiritual discipline and teaching called integral yoga, itself an integration of Eastern and Western thought. Its aim was the unification and divinization of spirit and matter. Sri Aurobindo had a distinguished scholarship of both Eastern and Western intellectual traditions and was a prolific writer and poet. His complete works comprise thirty-seven massive volumes, covering in vivid detail his spiritual insights and experiences, and illumining many other important fields of thought. The Mother's writings and recorded talks also comprise many volumes focused principally on psychological and spiritual development.

As I reflect on the life and work of Sri Aurobindo and the Mother, it recaptures the excitement of the moment I discovered their work in the dining hall at the ashram in Pondicherry. Their writings continue to nourish my mind and soul with a sense of spiritual foundations, orientation, and wonder, year after year.

Sri Aurobindo's writings convey his mystical insights with a flowery, poetic, and dense style making it most easily accessible from deeply meditative and highly concentrated states of awareness. This is reflected in the language used in this chapter which is, as the reader will undoubtedly notice, denser and less ordinary than elsewhere in this book. That said, I have tried to make it as accessible as possible.

INTEGRAL PSYCHOLOGY

The schools of psychology we have covered thus far convey partial understandings of human consciousness insofar as they stem from a foundation of cognition. Sri Aurobindo's edge is gained by the fact that his works do not originate in the mind, in cognition, but were first inspired by his divine perception and then structured in minutest detail to transmit them to seekers.

Sri Aurobindo's vast vision elucidates the psychological and mystical aspects of human consciousness. From a developmental perspective, they address our early life, the formation of our ego, sense of self, personal constructs, behavior, the functioning of the mind (our thoughts), emotions, and senses. Integral psychology explores consciousness in all its gradations from matter and intellectual development to a detailed examination of our spiritual potential. Beyond this, it tells us of higher and further possibilities that await us as both human beings and consciousness evolve. Sri Aurobindo felt that our highest potential was to transform the ordinary human consciousness and life into a spiritualized consciousness and a divinized life.

Planes of Consciousness

While his teachings do not only address our transcendent or divine nature, but "Sri Aurobindo has through personal exploration and experience mapped out and intimately described the entire terrain of consciousness in all its gradations."[3] A major element in Sri Aurobindo's thought and a reflection of his own inner journey is awareness of many levels of consciousness and the functioning at these levels. Sri Aurobindo briefly sketches out this wide, complex, and hidden terrain of our consciousness:

> There are three elements in the totality of our being: there is the submental and the subconscient which appears to us as if it were inconscient, comprising

the material basis and a good part of our life and body; there is the subliminal, which comprises the inner being, taken in its entirety of inner mind, inner life, inner physical with the soul or psychic entity supporting them; there is this waking consciousness which the subliminal and the subconscient throw up on the surface, a wave of their secret surge. But even this is not an adequate account of what we are; for there is not only something deep within behind our normal self-awareness, but something also high above it: that too is ourselves, other than our surface mental personality, but not outside our true self; that too is a country of our spirit. For the subliminal proper is no more than the inner being on the level of the Knowledge-Ignorance luminous, powerful and extended indeed beyond the poor conception of our waking mind, but still not the supreme or the whole sense of our being, not its ultimate mystery. We become aware, in a certain experience, of a range of being superconscient to all these three, aware too of something, a supreme highest Reality sustaining and exceeding them all, which humanity speaks of vaguely as Spirit, God, the Oversoul: from these superconscient ranges we have visitations and in our highest being we tend towards them and to that supreme Spirit. There is then in our total range of existence a superconscience as well as a subconscience and inconscience, overarching and perhaps enveloping our subliminal and our waking selves, but unknown to us, seemingly unattainable and incommunicable.[4]

Let us briefly analyze and elaborate on this passage to draw out more clearly its distinctions and implications. He first distinguishes the normal waking consciousness, which is made up of physical, vital,[5] and mental levels, from a more obscure subconscient layer of consciousness which is hidden from our normal awareness but nevertheless influences our waking state, particularly our body and life energies (i.e., the physical and vital levels). The subconscient can also cloud, influence, or overpower our mental perceptions and our rational thought and intelligent will.

The subliminal consciousness, like the subconscient, is also hidden from our normal awareness. Like the waking state, it is also comprised of physical, vital, and mental levels. These subliminal realms differ from the normal outer consciousness in that they are vaster, freer, and capable of greater and subtler powers. We sometimes get glimpses of these realms in vivid dreams, though dreams may also reflect influences or impressions from the more obscure subconscient layer. We may get glimpses of their greater powers in phenomena associated with hypnosis (such as superior memory, knowledge, and cognitive abilities), which utilizes this hidden, inner layer of the consciousness. Telepathy and premonitions also stem from this subliminal consciousness. Also included is our deepest inner psychic being or soul personality, which holds together and, as we evolve, increasingly organizes these various parts of the being around itself and guides their growth and evolution. Our waking consciousness is merely an outer fringe of this vaster, inner part of our being.

Finally, Sri Aurobindo distinguishes all these lower and mid-level parts of us from the superconscient realms of consciousness, which include several levels of a greater spiritual mind consciousness, but which soars even higher to a pure totality of awareness. Commonly defined as God, he refers to this as the supreme Spirit or Supermind. Thus, according to Sri Aurobindo, we are normally aware of only a small outer range of our total consciousness, but we can enlarge our consciousness both horizontally (inwardly and outwardly) and vertically (to higher spiritual and to lower subconscient levels), resulting in both greater awareness and greater powers, and unite with all in the consciousness of the supreme Spirit.

Lofty as this seems, when I take the time to penetrate into his readings, I feel myself connecting to a sense of direction, an upward and organizing pull, built upon an inner, spiritual structure. This quenches my thirst for universal truth. It puts into words, that which I have experienced, intuited and longed for while giving a map, that appeals to my intellect and makes it adaptable to the practice of psychotherapy. While some of the traditional schools which speak of truth vs illusion leave me with no sense of foundation, as I do not wish to identify with, what they call illusion, Aurobindo's model allows me to put my feet firmly on the ground and my head swimming deliciously in the clouds.

Liberation vs Transformation

Having briefly sketched Sri Aurobindo's conception of the ranges and realms of consciousness, it is important to clarify the aim of his path of yoga, which he said is "nothing but practical psychology."[6] He has made a point to distinguish his yoga from most traditional yogas in the sense that his aim is a *transformation of* the whole lower and outer consciousness, not merely a *liberation from* the ordinary consciousness by entering into the spiritual consciousness or pure Spirit while leaving the outer nature unchanged and relatively inactive. In India, for example, you may find spiritual masters who spend most of their life in an indrawn state of trance, called *samadhi*. Others may continue to live their outer life but inwardly live in a spiritual state of consciousness unaffected by what happens in the outer life. Outwardly they may live a life limited by ignorance and error, and subject to illness, disease, and pain, but inwardly their consciousness is liberated and unaffected. It is as if all this were occurring to someone else and not to them, for they are identified with the inner Spirit and not the outward life.

Sri Aurobindo made it clear that his yoga was different. His path takes liberation as a step on the way, ultimately seeking the complete transformation and divinization of the whole consciousness in the greater light and power of a dynamic spiritual consciousness (Supermind). This changes not only the aim but the very character of the practice. Usually in yoga, one aspect of our nature is selected to serve as a means of reaching the transcendent spirit. This aspect is then directed solely toward the aim rather than allowed its usual expression, and the rest of our nature is quieted down so that it does not interfere. Thus, our outer nature is reduced in its functioning to a thin strip of activity oriented toward the spirit. It may be through an exclusive concentration of the mind or the emotional nature through devotion to the Supreme Being or control of vital energies in the body through hatha yoga, specialized breathing practices, or other means. Typically one of these means is selected to the exclusion of others though sometimes several are combined. The aim of integral yoga is to make all of the daily activities a part of the discipline by bringing in a spiritual attitude while also utilizing practices of mental concentration, spiritual devotion, and the will to discipline and convert all the resistant and egoistic tendencies of our nature. The normal activities of life are not shunned, but they are changed and uplifted in their aim and character, with a goal to perfect them and shed their base and the forms of which we are less aware. Integral yoga does not seek an escape from life into an inner beatific transcendent state, but a divinized life on earth, one that is rich and varied, but also harmonious, beautiful, and full of delight. It aims not only at a spiritual change of one's own individual life but also of the collective life of humanity.

PRACTICES IN INTEGRAL YOGA

Sri Aurobindo described the broad lines of his discipline of yoga in *The Synthesis of Yoga* (1999), which like many of his other major works, first appeared as a series of essays in the journal *Arya* between 1914 and 1920. Much of Sri Aurobindo's discipline of yoga was based on his interpretation of the Bhagavad Gita, which he presented in a modern psychological language while also enlarging its aims and bringing out more fully its implications. From the Gita he derived a triple path of works, knowledge, and devotion which he synthesized in such a way that they became complementary and synergistic, both aiding and completing each other. In addition, he developed a new fourth limb of his discipline, which he called the yoga of self-perfection. This was largely an explanation of the discipline which he had worked out himself, or rather which was revealed to him in Alipore Jail, and which he later chronicled in his spiritual diary. This part focuses on the perfection of the mental, vital, and physical nature, as well as on the development of the higher planes of consciousness leading toward the Supermind, which makes the perfection and divinization of the former possible.

His exposition of integral yoga was not limited to *The Synthesis of Yoga* and his four-fold path. His small book, *The Mother*, further lays out the essence of his path in a powerfully concise way. He also comprehensively described the methods and practical issues encountered in the practice of the integral yoga in his three-volume *Letters on Yoga*, a collection of his voluminous correspondence with his disciples about their individual practices.

The three principal yogas of India are *karma yoga* (the yoga of dedicated work and activity), *bhakti yoga* (the yoga of love and devotion), and *jnana yoga* (the yoga of knowledge). All of these yogas can lead to God-realization, but they do not necessarily lead beyond that to what Sri Aurobindo calls the supramental consciousness, as they ordinarily aim at transcendence of all manifestation. Moreover, they are often pursued independently, in isolation from the others, rather than in combination or integrally. Sri Aurobindo's yoga includes all three and aims not only at transcendence of the lower consciousness but also at a transformation of the lower in the light and power of the divine higher nature. While his works give a philosophical basis and broad lines of guidance, they do not give much in the way of specific techniques or practices. In part this was because he emphasized that each person has a unique path, which must be determined from within, based on his nature and prior development; a standardized practice for all would be unsuitable. But, he also believed that each person must find the Divine within to guide him or her according to his or her own nature, or else accept the guidance of a living guru of one's choice who would perceive and understand their unique requirements. Outlined below is the four-fold path, with emphasis on the psychological implications.

Karma Yoga: The Yoga of Works

The essence of the first limb of integral yoga, the yoga of works, is the inner dedication in thought, attitude, and spirit of all of our activities to the Divine, the source and goal, and essence of all that is. This is a progressive undertaking; we start by making an inner offering of our actions whenever we remember. As our remembrance becomes more frequent, this increasingly becomes a felt, inner experience. This is because everything exists in the Divine, the Divine exists in all, and the Divine is all that exists. Through fragmentation of the Divine consciousness for the creation of this multitudinous universe, the consciousness of the oneness has been lost, hidden, and buried deep within. Each person and thing is, in reality, a different form and expression of the One Being, and the aim of the yoga is to recover this hidden consciousness of oneness and to bring out its ramifications and greater possibilities into the individual and collective life.

This practice of inner offering is a conscious acknowledgment to oneself, that in truth it is the Divine that acts through our acts. The source and substance of our individual vital energy, physical ability, and mental intelligence is the One Divine, who is all. Ordinarily we claim these as our personal possessions; we say it is *my* ability, *my* intelligence, *my* work. But when we look more deeply, we see that our intelligence and abilities are a function of our learning from others and from the world in which we live. They are also a function of our physiological constitution—the systems, organs, cells, molecules, atomic and subatomic particles of which we are made and which are in constant dynamic interaction with the environment and the world around us. They are also a function of the fundamental and constantly moving energy which pervades and drives all living and nonliving things and which changes from one form to another but is never lost or destroyed. We cannot honestly claim that all these things are "mine" or "me" in the ordinary sense of what we call ourselves, though it may be said that this greater, eternal, and universal energy and intelligence in which we live and have our being is our true self. Through our progressive inner self-offering, we weaken the false identification with our limited self, our ego, which is only a small, limited movement on the surface of this greater self.

Practically, this inner dedication to the Divine takes a variety of forms. There is, first of all, our attempt to discipline ourselves to remember and offer our work and activities. At first, one does this before and after our actions, but gradually with increased practice, a continual remembrance develops in the "back of the mind" during the activity itself. Thus, in a sense, it develops into a constant inner concentration on the Divine in the midst of our life activities. Further, this need not be restricted to outer activities; we can learn to offer our breath, the beating of our heart, our thoughts and feelings to the Divine, and increasingly sense that these occur as an outflow of the Divine life and mental energy within us. Moreover, we can learn to inwardly offer not only our own actions to the Divine but begin to perceive that the Divine is also working through all others and through all the activities and events that occur around us in the world.

While this inward dedication can be implicit in whatever action we may engage in whether sweeping the floor or composing a symphony, there is also a value associated with doing and offering work that may further the Divine's purposes in the world. For Sri Aurobindo, the world is a site for an evolution of consciousness. This evolution starts from inconscient matter, evolves through higher and higher life forms, eventually reaches self-awareness in the mind of human beings, and will continue to reveal higher forms of spiritual consciousness beyond the mind in higher forms of spiritual beings beyond the human being. The present humanity is at a pivotal stage in this evolution, for we can consciously participate in this evolution and contribute to its upward ascent. We can be an instrument for the Divine's efflorescence spreading influence in the world. We can work for the uplifting of human life toward the

Divine, work for the spiritual awakening of both ourselves and others, work for the establishment of a more and more divine life upon earth.

Jnana Yoga: The Yoga of Knowledge

The second limb of integral yoga is the yoga of knowledge. This part of the discipline hinges on a distinction at the very essence of the creation or manifestation. There is on one side a Being or Person within us who is the witness or conscious observer (*purusha*), and on the other side, there is an active dynamic nature that is constantly in movement (*prakriti*) and which can be witnessed or observed. This distinction runs from the highest, universal planes of consciousness down to each person on earth.

The yoga of knowledge focuses on the development of a witness consciousness. It is through this separation of the witness aspect that a spiritual liberation from our nature becomes possible. We can learn to see and sense that everything that occurs, whether in us or around us, is a part of one vast interconnected universal nature. Observation of our physical body reveals to us that it is merely our form, not truly who we are. Similarly, we may perceive emotions and thoughts rising in us. Often they may overpower our conscious sense of being separate from them, and we lose ourselves in their impulsive activity. Similarly, we observe the world around us and attempt to get some degree of conscious control over the things that most concern us.

We realize it is not so much that *we* think, but that thought occurs in us. Similarly, emotions occur in us and in those around us. Both thoughts and emotions are constantly flowing into us from others around us and going out from us to others. Even our physical actions take place independently of our conscious choice, and this becomes particularly evident with regard to automatic physiological processes or habitual actions that are counter to our conscious will. Of course, we can and do *will* many of our actions, but there is the deeper question whether our own will is entirely free and independent or is itself a part of universal nature, created, influenced, and shaped by mental and vital forces beyond our individual choice or control. We can learn to watch the various movements as if they were a movie taking place before our eyes.

For developing witness consciousness, Sri Aurobindo and the Mother recommended meditation and silent concentration, standing back from the thoughts, perceptions, and feelings. It is sometimes useful to first concentrate for a time on the breath, consciously observing the inhalations and exhalations, as this helps quiet the activity of mind and focus on the present moment. Gradually we may become aware of thoughts, feelings, or sensations rising in the consciousness. If we do not get involved in the thoughts, they tend to quiet down by themselves. It is possible and desirable, through this practice, to completely silence the mind. In that silence, it is possible to become aware of many aspects of consciousness. Before this inner witness, a greater and wider consciousness begins to reveal itself over time.

Bhakti Yoga: The Yoga of Devotion

The yoga of devotion focuses on the development and refinement of emotions, turning them from their usual aspects to love for an omnipresent Divine. An integral psychology must take note of all the parts of the consciousness and aim to eliminate their narrowness and blockages and perfect them. This is because all the parts of the consciousness are intimately intermeshed; the emotional and instinctual parts of our nature often distort the thought and spiritual perceptions or even push them aside altogether and temporarily dominate our awareness. The emotions are often unwittingly the field of dark and conflicting energies. Bhakti yoga aims to purify them and turn them to their highest possibilities.

In Sri Aurobindo's integral psychology, love and delight are essentially divine powers. Originating in the highest divine consciousness, they have become—here in the human consciousness—perverted by the darker powers born of the inconscience of matter into their opposites, such as hate, anger, fear, jealousy, and greed. However, they have the potential to be the most powerful of all unifying forces, not only in uniting individualities with each other but in uniting each one of us with the one divine existence that underlies all. Love is essentially a quest for union, a complete self-giving and losing of our separateness in a larger unified existence, whether of a united couple in the human sense, a higher cause or pursuit (e.g., justice, artistic beauty, knowledge), the fundamental ground of all existence, or the Supreme Being. In its origin, love flows out freely from the One Divine Being and permeates and progressively reunites this seemingly divided existence in its absolute delight and completeness.

In yoga this divine power of love becomes entirely self-aware and seeks its ultimate reunification with the One Divine Being, shedding its limited and degraded forms that it has taken in its upward evolutionary drive. Typically, human love is tainted by a hidden or unconscious self-regard; we love another person (or thing) on condition of a return of some kind, and when this return does not meet our expectations, it may fade or even turn to anger or hate. But the essence of the deepest spiritual devotion is a complete self-giving in which we lose our individual boundaries in the greater self.

Here the issue of impersonality *vs* personality arises. Some spiritual teachings say that the Absolute is an impersonal state of existence or consciousness, or even a nonexistence, an extinction of all perception, variation, or differentiation. Others, however, assert that the Absolute is not merely an infinite expanse of existence or nonexistence, but a Supreme Being. Sri

Aurobindo argues that personality and impersonality are two inseparable sides of the truth of existence. Throughout the hierarchy of existence, from the highest and most inclusive to the infinitesimal seemingly separate parts, we see that energies and forces take on embodiments, become unified wholes that are contained within larger wholes. The wholes represent the relatively self-conscious individual existence through which the one Supreme Person expresses itself.

According to Sri Aurobindo, the Supreme Being is fully capable of taking up a personal relation with us in whatever form or personality we conceive, whether Christ, Krishna, Hashem, Buddha, or human guru, just as we take up personal relations with others. The Divine surrounds us, interacts with us, and meets us through all human and nonhuman forms. If we conceive of him solely as the people and things of everyday life, we encounter existence in those limited terms; if we conceive of him solely as a vast impersonal energy constantly moving in the vastness of empty space, that becomes for us the impersonal, purposeless, cold reality of our existence; if we perceive him as a punitive extra-cosmic Godhead, he will train us through his punishments and rewards; if we perceive him as a Supreme Being of consciousness, love and delight immanent in the world as well as beyond it, he can greet us as a spiritual teacher, friend, father, or mother and lead us to him along the sweetest pathways.

Yoga of Self-Perfection

Whereas the first three limbs of integral yoga are largely based on Sri Aurobindo's interpretation of the Bhagavad Gita, the fourth limb takes up several aspects which are unique to Sri Aurobindo's path. According to him, this largely consists in purifying and elevating all the parts of the nature—body, life, and mind—to their highest possible development. At the summit of this process, this leads to their transmutation and divinization. This includes their development and refinement to the highest possible human limits but aims to go beyond these limits by bringing out their higher divine possibilities. This is clearly not possible through the power of human effort alone, so a complete opening and surrender to the divine power and its unimpeded reshaping of the whole nature is an important aspect of this part of yoga. Sri Aurobindo describes several layers of the higher spiritual consciousness above the human intellect, which he calls higher mind, illumined mind, intuition, overmind, and at the summit, the truth-consciousness or Supermind. Each of these levels of consciousness is essentially spiritual, but their corresponding knowledge and power become more embracing, powerful, and perfect with each higher level.

The realization of the Supermind or supramental consciousness is central to Sri Aurobindo's yoga. In a way, this is its ultimate aim because he viewed it as alone, capable of fully transforming and divinizing the lower nature, including the body. He viewed Supermind as the next emerging principle in the earth's evolution after mind, a radically new and divine consciousness, and envisioned that a new race of supramental beings would embody this consciousness and take the lead in the evolutionary ascent. His aim, which the Mother said was achieved in 1956 after he left his body, was to establish Supermind as a basic principle in the earth's evolution, and once "brought down," he believed it would gradually organize and reveal itself. He believed that humanity would progressively be radically changed by its emergence, and would serve as a kind of evolutionary bridge to the new supramental being, a passage or step for souls in their evolutionary upward journey. He envisioned that the human mind, in at least a portion of humanity, would become a "mind of light," almost an extension or outer fringe of the Supermind, lit up by its luminosity. The practice of these four limbs of yoga is aimed at purifying and elevating all the parts of the nature, mind, and being of the practitioner thereby preparing them and opening the way for a transformation of consciousness.

PSYCHIC TRANSFORMATION

Sri Aurobindo explained that the transformation of human consciousness into an essentially dynamic divine consciousness must occur through three stages, which although overlapping are basically successive. The first of these is the *psychic* transformation. He suggested that in each individual thing in existence, there is an essence which is divine; he called this the psychic spark or psychic entity. In the course of evolution through many lives an organized being develops around this psychic spark, which he called the *psychic being*. This psychic being although essentially divine is, at first, weak and clouded over by the outer self. Therefore, it is not able to express itself in the outer life of the individual; it remains behind a veil deep within the subliminal consciousness and influences the outer life only indirectly as far as it can through its instruments of mind, life, and body. Though hidden deep within from the external nature, the psychic being is the central organizing principle of the individual, leading it in its upward evolutionary ascent, persisting between incarnations, gathering new experience in each life, and organizing more and more of this experience around this divine center. This is in stark contrast to the ideas of Western psychology holding that the ego is the central force in human beings. On the contrary, Sri Aurobindo said that in most human beings it expresses itself in a tendency toward all that is true, good, and beautiful. He indicated that most people are not aware of their psychic being, and it is usually only through the practice of yoga that it reveals itself to the waking consciousness, at first intermittently and eventually more and more fully and permanently. As it comes forward, we surrender and allow it to take conscious control over our life, leading us directly toward its higher divine possibilities. It progressively organizes all the activities of the mind, life, and body around itself so that they reflect and participate in its spontaneous and inherent self-giving and opening to the higher divine consciousness. This process of bringing the psychic being forward and organizing all the nature of mind, life, and body around it is called in Sri Aurobindo's terminology the *psychic transformation*.

SPIRITUAL TRANSFORMATION

The psychic being is hidden from the waking consciousness deep within behind a veil or barrier and is brought to the forefront through sadhana or spiritual practice. The higher spiritual consciousness is hidden from us above a lid or barrier and its qualities and powers can be brought down into our waking consciousness through sadhana. The spiritual consciousness is essentially an infinite existence that is omniscient, omnipotent, and full of delight and secretly upholds, supplies, and makes possible the limited physical existence in which we live. It is possible to break through this veil and rise up into this infinity of consciousness. It is dangerous to do this prematurely. It is safer to call it down into ourselves, in which case it generally prepares the nature first and reveals itself progressively according to our preparation and ability to receive it. Sri Aurobindo also indicates that it is usual in his spiritual path to experience over time a succession of ascents and descents of consciousness, which progressively establishes spiritual consciousness in the outer nature. His vision is that the higher consciousness be brought down not only into the mind but also into all the being from the highest parts of the mind down to the physical body.

There are four primary powers of this higher consciousness: calm and peace, light, bliss, and power. These can descend and be experienced and become a permanent part of the outer awareness and life. Generally, a state of deep imperturbable calm and peace is established first. It is best to call for this first to descend because it makes the descent of the other powers safer. Another power that descends is the spiritual light, and this is not simply a mental illumination or clarity of thought though they tend to come together. It can be perceived through our subtle sight as a visible light descending into the head or body from above. Ananda or spiritual bliss again usually descends into the head first, but it may be felt anywhere in the body or even as occupying the whole of the body. There are different experiences of this; it is perhaps most often experienced as a quiet and peaceful delight, but it also may be perceived as an intense delight or ecstasy. The seeker may also experience a descent of power. This may be felt as a subtle stream of force, or it may take the form of an intense or even overwhelming force taking hold of the entire consciousness and into whose hold we must simply abdicate and allow it to do its subtle work in our nature. This power is sensed as coming from above or emerging from deep within; it does not feel as if it is our own personal power and is not to be confused with an egoistic sense of power that also may be experienced by spiritual seekers (see almighty syndrome, chapter 7). These descents are more likely to occur when the consciousness is drawn deeply within, either in meditation or sleep. In the latter case, we may become quite conscious and/or awake during the experience itself. They are also more likely to occur as a result or after a period of intense inner aspiration and devotion to the Divine.

While such experiences may, at first, be fleeting, they tend to have lasting effects on the consciousness, preparing it, refining it, and opening it in such a way that future recurrences of the experiences are more likely, as well as more frequent and lasting. It is through such descents from the higher consciousness that the whole waking consciousness and lower nature is progressively transformed into a kind of outer annex of the limitless and more powerful spiritual consciousness above. It is part of the spiritual transformation. One feels their consciousness centered in the freedom and infinity of the spiritual consciousness above, with the physical and body consciousness merely an extension and outer vehicle for physical expression and action.

SUPRAMENTAL TRANSFORMATION

There are several levels of the spiritual consciousness between the intellect and the Supermind, and in the course of integral yoga, each of these levels is scaled and; their successively greater illumination and powers realized. The succession of ascents and descents of the consciousness is an important part of this process. The consciousness ascends to a certain height, and then its light and power is gradually assimilated into the lower nature, and as this assimilation proceeds, it may feel as if we have descended again into the lower consciousness. I like to use the imagery of climbing a spiral staircase here. This roadmap helps us keep our apparent ups and downs in perspective and, in turn, gives us the understanding we need to hold our course in the face of challenges. If the aspiration to go higher is maintained, the periods of assimilation may be relatively shorter and unperturbed. Higher ascents of consciousness can follow. These are an opening to greater knowledge and powers, which come down to change our outer life and nature. It is after a long process of such development that the consciousness may ascend to the Supermind and, in turn, its more powerful transforming effects are brought down into our life.

Unlike the other intervening levels of the spiritual consciousness, the Supermind is essentially omniscient and omnipotent. Sri Aurobindo calls it truth-consciousness. It operates under a different principle than mind; even the higher levels of the spiritual mind. The Supermind does not seek ignorance or knowledge from outside. In simple terms, it *is* everything and so knows everything as itself. It can also put a certain part of its knowledge or its being in the front of its consciousness, keeping the rest behind, but this is a voluntary action and not a fundamental division. If desired, it can bring forward whatever knowledge or powers are required for its immediate purpose. Similarly, its will is not divided within itself like the human will; neither is it divided from the universal will of the Divine. Thus, it does what must be done perfectly. It expresses perfectly what must be expressed, according to the universal will at the appropriate time and place. Its will is fundamentally and perfectly in sync with the truth of existence, and it reveals its greater powers which it keeps behind when and in the manner in which it is appropriate to do so.

Sri Aurobindo believed that it was only this supramental consciousness that could finally and radically transform the lower nature. The intervening levels have a successively greater power and transforming effect on our nature, but they cannot in themselves finally deliver it from the grip of its fundamental ignorance and incapacity. The physical body is particularly resistant to the intermediate spiritual powers to transform it and remains subject to illness, pain, incapacity, and death. Sri Aurobindo believed that the supramental power could enable the individual to become free from these shackles. This does not mean that we would be condemned to live eternally, but that leaving the body would be an act of will rather than an imposition by nature. Of course, even in the intervening levels of the spiritual mind, the substance of the person's consciousness would perceive its immortality, and the death of the body would be more or less like changing clothes. But Sri Aurobindo suggested that the Supermind would bring fundamental changes to the body's functioning and appearance, a greater lightness and plasticity, as well as harmony and perfection in all its movements.

PSYCHOPATHOLOGY AND DIAGNOSIS

It is possible to use Sri Aurobindo's framework to more deeply understand pathologies according to the level of consciousness at which they occur. Each individual's consciousness is composed of many layers which are in dynamic interaction with each other. Each of these layers contributes characteristic qualities to the whole personality which create imbalances in the personality, when they are either too weak or too dominant. Using Sri Aurobindo's framework and insights, clinical psychologist A.S. Dalal[7] has delineated many psychological problems that are associated with imbalances of these various levels of the consciousness, and the following is a brief summary of his findings.

Mental Disturbances

One of the foremost features of the human mind is that it has the ability to observe its own state, including its thoughts, perceptions, imaginations, and memories. It is this characteristic which makes it aware that it is experiencing a psychological disturbance in the first place. While the mind may be acutely aware of a psychological problem, it may feel powerless to solve or remove it, exacerbating the pain associated with it. Further, due to its ability to imagine and anticipate the future, the mind may imagine problems which are not there, exaggerate small problems into bigger ones, and become convinced that terrible events will occur which may never come to pass. It also has the capacity to look back in its memory at past events—and with the intrusion of certain negative tendencies of the vital nature—experience these memories with sorrow, regret, or remorse. Thus, the psychological pain associated with worry and anxiety, on the one hand, and regret and remorse, on the other hand, are due in large part to an unhealthy functioning of the mental consciousness.

Further, the mind has the troublesome ability to avoid seeing problems which are painful or inconvenient to admit or to face. This short circuit creates defense mechanisms such as rationalization, in which the mind finds excuses and justifications for gratifying the inappropriate impulses and desires of the vital nature; projection, in which the person attributes negative feelings or motives they are resisting to another person or thing. Here the cognitive functions of perception and judgment are distorted by unconscious feelings and impulses. We create defense mechanisms to survive perceived threats to our physical, emotional, or mental being. We then build a particular, but precarious psychological balance around that mechanism. Therefore, it may be dangerous to prematurely expose or remove them until we have the strength and balance to address the core issues. At the same time, our defense mechanisms prevent us from confronting and overcoming problems that may be impeding growth and psychological health.

Another type of disorder, associated with what Sri Aurobindo calls the physical mind, is unwanted mechanical thoughts which keep repeating themselves even though they serve no useful purpose. They may also be disturbing or destructive. For example, continuous repetitive thoughts of being worthless or having committed some serious offense are of this character and are common in severe depression. Similarly, repetitive thoughts that something terrible may happen often occurs in some anxiety disorders. More commonly, people may become obsessed with guilty, hostile, or lewd thoughts. Many others experience a restless, chaotic activity of the mind, such that it becomes like a busy marketplace, constantly active and shifting with no steady direction or purpose, and which interferes with concentration and goal-directed thought and behavior.

I once went on a meditation retreat after a particularly busy period in my life. I was amused to find that in place of the silence, peace, and life-changing insights I normally enjoy, my mind was like a heavy metal concert. Even though the content of the noise was entirely positive, it was if it had a mind of its own. It was only through perseverance and objectivity that, after a few days, I managed to allow the noise to drop away and enjoy the rest of my retreat in silence.

Vital Disturbances

Perhaps the most characteristic feature of our vital nature is desire. Desire itself is a state of disturbance though it may not be recognized as such by most people. Desire, craving, and the sense of *needing* something cause restlessness and agitation. At extreme levels, this becomes a kind of anguish and emotional suffering. Desire is always in the background of ordinary human functioning. When it gets out of line and becomes a predominating factor in the personality, it leads to a constant, restless striving and dissatisfaction with ourselves and our situation. Because the nature of desire is to want instant gratification, desire is also associated with impatience. When desires remain unsatisfied for too long, they may result in depression or anger. Fear and apprehension about big or small things is a common cause of suffering in normal psychological functioning. In their extreme, they may become exaggerated, painful, and paralyzing. Fear is commonly related to desire and attachment. We fear that our desire for some thing or condition will not be fulfilled.

Disturbances of the Physical Consciousness

The physical consciousness is characterized by inertia, commonly associated with weakness of the will. This malady contributes to addiction, laziness, and indolence. The physical consciousness is inert and does not want to move of its own accord, but rather is passive to whatever forces may act on it from outside. These are most often the ordinary forces of the lower vital nature—lust, anger, fear, despondency, desires for food and drink, and the like—responding to higher forces such as the directives of the mental will, the soul or spirit, which generally require a conscious choice and subtlety of response. The physical consciousness does not ordinarily have this until it has been disciplined and trained. Therefore, part of what spiritual practice is designed to achieve is training of the physical consciousness to automatically respond to the higher spiritual forces rather than to the lower forces of our ordinary vital nature.

A predominance of the physical consciousness leads to a general dullness and slowness in reacting to stimulation. It imparts insensitivity and coarseness. Due to its inertia, strong stimulation is required to move it. Hence, we are driven to seek strong stimulation, such as intense excitement and drama in order to feel something. Thus, it may contribute to extreme actions such as murder, suicide, cruelty, and violence, and on a smaller scale, fights, quarrels, and dramatic emotional upheavals.

Disturbances of the Subconscient

This part of the consciousness is associated with the purely physical and vital elements of the bodily life, a very obscure part of the consciousness which is unobserved by the mind and uncontrolled by it in its actions. It controls the processes and automatic responses of the hidden consciousness which operates in the cells, nerves, and the primitive functions of the senses and sense-mind which records and stores impressions of various stimuli acting on the individual. As recognized by psychoanalysis, the subconscient is the storehouse of things which have been repressed and kept out of conscious awareness, but which remain buried and continue to surreptitiously influence the consciousness and actions of the person. It is behind all habitual movements, especially of the physical and vital nature. Because the subconscient retains these habitual tendencies in its hidden storehouse, it is able to revive them even after they have been eliminated from the conscious part of the being, thus making habits particularly difficult to break. In this manner, the subconscient contributes to all types of addictions and maintains their repetitive movements even when the conscious part of the being wants to be rid of them and when they lead to disease or suffering.

The subconscient also retains all kinds of impressions from the environment which may influence the individual. The state of consciousness of the parents at the time of conception is considered in integral yoga psychology to leave a strong stamp on the psychology of the individual. Similarly, the states and behavior of the parents in the presence of their infant and young child are apt to leave lasting impressions in the subconscient, which continue to exert their hidden influences throughout life. The most serious forms of psychological disorder are often associated with early childhood neglect, abuse, or trauma. At the same time, the subtle influences of others in the family, community, and the culture as a whole in which the child grows up leave their impressions in the subconscient. This is significant given the violence, degradation, and deprivation endemic in many communities. Finally, the activities and subtle vibrations of the physical and social environment in the present as well as in the past are continually leaving their impressions in the individual's subconscient and exert their influences on the consciousness and actions of the person without his or her awareness of their source. This is perhaps why many spiritual disciplines emphasize the need for care in selecting one's associates and in creating and maintaining a healthy spiritual atmosphere in which to live.

Vignette—Spiritual Self-Delusion

Dr. Soumitra Basu and I facilitated bi-yearly three-day workshops in Paris over a period of several years on the theme Evolving in Consciousness. *On this particular occasion, there was a massive transport strike and Dr. Basu and I enjoyed long walks to and from the workshop venue, in the icy cold. After the workshop, we hosted a series of evening discussion groups to support the participants in a continual integration of the material covered. Arlette, one of the participants, had convinced herself, based on her reading of Sri Aurobindo's works that she had realized the Supermind. She outright expressed this with an angry defiance that was incongruent with her claim. I tried to give her a little extra attention as her behavior was somewhat disruptive to the group. After the evening's discussion group, we enjoyed a light supper. The conversation was engaging, and while no one was paying attention, Arlette gorged herself on wine and started to become obnoxious. The mind is a tricky thing. It becomes even more slippery when we venture into spiritual pursuits. Fortunately, I don't think anyone apart from Dr. Basu and I noticed Arlette's tomfoolery. As painful as it is to observe these types of situations, the combination of her defiant and self-righteous attitude and claims and the context of a group discussion, a confrontation would have been inappropriate and ill-received. I felt the best approach would be to reflect a higher possibility to her. I expressed warmth and compassion, speaking with her in a gentle and reassuring way. She seemed to calm down. I believe in respecting the individual choice and path of each person while gently inviting them toward healing and evolution.*

Adverse Forces

According to integral yoga psychology, adverse forces, also called hostile forces, are subtle entities and forces which exist in dimensions in the vital realms which are beyond the physical world. They exert their influences here in the physical world on people and events. They are recognized in most religious and spiritual traditions and are commonly referred to as demons. In the Indian tradition, three main types are distinguished—*asuras, rakshasas*, and *pishachas*, corresponding respectively with a predominance of mental, vital, or physical propensities. Marked physical or psychological weaknesses in a person can create an opening for adverse vital forces or beings to influence, attack, or even possess (completely or partially, momentarily or permanently), leading to various kinds of psychological disturbances. According to integral yoga psychology, psychotic disorders are typically due to possession of a person by a hostile entity. Such forces are said to be antidivine, and consciously opposed to spiritual growth and transformation. Thus, they tend to attack persons who are consciously pursuing a spiritual discipline. Wherever there are psychological weaknesses, hostile forces tend to influence the person through them and exacerbate the problems and severity associated with them. Excessive severity of otherwise ordinary psychological problems (e.g., anger, fear, lust, greed, egoism, etc.) may be a sign that adverse forces are at play. Focusing on developing objectivity and perseverance is helpful in building and strengthening our psychological makeup warding off such difficulties.

The Role of the Psychic Being in Mental Health

The psychic being, popularly referred to as the soul, is the divine element within each individual, the part that is immortal and reincarnates in successive human births, developing and evolving the outer nature so that it may become a suitable and expressive instrument of its governing influence and control. This part of the being is usually hidden deep within and only influences the outer nature indirectly through those parts that have become open, receptive, and resonant to its subtle directives and influences. It is mainly through prolonged spiritual discipline that it comes into the person's conscious awareness and begins to govern the outer nature directly and progressively more completely. It is not the origin of particular psychological disturbances; on the contrary, it is the seat of psychological health, balance, harmony, growth, and integration. It is noted here because it is through a progressively increasing openness to its influence that psychological health and integration can best be facilitated. Thus, methods that facilitate this opening and the psychic being's influence in our nature are among the most potent for achieving optimal and sustainable psychological health.

Vignette—Levels of Consciousness: Multidimensional Diagnosis and Treatment

Lakshmi was twenty-six when she came to me to help her overcome her resistance to marriage. There is a lot of social pressure in India for women to marry well before the age of thirty. Lakshmi's friends helped her to understand that her resistance was psychological and convinced her to start therapy.

Lakshmi came from the growing upper middle class of urban India. Her family placed high importance on social status and achievement, and yet, maintained a connection to their spiritual roots in the form of observance of major holidays and ritual practices. There was no focus on inner development. We started exploring her past from the perspective of her storyline and the scripts and beliefs that were formed as a result of her experiences in her youth. Lakshmi's father was both very strict and often absent due to his work. This left her with the impression that men are unfair, domineering, and abandon those they love.

Very early on in our therapeutic work, she went on a pilgrimage to a renowned holy place with her family for a religious festival. While in the temple, she began receiving inner guidance to clean up her life. Consistent with her interpretation of what the voice was telling her, Lakshmi returned home and began systematically cleaning out her apartment from top to bottom, inside and out.

There was no doubt in my mind that what Lakshmi was experiencing was not pathological as she had no history of hearing voices, mental imbalance, or instability. I felt she had had an experience of opening to subtle levels of consciousness and received this inner guidance. But when we have experiences of an inner voice, whether it is our own conscience (the voice of the soul) or some divine intervention, we may not necessarily have the capacity to grasp it in the way it is intended. The way each of us experiences our spirituality is, in fact, determined by our sociocultural context, our ego structure, as well as our level of maturity and evolution.

Lakshmi was just beginning therapy and had very little self-knowledge or capacity to understand her inner self. She was extroverted, tending to look outside herself to find the answers to her questions. Therefore, when she had this experience, instead of delving into a quest for inner purification and cleansing, she gave it an external interpretation. Her apartment cleaning was systematic and thorough, yet she continued to hear the voice telling her to clean up her life. Therefore, once she had completed a thorough clean out, she started cleaning her apartment again. The voice rang true for her and yet she had neither the means to interpret it properly nor apply it at the level at which it originated.

When I realized that this experience and subsequent guiding voice was turning into an issue, I pondered on ways to get her back in her body and ground the experiences she was having. Every morning when she got up, I recommended that she take a cold sitz bath. The effects were immediate. She ceased hearing the voice. We were able to resume her course of therapy on a step-by-step basis. I had complete faith that, as she began to unpeel the impressions from her accumulated life experiences, structure her self or ego in a way that was more conscious and aligned to her inner self, she would again receive guidance. In that case, she would be able to ground and follow that guidance according to a higher level of integration and maturity. I reflected on how modern psychiatry or practitioners who do not recognize higher levels of consciousness or transcendent experience may have perceived Lakshmi's experience. There is every chance she would have been diagnosed and medicated, thereby changing her life course forever with little chance of working through her childhood issues and opening a way to find the stable and nourishing marriage she desired.

INDIAN SCHOOLS OF INTEGRAL THOUGHT

At the same time as Aurobindo was elaborating upon his work in India, there were other thinkers and philosophers exploring along the same lines. Some of these Indian thinkers were inspired by the teachings of Sri Aurobindo. Others came upon similar views on their own. This seems to indicate a collective realization of the integral nature of consciousness.

Indra Sen

In the 1940s, Indra Sen,[8] a psychologist and devotee of Sri Aurobindo, began systematizing Aurobindo's views of psychology, his observations of existing models, and developing it into a model of psychology. He coined the expression "Integral Psychology" in a series of lectures and essays written in the 1940s and 1950s covering the works of Sri Aurobindo. Though Sri Aurobindo never used the term integral psychology, it emerges from his system of integral yoga, which is essentially a complex and mystical psychology.

In his book *Integral Psychology*[9] based on Sri Aurobindo's teachings, Sen describes the standpoint of Sri Aurobindo's psychology as empirical, evolutional, and personal growth–oriented, utilizing introspection (self-observation) as its primary method which allows immediate knowledge of psychological data.[10] Sen presents integral psychology as an empirical approach based on direct experiential knowledge, which unlike Western empiricism, does not confine itself to sensation, perception, and cognition.

Haridas Chaudhari

Haridas Chaudhari[11] is the author of many books and the founder of California Institute of Integral Studies (CIIS), a private educational institute in San Francisco. CIIS offers accredited graduate programs in counseling psychology and clinical psychology and has a school of consciousness and transformation. CIIS employs and educates scholars in the field of integral psychology like Brant Cortright, Paul Edwards Herman, and Bahman Shirazi. Though Chaudhari was influenced by Sri Aurobindo, his work was not confined to his ideas and teachings. Chaudhari proposed an authentic and unique version of integral psychology, which brought together both Eastern and Western psychological systems.

According to Shirazi, Chaudhari's attempt at integral psychology may be summarized in terms of his triadic principle of uniqueness, relatedness, and transcendence as well as his proposed tenets for an integral psychology as follows:

(a) Need for personal integration—It is crucial to understand the self and go deeper into the psyche. Only then can the diverse components of the human personality be integrated.
(b) Integral self-realization—Self-realization is the highest and deepest potential of the human being.
(c) Transformation—Transformation of baser qualities into positive, desirable qualities replaces withdrawing from the world for a psycho-spiritual quest. This transformation is achieved through discipline.
(d) Ontomotivation—In the journey towards self-realization, the ego is gradually replaced by the happiness and joy of uniting with the Supreme Being.

In addition to these foundational principles of his vision, the qualities of "uniqueness, relatedness and transcendence correspond to the three domains of personal, interpersonal and transpersonal psychological inquiry ... which are equally important and essential aspects of the personality."[12] Chaudhari believes that every individual has a unique set of qualities and characteristics, and a unique path of growth and development, which cannot be found in any other person. Most Eastern spiritual traditions undermine the individual aspect as individuality is often equated with selfishness and disregard for the harmonious functioning of society. In contrast to uniqueness, relatedness is also important. "Just as an individual needs to maintain harmonious intrapsychic dynamics, she or he needs to also maintain balance and harmony with others and with nature."[13] The transcendence principle refers to the human urge toward transcending the limitations of human existence.

A.S. Dalal

A.S. Dalal[14] studied philosophy before becoming an inmate of Sri Aurobindo Ashram from 1952 to 1959. He went on to study psychology, clinical psychology, and psychoanalysis holding several positions in the United States. Primarily a researcher, since that time he has written several books on Sri Aurobindo's integral yoga psychology, an entire series of works compiling Sri Aurobindo's thoughts into succinct works according to topic and a work comparing the approaches of Sri Aurobindo with those of Eckhart Tolle. His compilations of Sri Aurobindo's teachings make Aurobindo's otherwise dense writing style more accessible.

Dr. Brant Cortright, Dr. Soumitra Basu, Michael Miovic, Arya Maloney, Dr. Alok Pandey, Bahman Shirazi, and Matthijs Cornellisen are some of the most well-known practitioners, authors, and academicians whose works are inspired by the teachings of Sri Aurobindo.

LIMITATIONS OF EASTERN APPROACHES
TO INTEGRAL PSYCHOLOGY

The path of unfolding to our inner self holds hidden risks. If we are not careful, certain aspects of spiritual growth can lead to building an ego rather than transcending and transforming the ego. Reading spiritual books and experiencing expanded states of awareness can lead to the development of a "spiritual ego" if we lack such qualities as maturity, balance, and discernment. In an inflated sense of self, we believe we are special; we are the one who understands, and we may believe we are spiritually realized. This may effectively block the way to spiritual progress and possibly lead to abuses of our expanded but still egoistic abilities and powers, especially over those who may look to us for spiritual inspiration or guidance. Spiritual growth is safest when accompanied with spiritual humility. Clear objectivity and discrimination with regard to our own spiritual development gives us the ability to accurately assess our shortcomings, weaknesses, and defects, and not become inflated by our inner experiences which may be temporary and have limited effect on the change of our outer nature or the sublimation of our ego. This topic is further developed in chapter 6.

STEPPING STONES FOR INTEGRAL PSYCHOLOGY

Sri Aurobindo's yoga extends beyond the ordinary aims of psychological health. It suggests, in modern psychological terms, the highest possibilities of human psychological health as well as concrete approaches toward achieving it. The integral approach of Sri Aurobindo and the Mother offers a very broad framework for integrating the insights of modern psychologies that are open to the spiritual possibilities of humankind with the spiritual findings of sages and mystics. According to Dalal,[15] Sri Aurobindo spoke about "psychological methods of discipline by which man purifies and perfects himself—the work of psychology, not as it is understood in Europe, but the deeper practical psychology called in India yoga." Dalal adds, "In presaging the emergence of psychology as a science of consciousness and a self-knowledge discipline lies perhaps Sri Aurobindo's greatest relevance to modern psychology."

According to Sri Aurobindo, all psychological phenomena begin in the subtlest levels of our consciousness. For example, illness or mental imbalance starts out as a shift or deviation at the subtlest level of our consciousness. As time goes on, it becomes denser and eventually, if it is not harmonized in the meantime, manifests in the surface awareness of the individual. If the person is less sensitive, it may take longer for them to recognize and address the problem. Once we are in an emotional crisis, it is because that subtle imbalance has already been able to densify all the way down into the emotional level of consciousness where we finally begin to perceive it. The practice of meditation helps us develop our subtle perception and develop the power to correct issues before they become crystallized. On the other hand, in a less subtle mind, it might take a meltdown before the person realizes that something is out of harmony in their psyche. The same applies to physical illness.

Similarly, while the physical level can sometimes be measured, compared, and proven, the emotional and mental levels although observable are already less tangible and more subjective. The higher experiences of the subliminal and spiritual consciousness can only be felt, related to, and conveyed by subtly tuned minds. Nevertheless, we have no reason to believe that the subtler levels are not just as real. This is how psychics and mediums work. They tune into levels which are sometimes beyond the level of perception of the people they read. Something can be clear as day to them and, yet, not perceived by their subject.

CONCLUSION

Sri Aurobindo's teachings, while built on deeply mystical foundations, give us practices and a roadmap to help us to understand and transform the psychological aspects of our being into a path and a means to achieve our higher, divine calling as human beings. Unlike many other yogic philosophies, Sri Aurobindo calls on us, not to retreat from the world into spiritual heights that have no grounding or call to action in the world, but rather to transform our consciousness and then, let that transformation come down into the earthly plane to bring the inner light into our actions in the world.

Aurobindo's unique contribution is not only to tell us that there is a capstone, an inner light to which we can align, but that what we gain in this inner transformation is then to be brought into the world. It is based on a transformation from ego consciousness to soul-consciousness and not, as in the West, the other way around. In contrast to Aurobindo's mystical or inner vision which channeled down into an approach to psychology, Ken Wilber developed an intellectually based model that we will explore in the next chapter.

NOTES

1. Born Aurobindo Ghose, 1872–1950.
2. 1878–1973.

3. A.S. Dalal, *A Greater Psychology: An Introduction to the Psychological Thought of Sri Aurobindo* (2001, Pondicherry, India: Sri Aurobindo Ashram Press), p. 581.

4. Sri Aurobindo, "The Life Divine," in *The Complete Works of Sri Aurobindo*, Vols. 21–22 (2005, Pondicherry, India: Sri Aurobindo Ashram Press), p. 581.

5. The vital level includes our automatic physiological processes, instincts, sensations, desires, energies of action, cravings, and emotions.

6. Sri Aurobindo, "Synthesis of Yoga," in *The Complete Works of Sri Aurobindo* (1999, Pondicherry, India: Sri Aurobindo Ashram Press), p. 44.

7. A.S. Dalal, compiled, *Psychology, Mental Health and Yoga* (1996, Pondicherry, India: Sri Aurobindo Ashram Trust).

8. 1903–1994.

9. 1986.

10. 2001.

11. 1913–1975.

12. Bahman A.K. Shirazi, "Integral Psychology Metaphors and Processes of Personal Integration," in Matthijs Cornelissen, ed., in *Consciousness and Its Transformation* (2001, Pondicherry, India: SAICE), p. 37.

13. Shirazi, 2001, p. 37.

14. 1926–.

15. A.S. Dalal, *A Greater Psychology: An Introduction to the Psychological Thought of Sri Aurobindo* (2001, Pondicherry, India: Sri Aurobindo Ashram Press), p. xx.

Chapter Five

Ken Wilber's Integral Psychology

In the 1970s, Ken Wilber began writing books that explored ways to find common ground and integrate various disciplines related to science, spirituality, and psychology. His early quest for unifying principles led him to study Sri Aurobindo's work, the Tao Te Ching, and other Eastern and Western philosophies. Wilber published his complex and comprehensive work *Integral Psychology*[1] in 2000. He attempts to create a congruent, interconnected, evolutionary platform paving the way for a new vision for psychology. With far-reaching intellectual insight and detail, Wilber describes this new force or trend in psychology as a theoretical means of examining, quantifying, and defining all aspects and all levels of human experience: body, mind, soul, spirit, nature, and society. Wilber claims to be the most widely published philosophical writer of our times. At the time of his publication of *Integral Psychology*, he had published twenty books in thirty-four languages. Today, those numbers stand at thirty-four publications.

While Wilber's approach to integral theory and psychology does not start or stop with the material in this chapter, and it is still being elaborated by him, his collaborators,[2] and his critics, I have chosen to content myself with a broad overview of its foundations such as they were laid out in *Integral Psychology*. I will attempt to encapsulate Wilber's work while focusing on what I feel are the key aspects for the more mystical and practice-based approach I will be presenting in the last four chapters of this book.

During my studies at Durham University, I ventured out of my purely clinical practice into the extant literature in the fields of humanistic and transpersonal psychology. I devoured the writings of Carl Rogers, Abraham Maslow, Colin Wilson, and other humanistic thinkers enjoying and feeling nurtured by the gentle and soothing, yet structuring worldview. My quest for transcendent meaning led me to take in, with an even greater thirst, William James, Carl Jung, and other transpersonal pioneers, eventually reading what was the entire works in the field of transpersonal psychology at that time. I was fueled by a passion for studying the mysteries of psychology and consciousness and yet, I cannot deny that in spite of all the reading and the clinical training which was the focus of my course, I found myself occasionally touching the edges of the possibilities of these schools, much like Jim Carrey in *The Truman Show*. Living an apparently ordinary life, he increasingly suffers from a sense that something is amiss; there must be more to life than what he is experiencing. He finds the answer when he accidentally discovers that his whole life has been staged for a reality TV show. His desire to discover what is beyond the pseudo life he has been living is so strong that he is willing to do whatever it takes to discover what is real.

After my second semester at Durham, I spent my summer break in Del Mar, California. A lengthy visit to a local independent bookstore resulted in a stack of books on my bedside table, a task that would be undertaken horizontally from my beach towel. One day, while reading Wilber's *No Boundary* and avoiding kids kicking sand into my face, I had an epiphany. Wilber was attempting to join the dots. I was converted. I was so excited that I ran down the beach and into the ocean to exclaim to my friend Claude, who was visiting from France, "It doesn't have to be either-or!! Each school has its place in a larger, more inclusive context of psychology and consciousness!" Much to his credit, Claude feigned excitement and understanding and let me rant and rave until the fire was under control. I took a nice long dip in the Pacific and ran up the beach to dive back into Wilber.

THE GREAT NEST OF BEING

A common core in many spiritual belief systems is the "great chain of being," a Western perspective on the more Eastern-influenced perennial philosophy. It views consciousness as having levels of being and knowing that range from "matter to body to mind to soul to spirit. The first important great chain system is in the Vedas (1800 BCE), where we find the first distinction between states, bodies and structures of consciousness."[3] Early descriptions of hierarchies of beings are also found in both Plato and Aristotle's writings.

Wilber adopted the term "great chain of being" which he feels is more suitable because each level is a whole unto itself and is enveloped by the next, thereby creating a great chain. While some levels of development in the great chain are givens, others are potentials, which are accessible, but must be developed. Each level of consciousness is nested in the level above or beyond it in an "asymmetrical hierarchy of increasing holistic capacity ... each senior level transcends and includes its juniors, but not vice versa."[4] Wilber's approach does not consider only levels that are ranked in terms of hierarchy (dimensions of hierarchical importance) or levels that are ranked in terms of heterarchy (dimensions that are mutually linked). Neither approach is sufficient to give a fully integral explanation of development. Instead of these limiting, restrictive terms, Wilber uses the concept of holarchy, a blend of both hierarchy and heterarchy that carries a greater capacity for addressing multidimensional realities.

UNITY IN DIVERSITY

Some schools of thought are absolutist, claiming to hold the only valid worldview. Yet others seek to integrate and unify different psychological and philosophical schools and ideologies. Perhaps the most common method has consisted of selecting a homogenous blend of different elements chosen from each of these schools or ideologies and combining them to create a new approach. Wilber makes it clear that such an approach, has no place in an integral psychology. Wilber is not seeking to create homogeneity, but rather a unity in diversity of methods, applications, approaches, and levels of development and consciousness. The concept of unity in diversity allows mutual acknowledgment and respect for similarities and differences and creates a vision of a complex world in which there is room and stimulation for evolution. Homogeneity, while reassuring to some, is not harmonious with the very life force that animates us. Indian society is a living example of unity-in-diversity, which stems from Sanatan Dharma, the philosophical precursor to Hinduism.

In *Dictionnaire Amoureux de l'Inde*,[5] Jean-Claude Carrière astutely observed the unity in diversity of the Indian people. While there are increasingly modern aspects of society developing in India, for example in information technology, international business, and even the films of Bollywood, the modernisation is not uniform. Even back to the earliest history of India, as each new people, ideology, or lifestyle comes into existence, it does not take over its predecessors, but finds its place and coexists alongside them. The transition is neither linear nor homogenous. There are periods where one philosophy, say Buddhism or Vedic thought, is predominant over another. Unlike in other countries, apart from rare periods where invaders have come in and taken over rule by force, change in predominance of one religion or another has mostly happened through new settlers coming in. They bring their worldview which takes root sometimes fully and at others, leads to emergence of sub-communities, for example, Parsi, Jewish, Christian, and Muslim.

Wilber seeks to explore consciousness and psychology. Rather than create a synthesis or blend from them, he aspires to recognize the wisdom each one brings to mankind for his understanding and development. Wilber refers to the fact that no individual or school, despite what they would like to believe, holds the entire truth. Each school holds a partial truth. The concept of "partial truth" is found in the teachings of Sri Aurobindo and can be traced back to the early Western mystical school of Hermeticism. Wilber painstakingly distinguishes the contributions of each school and their place in respect to the hierarchy of levels of consciousness and the scheme of human development. Then he demonstrates how the different schools relate to one another creating a complex and multidimensional interrelationship resembling the very complex nature of man and consciousness. I like to use the image of a large multidimensional picture puzzle, unassembled in its box. As each school begins to find pieces that appear to go together, they create their theory of human consciousness based on the piece they are holding, or the little section they have managed to put together and generally work within one of the many dimensions of the puzzle. It is not until the whole puzzle has been put together that we can see the image it depicts in all of its aspects and dimensions. Science puts together the pieces of the puzzle by painstakingly testing each match, each section, sometimes stopping at a little section and taking it for the whole. The thing about an integral puzzle, to continue my analogy, is that it is never complete. It keeps evolving.

SPIRAL DYNAMICS

Spiral dynamics is a theory of human development that demonstrates how humans and society adapt and evolve with the changing times. It is based on the theories of psychologist Clare Graves and developed into a system by Don Beck and Chris Cowan. The spiral shape symbolizes how each era and its corresponding worldview evolve out of previous periods. Society evolves collectively in memes, little steps toward a greater worldview, and tiers which represent a change in paradigm toward a more universal consciousness and fundamentally more holistic and inclusive ways of functioning. It is applied in such areas as coaching, consulting, and conflict resolution.

PREMODERNISM, MODERNISM,
AND POSTMODERNISM

Wilber talks about the development of civilization in terms of three major eras: premodern, modern, and postmodern. The premodern period refers to the time when the various interpretations of the great chain of being or the perennial philosophy were the primary means of interpreting man's development and potential.

In the age of modernity, humanity focused on elaborating the faculty of cognition and the effects of physiology on our mental functioning and animal nature. The focus on physiology became a bigger fish than more holistic views and big fish do have a tendency to eat smaller ones. Through this focus on physiology, we lost sight of our potential for transcendence and fell into reductionism. Mainstream thought developed an increasingly rationalistic means of defining consciousness. It is useful to gain an intellectual understanding of ourselves. According to Sri Aurobindo, this was a necessary step in the evolution of consciousness. Falling into reductionism implies falling out of touch with the more subtle, irrational aspects of consciousness that are essential for balance and continued development. In this period, all levels of development beyond cognition lost their validity; the modern definition of reality was defined more through the mind and no longer through intuition or spiritual experience. Modernism added the interpretive tool of epistemology to the repertory. It left behind the previous ontological approach that embraced the valid and valuable contributions of intuition and spiritual experience and began sinking into a perception of reality that was limited and confining.

The postmodern era is characterized by a tendency to perceive all things as being equal. Denial of the higher states of being and search for satisfaction of our outer needs—body, emotions, and mind, has resulted in compartmentalization and fragmentation of our beings and loss of our spiritual worldview. We fell into a spiritual "dark age" where rationalism and egoism reign. This corresponds to the ancient Vedic vision of the last phase in the cycle of ages through which humankind passes, called the kali yuga, an age of ignorance of our true or divine nature. While the kali yuga is traditionally associated with ignorance and degradation, Sri Aurobindo describes it as a period of destruction of old forms to make room for renewal.

The imbalance created by a reductionist view is clearly visible in the numerous breakdowns occurring at all levels of society. The worldwide ecological and economic crises are manifestations of our current, limited perspective on life. These crises are a result of both a lack of ethics and an ethics that is not aligned to our inner truth. The results of this ethical crisis are greed, short-range thinking and acting, disharmony, and ethical, ecological, and economic crises.[6] One way this issue could be explored or brought into balance is by addressing the needs and potentials of both the logical, linear, and rational approach to life and the inner, intuitive approach.

ALL QUADRANTS—ALL LEVELS (AQAL)

AQAL is a complex theory putting emphasis on four perspectives of self which lead to a much more intellectually based foundation than the mystically based Aurobindo (table 5.1). AQAL is designed to help the integral thinker adopt a wider view. The four quadrants describe the interior (left) and exterior

Table 5.1 AQAL Model

Upper-Left Quadrant-the interior of the individual, subjective feelings and how we experience the world	Upper-Right Quadrant-the exterior of the individual, objective aspects of our self that are apparent to others
Lower-Left Quadrant-the interior of the collective, subjective aspects of the society	Lower-Right Quadrant-the exterior of the collective; objective, measurable aspects of society

(right) aspects of individual self (top) and our collective self or society (bottom). This system shows four different aspects of our integral existence which helps to eliminate the possibility of viewing things from a singular or less balanced perspective.

I choose to put my main emphasis on the upper left or inner subjective quadrant, our fundamental relationship to ourselves. Our inner subjective perception sets the tone of what we feel, experience, and do in the world. Everything stems from this inner core and must ultimately be addressed and transformed at this level. It is not that we should ignore the rest, but neither should we get distracted in it. We can, very constructively and substantially use it as our mirror and gauge for understanding and working with the inner self. I hate to admit it, but although I try to understand an experiential application of the AQAL theory, it seems like an external construct floating out there in space. The upper left quadrant is analogous to the rudder of a ship. Putting an equal accent on all four quadrants feels like a dilution or a distraction from our inner, mystical core. Furthermore, AQAL leaves me with some questions: Can each of the four quadrants also be fit into a model of levels of consciousness? Personal unconscious, physical unconscious, conditioning, karma, super-conscious, supraconscious. … For example, does intuition exist in the four quadrants, is there a type of intuition linked to each quadrant? Does the AQAL model extend beyond a consciousness-based approach or is it more confined? As a practitioner and yogi, whose main aspiration is the transformation of consciousness, elaborate intellectual theories, whose applications I cannot grasp, do not shift my worldview or consciousness. Furthermore, I cannot see the practical application in terms of healing and transformation. I have no choice but to leave AQAL up to the theoreticians.

PSYCHOLOGICAL DEVELOPMENT AND INTEGRAL PSYCHOTHERAPY

Seventy years after Piaget and Vygotsky, Ken Wilber has developed a new and more poignant vision for developmental psychology. He added psycho-spiritual "states, waves and lines" of development to the staid givens of mechanistic development covered by existing models of developmental psychology. He further pointed out that while basic development is a given in normal, healthy individuals, psycho-spiritual development is not. These higher levels of development depend on an individual's drive and natural inclination to move toward self-actualization. Maslow's theory of self-actualization would add that this is more or less dependent on a conducive environment in addition to the strength of the individual's drive. Jung, however, felt that reflection (religious urge) and creativity were just as instinctual as the basic drives of hunger, sex, and activity.

Forman[7] describes Wilber's developmental model in terms of cognitive lines of development (Piaget), identity development, and maturity. In Wilber's view, development occurs through both ascending and descending drives. The ascending drive reflects the quest for transcendence, universality, and liberation, whereas the descending drive reflects the quest for embodiment, psychological wholeness, and fulfillment of social or societal needs.

Developmental psychology has sometimes been criticized for being too theoretical and linear and therefore not corresponding to what clients actually go through in their therapeutic process. Yet, it can prove useful for understanding and situating the process of psychological and therapeutic unfolding. In general, it states that individuals seated in the lower levels of development will have a more limited and fragmented perspective. As they evolve, their level of functioning and worldview become more holistic and integrated. They are able to get a better sense of the big picture. But models of development should not be taken too literally or linearly. They provide a platform, a general contextual understanding and do not necessarily reflect a person's lived experience. The actual process of unfolding is less consecutive and linear. As we integrate higher stages, we do not leave behind the previous ones. They remain a part of who we are. In reality, we may be working on various elements of different levels of development at once. Therefore, a person's stage of development is looked at in terms of their predominant level of functioning at the given time.

Forman points out that when a stage of development no longer fits and becomes too confining, we begin to differentiate by seeking new experiences and attempting to integrate a new level of development that encompasses even while it transcends our current level. This transition can be difficult, painful, awkward, or fluid depending on our attitude and mindset. In the transition, some clients experience discomfort and want more out of life, whereas others may resist making needed changes. In this situation, the therapist has a dual role. First, he can accompany the person through the transition, helping to ease the symptoms and facilitate the process. At the same time, he can help the client see the meaning in the discomfort, which is a natural experience in times of transition.

Wilber notes that the entire spectrum of development is also a spectrum of pathology. Trauma or other occurrences that we experience during the different phases of our development affect our congruence at that level. Forman sees developmental psychology as a pillar of integral psychotherapy, assessing and working with clients' challenges and pathologies using various treatment modalities.

Forman likens the process of development to that of walking a labyrinth. I believe it also has both a cyclical and an evolutionary direction. We delve into the dark depths, the subconscious, shadow, or unconscious, in which earlier perspectives or memories are revealed to us. As we work with and integrate this material, we reemerge into a phase of outer focus and action. Later, we cycle back around to the dark, inner world again to become aware of and integrate other subconscious material into the outer life.

During the therapeutic process, we become aware of our potential on the upturn and then get called down into our subconscious layers to address core conditioning and wounds that inhibit us from coming to terms with and thus integrating them. As we start to liberate the energy invested in the wounds and conditioning, we experience a sense of lightness, freedom, expansion, and aliveness. We uncover insights about ourselves, our life story and perspectives of which we were not previously aware. Forman noted that "the greater the wounding at any given stage of a person's life, the greater the developmental distance he or she will need to traverse in order to address it deeply."[8]

Vignette—Healing: An Upward Spiral

Jennifer came to see me because she wanted to address the problem of hoarding. She was well aware that her chronic habit of saving everything and being unable to let go was imploding on her. It became an all-consuming obsession and served as an excuse not to go out and engage in life. We explored her history of hoarding and an overview of her life as well as the psychological and metaphorical symbolisms in her behavior, revolving around the fear of lack. If we translate this to the level of core needs, we can look at it in terms of a fear of lack of love and acknowledgment. Our work focused both inwardly at the core, emotional wound and outwardly at her goal of de-cluttering her house. We addressed the core wounds from not having felt loved in her childhood and saw how this experience led her to create a belief that she would never be loved. Relationships are mirrors of our light, but also our shadow. Her relationships reflected her core belief and were short-lived and painful. Material things gradually began to replace human love. It is much easier to control things than people. Things do not abandon us. The impulse to control is a way we compensate for, rather than address, our vulnerability and pain.

During our work together, her son offered to move in with her and help her clean out her house. We reflected on the meaning of his actions, the inherent gift in the fact that her son, of his own choosing, had offered to give his time and love to her. She had difficulty letting go of old newspapers, articles and items she had collected throughout her years. She struggled and fantasized about going out and digging in the bins to get her stuff back. Every once in awhile the positive impact of her efforts, a sense of lightening the load, would dawn on her. When she plunged back into the struggle, she would lose sight of all the [inner and outer] progress she had made.

About one-third of the way through the process, she began having her own momentum. One day, while her son was out she spontaneously started cleaning out a section of her house on her own. The project of cleaning her house continued. Jennifer experienced periodic moments pedaling ahead with her son, and ultimately with herself, on the project. At other times, she regressed, resisting the project by wanting to hold on to things, and again, fell into believing that all was lost. In session, I pointed out to her the cyclical nature of the healing process. When we plunge down into the difficult moments, we see only darkness. We forget how far we have come and lose sight of the fact that, despite the moments of struggle, those moments are shorter lived. We have more objectivity and more strength to go through them gracefully, not spiraling downward. I pointed out to Jennifer that as we become free from the holds of our negative patterning and emotional wounds, our natural élan toward healing and wholeness reawakens.

SPIRITUALITY IN WILBER'S INTEGRAL PSYCHOLOGY

Integral psychology addresses spirituality as a potential in consciousness toward which we can aspire, evolve, and realize. For Wilber, our spiritual development involves working on all levels of development and all four quadrants of experience. Therefore, integral therapies work from an understanding of subtle dynamics and higher potentials, not a cognitive psychology of religiosity. Spiritual pursuit carries its own set of challenges, imbalances, and pathologies. The integral therapist, through their study of models and inner work, develops the ability to recognize and work with both healthy and imbalanced expressions of spirituality and altered or expanded states of consciousness. They can learn to detect the various pathologies that can manifest as a client develops spiritually. These may occur during intentional cultivation of spirituality or through spontaneous or crisis-provoked experiences, such as near death experiences (NDEs) or spiritual emergency. Even healthy nonordinary and spiritual experiences can be powerful and destabilizing. Therefore, being able to share them with a competent professional can help the client derive meaning from the experiences and integrate them.

All spiritual experiences are not created equal. One of Wilber's most important theories is the pre-trans fallacy. He distinguishes between childhood spirituality, marked by a preindividuated innocence, and an adult, postindividuated spirituality in which the ego has been developed, strengthened, and transcended. This distinction helps us understand and work with individuals, both in terms of their psychological and spiritual experiences, in a more informed and adapted way.

At the top of the climb, in Wilber's view, is nonduality. Nonduality is neither an altered state of consciousness nor is considered to be a stage of development. According to Forman, it is "one's true identity at all times, even as we are deeply unconscious of it. ... One would therefore not *develop* into nondual realization so much as one will simply *recognize* or become aware of it at a given point during the climb."[9] Sometimes, states of nonduality can be experienced while one is in an early stage of development. They are always there and can reveal themselves to us at any time along the way, though integrated individuals are more likely to experience them.

PERSONAL DEVELOPMENT—
INTEGRAL LIFE PRACTICE (ILP)

ILP, based on Wilber's AQAL model, addresses our development in terms of lines of development: body, mind, spirit, and shadow (therapy). There are various approaches and systems to our integral development such as integral lifework, integral transformative practice, and holistic integration.

Their aim is to provide a means for putting integral theory into practice in our daily lives for personal and societal transformation. ILP provides a vision and means for whole life development. Wilber[10] claims that while all schools address some of the areas addressed by ILP, they usually do not include all four core modules that enable integral development. Forman points out that we can follow ILP in two ways, by implementing a regimented and disciplined system or by letting our intuition guide us in our daily practice rather than our minds. It is not like a supermarket where we have to go up and down each aisle scouring the shelves and checking items off our list of issues to address and levels of consciousness or types of powers to develop. Instead, we can follow the callings awakened in our day-to-day experience, taking on and working with issues and insights as they arise.

Letting our intuition be our guide in our ILP requires a level of healing and mastery over our shadow. Qualities such as surrender and sincerity will naturally emerge and hopefully alleviate the tendency toward dogmatism or spiritual materialism—engaging in development or evolutionary practices for what we can get out of them. While this is natural, as we evolve, many people might observe that we have the tendency to seek self-satisfaction, power, gratification through our spiritual pursuits. As we develop, this tendency gradually loosens.[11]

While visions for fostering our development have existed since time immemorial, integral transformative practice seeks to be truly holistic, cultivating multiple dimensions in a complementary way to facilitate our balance and evolution. Forman[12] looks at integral transformative practice in terms of the AQAL framework:

In the West, application of integral psychology for personal development involves integral growth, discovering, developing, and balancing all aspects of self: mind, body, and spirit. Focusing on the conceptual or theoretical aspects of growth and development develops our intellect or outer knowledge and gives us a framework. We develop the outer self through conscious choices and our inner self through the practice of spiritual disciplines, going within, learning through feeling, perceiving, and inner realization. We liberate the inner self from the confines of our ego with its psychological structure, attitudes, fears, attachments, and desires, and come home to our most profound experiences and realization of oneness with the Divine. Through integral growth we discover who we are, in all of our dimensions, from instinct to intuition, to oneness with the infinite.

Jorge Ferrer lays out interrelated guiding principles of integral growth: "Integral growth is co-created by all dimensions of human nature. ... Integral growth unfolds from within, grounded in our most vital potentials. ... Integral growth balances the feminine and the masculine."[13] Holistic integration involves interactive embodied meditations, multidimensional contemplative practices, individual integrative practices, and work in everyday life aimed at the following:

(a) differentiation, maturation, and integration of all human dimensions (body, instincts, heart, mind, and self-consciousness); (b) making these dimensions more porous to both immanent and transcendent spiritual energies; (c) differentiation, maturation, and integration of the "masculine" (agent) and "feminine" (receptive) capabilities at all dimensions; (d) healing and transformation of wounds, conflicts, or dissociations stored at deep energetic layers of these dimensions; (e) creation of spaces for the natural emergence of new capabilities, qualities, or potentials from within those dimensions; (f) training in the development of these emerging capabilities, qualities or potentials; and (g) integration of polar realities, such as mind/body, sexuality/spirituality, masculine/feminine; individual/community, or strength/gentleness.[14]

Vignette—Collective Healing

In 1992, I visited a beautiful ashram in Tamil Nadu, India called Shantivanam. The ashram was headed by Father Bede Griffiths, a wise and loving Benedictine monk, originally from Great Britain and the author of many books on East-West spirituality. The day before I planned to leave, I had a private audience with him. I told him about the way I work with the breath to help release deep-seated emotional issues and help people unfold to their inner self. He asked me if I'd

Table 5.2   Integral Transformative Practice: AQAL View

UL	UR
• Personal therapy • Meditation (mindfulness, concentration) • Altered states (to facilitate deep healing) • Typology • Creative expression	• Action • Physical development (preferable holistic/proprioceptive activities • Biological & neurological
LL	LR
• Group process (challenges assumptions about others) • Multicultural exposure & teachings (questions our assumptions and worldviews) • Relationship with spiritual teacher as model or guide	• Service • Community/political involvement

like to hold breathwork sessions for the people staying at the ashram. I was fortunate to have every liberty to change my plans, and I accepted his invitation. Every day for about one week, I offered a breathwork session, after the postlunch rest time. The sessions took place in a simple gazebo with waist high walls leaving a beautiful view of the surrounding rice paddy fields and banana trees and a thatched roof overhead to protect us from the sun.

Every day, about twenty people from all over the world would come for a breathwork session. Due to the peaceful and communal environment, we did not need ice breakers. We began immediately exploring deep issues in the 3–4 hour sessions. On one of the days, a special session was organized for twenty young Indian nuns. I introduced the context of the workshop and then we went around in a circle. Each participant gave a little introduction about themselves. Their shyness and reluctance to talk about themselves is quite typical of women in Indian society which encourages males to be assertive and females to be subdued. Everyone chose a spot and laid down on their backs for the breathwork.

I explained the technique and began guiding the nuns to let themselves open up to the breath, to feel and surrender to the breath, to open up the entire chest and lungs. After 5–10 minutes, most people begin to reach the phase where the consciousness begins to open. At this point, one of the women started to laugh. I could sense she was trying to hold back the laughter and encouraged her to just breathe and enjoy, let it flow. I knew from experience that laughter in a breathwork session can mask discomfort so we don't have to face it and, also, to cover up our vulnerability in front of others. I kept encouraging the women to breathe deeply, openly, with surrender. Before long, there were other snickers, and then more. Soon, twenty nuns were rolling on the floor with laughter. It was quite a scene. I encouraged them to let the laughter flow and keep breathing into it.

Within a few minutes, one of the nuns had a pained look on her face, tears followed within seconds. I encouraged, "Whatever you are experiencing, just keep letting the breath take you into it." Before long, the barriers were broken. The mass laughter turned to mass tears. In a gentle, reassuring voice, I kept encouraging the women to just let the breath take them into their experience. When running groups, there is usually an underlying theme that emerges. Something that is beyond explanation. It leads one to believe there is an underlying reason each group comes together, a group theme and a magical experience of the group dynamic. And yet, never before had I seen such deep group cohesion. There were deep sobs, profound release, total surrender. This went on for awhile and then gradually subsided. The profound sadness was gradually giving way to peaceful, serene looks, looks of openness.

This is a typical pattern that occurs during breathwork, both in individual and group contexts. As we breathe, we begin to reinforce our relationship to prana, life force. Any issues we are ready to work with emerge from our subconscious so that we can release them. As we release the blocked energy, we can have experiences of openness, surrender, and strong feelings of love, gratitude and oneness. At the moment of final release of the negative or blocked emotions, it is not uncommon for people to get deep insights into themselves, opening up the way for both inner and outer self-transformation. Breathwork has a natural cycle of 60–90 minutes. This time usually feels like 15–20 minutes as we are deep in our inner worlds, beyond any sense of space or time. At the end of the cycle, the nuns began stretching, opening their eyes, coming back into contact with the outside. I exchanged a few quiet words with each nun as she emerged from her session until everyone was finished.

At the end of a group session, it is important to share our experiences. Understanding that we are not alone is a very healing part of psychotherapy. It takes the charge out of our experience and helps us assimilate it. Within a short while, everyone was sitting in a circle with open, glowing faces. Warm looks were exchanged. Hands were held in a gesture of sisterhood.

One by one, they shared their experiences, their realizations and their stories. There was a clear-cut common theme that ran through the heartfelt sharings. Each woman had experienced a sense of inferiority at being born female in a society that has a clear preference and advantages for male children. Perhaps that experience was not fully conscious as it is a cultural norm. Rather than being taught to listen to and honor their innermost feelings, they had learned to be obedient, submissive and cooperative in their families, their schools and their roles in society. It was a very powerful sharing session, with open hearts and poignant honesty. Even though the motivation at the onset may have been through inner pressure or outer coercion, the session had led each woman to deeper understanding as to her choice to become a nun and had opened up a greater sense of connection to their vocation, both on a personal and spiritual level.

I facilitated a few sessions during my stay at Shantivanam, but this one was particularly touching and remarkable. For the rest of the week, one or another of the nuns who had participated in the session would come to my room and confide more to me about their life and the insights and experiences of their breathwork session.

DIAGNOSIS IN INTEGRAL PSYCHOLOGY

The practice of diagnosis is reflective of an allopathic conception of health which, to fit into scientific reasoning, must separate itself out from the whole. Where the current psychopathology model in the science-based *Diagnostic and Statistic Manual* (*DSM*), describes dysfunctional personality traits as being disorders, Ingersoll[15] suggests using the term style instead of disorder. This simple change in wording removes the stigma and terms what has traditionally been labeled and shelved as a disorder, as an opportunity for acknowledgment, healing, and growth. We reintegrate the notion of empowerment, responsibility, and honoring the sometimes bizarre, but inherent, wisdom in our experiences and the way our lives unfold that science took away from us in the not too distant past. Ancient practices, coming from wholeness and oneness were more in the lines of accompaniment and healing the whole self. Wilber, in his inclusive style, acknowledges the usefulness of the *DSM*, the predominant system in the West. He then shows us how to go beyond its partial, but valid point of view and to work from a larger perspective. This includes transpersonal levels of consciousness and corresponding imbalances.

The DSM's standpoint, in Wilber's view, is what he calls the "eye of flesh," "an eye that looks at the objective, measurable physiosphere and biosphere of the client. ... The three 'eyes' are metaphors for epistemological tools that we can look through to gather knowledge about psychological disturbances."[16]

Each eye is increasingly subtle, like layers of consciousness, and therefore more difficult to perceive and to diagnose for patient and therapist alike. At the same time, like layers of consciousness, each eye perceives the levels beneath itself, and therefore, the vision of each eye as we go up on the scale becomes more holistic than the eye beneath it.

The "eye of the mind" is observed through dialogue which develops a picture of the client's world, its structure and how they experience it. The "eye of the spirit" is the most subtle eye and therefore the most difficult to bring into the therapeutic setting. There are, however, often blatant experiences which bring this eye into perspective, such as premonitory dreams, out-of-body experiences and nonordinary or transpersonal states of consciousness. The "eye of the spirit" is the eye of ultimate meaning and transpersonal or all-encompassing aspects of consciousness. Like any other experience of a broadened vision, the "eye of the spirit" puts things into a larger perspective for the client and the treating therapist, thereby opening up to whole new means of personal growth and development.

WESTERN SCHOOLS OF INTEGRAL THOUGHT

The earliest known thinkers of the West whose thoughts on the nature of consciousness and human evolution reflect integral consciousness are Teilhard de Chardin and Jean Gebser. In addition to Wilber and other theorists mentioned in this chapter, some of the most well-known integralists are, Don Beck, business consultant, professor, and coauthor of spiral dynamics is also a close collaborator of Wilber and contributor to integral theory (politics), Ervin Laszlo (spirituality and consciousness), Mark Forman and Elliott Ingersoll (psychology), Brian Swimme (cosmology), Sean Esbjörn-Hargens and Michael E. Zimmerman (ecology), George Leonard, Michael Murphy (integral transformative practice). Integral theory is increasingly popular in the fields of consulting and coaching with the number of practitioners growing by the year.

LIMITATIONS OF INTEGRAL PSYCHOLOGY

Wilber is both highly appreciated and highly criticized. His critics take apart his theories and demonstrate their weaknesses with great mental dexterity.

Shirazi[17] thinks that the AQAL model complicates rather than helps. He feels that although Wilber acknowledges the contribution of the different schools in the East and West, he is ultimately trying to fit them into his *own* model. Shirazi puts it succinctly,

> It is true that one might conceive of a state of consciousness from which all realities are visible as one interconnected reality. It is also conceivable that one might be able to develop a map inspired by such state of consciousness, that would translate that experience into a cognitive expression. However, this does not mean that such a map is derivable through superimposition of various psychological maps hitherto developed by various thinkers and practitioners. In a nutshell, Wilber's integral psychology is too complex to be useful in praxis. It remains, at best, a form of philosophical psychology.[18]

In applying integral psychology with its multiple facets for our personal growth, one must be careful not to become scattered in all of its aspects. Rather than focusing on the many different aspects of our development, the key is to let the higher aspects provide the guidance while acknowledging and working through the various lower aspects as needed. If we do not place importance on the development of the center or soul as the aim of our development, and instead focus on external aspects, we can be distracted from finding our inner self. When we focus on the outer self, we may untie knots and give the impression of getting somewhere, but ultimately it may lead to going round in circles. I like to use the analogy of our lives and spiritual evolution as being like a ship. If the ship's rudder is aligned to the ego or outer self in the forms of the physical and material plane, our ship becomes a tugboat since the physical, being the densest level of consciousness, is slow to change and carries a heavy load. If it is the emotions, we can be sure that the ride will be on a faster boat going through the storm, the tumultuous nature of our emotions when they are untethered. If the mind is the rudder, we can picture this as a lifeguard rescue boat due to the mind's capacity to act quickly with a tendency to go into fight or flight response, either speeding up to get away from danger, or engaging in quick, survival tactics to talk or reason ourselves out of danger. If on the other hand, the soul is the rudder, you will have a pristine, state-of-the-art vessel that will sail smoothly, guided by wisdom, a larger perspective, self-mastery, and similar qualities, no matter in what conditions it is sailing.

Wilber's objective is to address the full spectrum of human consciousness in a way that is inclusive and aspires to create a more functional and congruent world. His theories are intellectually stimulating and capture the imagination and passion of many aspiring spiritual revolutionaries. Some have said that what is missing in order to transform his teachings from theory into a genuine spiritual path is the point of light which unites the whole—a trickle down of something genuinely beyond the human ego and intellect. Without that, one can have the most seemingly perfect theories, but they are subject to the corruptibility and imperfections of the human ego.

There is a particularly trendy and hip tone to a lot of Wilber's work. While this gives it a seductive and provocative appeal replete with swear words and brash rebuttals to his numerous critics, these are cause for wariness, or better yet, discernment. A mature seeker is not lured by outer displays of outrageousness and intellectual acrobatics. He will take a step back from these outer phenomena and seek to determine the essence of the message and the purity of intention. In the end, we must ask whether Wilber's brand of integral psychology resonates with the inner calm that leads to transcendence and transformation or does it overflow with the excitation and the seduction of intellectual rapture? The essence of integrality is that transformation and transcendence occur through direct inner experience and not through the intellect alone.

Wilber is continually reevaluating his thinking. Yet, he still seems to miss out on the point that no amount of intellectual understanding or exploring of things will lead to the highest transformational realities that can only be attained through concerted spiritual discipline.

I am not an intellectual but a seeker of truth, a believer that truth is found through inner experience. In my work as a therapist, my role is to help bring the light of truth into our dark places to facilitate the way for an evolution in consciousness; awakening and aligning to our inner truth. While Wilber's incredibly complex and far-reaching theory is indeed impressive, I prefer to simply meditate and realize the truth within. In terms of practical application, presence is by far a more powerful force in helping others (and ourselves) address their issues and become whole, than any theory I have ever come across.

STEPPING STONES FOR AN INTEGRAL PSYCHOLOGY

This life is full of challenges and lessons. Most of the time we are facing challenges and occasionally we get to reap the benefits of learning from them. Even if one begins therapy with the simple, human goals of managing ordinary life situations or seeking greater happiness, this quest may lead to a quest for or discovery of a spiritual dimension.

While Wilber's copious writings achieve an intellectual feat, now it is time for us to find a means of integrating this information and applying it in our lives and therapeutic approaches. Wilber says that, "integral doesn't change what you're doing, it simply helps you look at what you're *already doing* with a wider set of perspectives, explains how those perspectives relate to each other, and then gives you a language to talk about all the cool new things you can see."[19] Integral philosophy gives us a common language and map that help us situate and understand the inter-relationships of each school.

Psychoanalysis and behaviorism due to their more limiting views on man's functioning and potential often may suppress ideas or experiences that are out of their scope. The schools of psychology which focus primarily or only on the outer self (ego) without a higher, centralizing principle, may be productive for short-range goals. Once the patient has reached a certain level of self-knowledge, balance, and congruence, pursuing a purely horizontal approach to psychology runs the risk of becoming a distraction or a mental hamster wheel.

Despite the broader range addressed by holistic therapies, if they focus on mid-way experiences such as emotional release or altered states of conscious-ness without our higher potential in scope, it is like delving into the jungle without a map. The client may find interesting experiences, but unwittingly remain lost. In any case, eventually, through unleashing our natural drive toward evolution, our conscience or soul will call us back on track. Therapy, to me, is a spiritual path. It encompasses psychological balance, growth and self-knowledge, but it goes beyond these toward realizing our highest spiritual potentials.

Each successive movement in psychology is a further step toward encompassing and embracing our entire nature and the spectrum of consciousness on our way to becoming truly integral. The integral view invites us to go ever further in embracing our multidimensional and nonlinear consciousness, reclaiming our right to be fully human—body, mind, soul, and spirit. The metaphorical significance of the emergence of thinkers such as Wilber is the strengthening of mankind's drive toward evolution. This leads to an increasing wholeness, deeper congruence, and desire for harmony between all the parts of our being, society, the planet, and the universe. As with all preceding schools and trends of psychology, it is important to acknowledge that we are always on the way to realizing our ultimate potential of understanding and merging in the infinite, and also realizing that we are not yet there. This will ensure that we do not assume we have arrived at our goal and, therefore, we must continue to strive.

CONCLUSION

Wilber's *Integral Psychology* is one of the most far-reaching books in its thought that I have come across. It clarified misconceptions and confronted my value judgment-laden view that divided all schools and ideas of psychology into right and wrong. It made me see that there is a place for everything and everyone at their level of development. "The goal of an 'integral psychology' is to honor and embrace every aspect of human consciousness under one roof."[20] Instead of dividing the different ideas and schools of psychology into right and wrong, Wilber explores how each one contributes a partial truth to the bigger picture created by his "meta" approach to psychology. This reminds me of a traditional Indian story: Six blind men are walking through the jungle and come upon an elephant. "It is a pillar," said the first man who touched its leg; "No! It is a rope," said the second man who touched the tail; "Oh, no, it is the thick branch of a tree," said the third man who touched the trunk; "It is a big hand fan" said the fourth man who touched the ear. "It is a huge wall," said the fifth man who touched its side. "It is a solid pipe," said the sixth man who touched the tusk. Each one believes he has the whole picture whereas, in reality, it is only through creating a comprehensive and collective view that the whole can be perceived in its entirety. Perhaps the whole can only be seen by the transcendent onlooker who observes this cosmic event.

Integral psychology has two main schools: the earlier Eastern approach stemming from the teachings and perceptions of Sri Aurobindo and the contemporary Western approach developed by Wilber and his associates. The former, steeped in mysticism, represents an in-depth perception of universal concepts and principles channeled down from the subtle realms and made accessible and applicable to all levels of our existence, giving us a possibility of evolving toward our highest reaches, meaning, and congruence. The latter is Western and pragmatic and sees itself regularly applied to practical fields such as psychology, conflict resolution, coaching, and business consulting.

This brief overview of some of the most important schools of psychological and spiritual thought has laid the foundations and context for the development of a practical approach to integral psychology. Aiming to maintain the sense of meta-theory, I have been trying to weave together and we will take with us some of the theories and principles into an exploration of techniques and practical applications.

NOTES

1. Ken Wilber, *Integral Psychology: Consciousness, Spirit, Psychology, Therapy* (2000, Boston: Shambhala).

2. For example, R. Elliot Ingersoll and David M. Zeitler, *Integral Psychotherapy: Inside Out/Outside In* (2010, New York: SUNY Series in Integral Theory), and Mark Forman, *A Guide to Integral Psychotherapy: Complexity, Integration, and Spirituality in Practice* (2010, New York: SUNY Series in Integral Theory).

3. Wilber, 2000, p. 12.

4. Wilber, 2000, p. 31.

5. Jean-Claude Carrière, *Dictionnaire Amoureux de l'Inde* (2001, Paris, Editions Plon).

6. See Nandram and Borden, 2009.

7. Mark Forman, *A Guide to Integral Psychotherapy: Complexity, Integration, and Spirituality in Practice* (2010, New York: SUNY Series in Integral Theory, SUNY Press).

8. Forman, 2010, p. 168.

9. Forman, 2010, p. 160.

10. Ken Wilber et al., *Integral Life Practice: A 21st-Century Blueprint for Physical Health, Emotional Balance, Mental Clarity, and Spiritual Awakening* (2008, Boston: Integral Books).

11. Wilber, et al., 2008, p. 5.

12. Forman, 2010, p. 295.

13. Jorge N. Ferrer, "Integral Transformative Practice: A Participatory Perspective," *Journal of Transpersonal Psychology*, Vol. 35, No. 1) (2003), pp. 28–29.

14. Ferrer, 2003, p. 34.

15. Ingersoll and Zeitler, 2010, p. 14.

16. Elliot Ingersoll, PhD, PCC, "An Integral Approach for Teaching and Practicing Diagnosis," *Journal of Transpersonal Psychology*, Vol. 34, No. 2, (2002), p. 5.

17. Shirazi Bahman, "Integral Psychology Metaphors and Processes of Personal Integration," in Matthijs, Cornelissen Ed., *Consciousness and Its Transformation*, (2001, Pondicherry, India: SAICE).

18. Shirazi, 2001, p. 37.

19. www.integralnaked.org.

20. Wilber, 2000, back cover.

Chapter Six

An Integral Approach to Psychology
Theoretical Considerations

Truth does not pay homage to society. Society has to pay homage to the truth or perish.

Swami Vivekananda

In keeping true to my role as a practitioner and my aspirations as a spiritual seeker, it is time to put forth the fundamental ideas that distinguish and define my integral approach to psychology. I aim to keep the theoretical aspects basic and simple, to pose a necessary structure and foundation, one that is an invitation rather than a declaration.

We have covered the history of psychology in the East and the West, emphasizing the evolution in the West from early mystical worldviews to increasing emphasis on intellectual perspectives and consequent exile of the unseen dimensions. Material foundations pose the predominant worldview in the West, and yet, they are not as absolutist as they seem. While there have always been a few who have resisted reductionism, the emergence of humanistic and transpersonal psychologies has ended the authoritarian rule of the reductionist mindset. Reintegration of more human and subtle aspects of human experience is undeniably here to stay. They stake their claim and hold their own in the face of the reductionist schools, more or less aspiring toward increasingly holistic ideals.

Now we turn to the Eastern mystical schools of thought, which descend from the great rishis or seers who tell us of the mysteries of the universe through their direct experiences and perception. The sacred texts conveying their insights draw on psychological self-knowledge as a path to transcendence. The belief was that this earthly plane was nothing but illusion. Dissolution of the self and transcendence were the supreme goals.

Sri Aurobindo brought in the Western concept of evolution which began as a metaphysical, then philosophical, and then physical quest. The potential for evolution in consciousness gives fresh light and accessibility to a truly integral psychology. Before his time, the focus of mystics and philosophers of India was traditionally transcendence or verticality. Aurobindo, in telling us that our greatest quest was not to eliminate the ego but to align the ego with the soul or inner being, introduces a possibility of horizontal development. Ken Wilber invests Aurobindo's integral perspective with intellectual foundations. His work pragmatically integrates East, West, traditional, modern, postmodern, and multidimensional consciousness.

Psychology is evolving and, one might dare say, moving in the direction of integrality which takes the entire matrix of the East and the West, past, present, and future, to the next level. We begin with acknowledgment of multiple levels of consciousness and ultimately transcend the confines of the mental, shifting our inner axis of consciousness. Integral evolves and stems from the essence of our being. From the matrix of the whole emerge new possibilities in consciousness, an entirely new paradigm. Before we dive into the theoretical constructs of integral psychology, let's look at where we currently stand, what is missing, and how an integral approach paves the way forward.

EVOLUTION OF PSYCHOLOGY
"DEVELOPMENTAL ISSUES"

Western psychology stems predominantly from intellectual and scientific worldviews. This is reflected in the way we perceive human potential and the corresponding goals and techniques of psychotherapy. Western psychology's strength is in the outer self and the self in the world. Its goals, in evolutionary order, are the scientific deduction and medical treatment of mental imbalances and suffering. Cognitive approaches seek to identify, quantify, and categorize the outer, observable self; manage psychopathology; and build a healthy ego and capacity for personal and social adaptation to overcome neurosis and suffering. In its outer reaches, it begins to veer from a pathology-based approach toward human potential in aiming to help us break away from limitations and engage in self-discovery.

In the expansionist schools, humanistic psychology explores the possibility of self-actualization. The transpersonal schools, although remaining on the fringes, reach higher heights by studying nonordinary and transcendent experiences.

At its greatest heights, there are deep perceptions, intuitions, and insights into our ultimate potential and the functioning of consciousness, but despite its sincere efforts, Western psychology has not yet succeeded in creating the perfect fusion—an unfragmented vision—of mind and spirit centered around the highest common denominator. Perhaps it's time to put Descartes in his place and get out of our heads!

Where Do We Go From Here?

The efficacy of Western approaches is unquestionable. However, working with approaches and belief systems more limited than our actual potential puts a ceiling on the possibilities. We may end up identifying with a restricted aspect of our nature such as a childhood drama, our wounds, the ways in which we were victims, or the stigma and reductionism of medical diagnoses.

No matter how far ordinary psychology takes us, we have an infinitely greater potential that can be discovered beyond the reach of the all-consuming mind. The intellect is inherently fragmented and cannot see beyond itself. In ordinary consciousness, everything gets mixed together with no apparent order or guidance. We can add in elements, address new diagnoses, and develop new tools as we discover new forms of suffering, but inherently, our approach will remain fragmented. Everything we develop at this level, no matter how innovative or revolutionary, amounts to nothing more than incremental change. Why? Because the foundations are still in the outer self, the ego which is finite, limited, and external. We may have all the outer elements at the physical, emotional, and mental levels, but these disparate parts of the self require something greater, something beyond, to bring them into harmony with one another.

EASTERN CONSCIOUSNESS PERSPECTIVE— EVOLUTION OF CONSCIOUSNESS

The Eastern approach to psychology has been spiritually rooted in yogic philosophy, the mystic core of Hindu tradition.[1] It is relevant here to elicit a key difference in the development of Eastern vs Western spiritual and philosophical foundations. In India, although the interpretation and practices have undergone evolution and, prior to Adi Shankara's reformation, a period of hibernation, the spiritual foundations have been unbroken since their origin; they reflect an age-old continuum.

In contrast, in the West, the Age of Enlightenment reflected the split between spirit and matter. It not only emphasized and deified the rational mind, it presumed absolutism. Although there is a strong wave of rediscovery or rekindling of spirituality, our roots, worldview, and functioning are predominantly cognitive. We reflect on our spiritual aspects rather than experiencing them.

The focus of traditional Indian spirituality is vertical. It emphasizes transcendence, surrendering our ego and aligning it to the divine consciousness or the highest reality. The Eastern practitioner, in pursuing this lofty goal, will identify and progressively disentangle himself from aspects of the ego that retard his spiritual progress.

The Eastern focus on spiritual and inner dimensions, for those who resonate with them, brings meaning, purpose, and inner peace. It puts our worldly trials and challenges in perspective, showing us that they are an opportunity for growth (learning) and evolution (acceptance and attitudinal shifts). According to most psycho-spiritual aspects of yogic philosophy, human life is a trajectory of evolution from entanglement in our human state toward spiritual realization and liberation, the goal of all human life.

SRI AUROBINDO'S AND KEN WILBER'S INTEGRAL PSYCHOLOGIES: EASTERN AND WESTERN PERSPECTIVES

Spiritual psychologies in the West delve into the depths of the subconscious and to our greater potential. In my personal view, no one seems to integrate the two poles of psychology and spirituality better than Sri Aurobindo's integral yoga psychology. By exploring our body, mind, and emotions, we gain an understanding of their functioning. This helps us to identify and heal the wounds that cause us to go off track. Yet, the psychological dimension need not be an end in itself, but a gateway leading to our highest potential through discipline, aspiration, meditation, the cultivation of wisdom, devotion, direct experience (inner self-discovery), and, hopefully, a healthy dose of grace. The transformation of consciousness we attain is then channeled back down to the worldly plane, where we aspire to bring spirit into matter.

Sri Aurobindo's work lays the capstone for an integral perspective, embracing our inherent mystical nature and potential horizontal and vertical. Wilber adds intellectual foundations with his multidimensional, inclusive, and pluridisciplinary understanding of psychology. The wisdom of the East, and, in particular, Sri Aurobindo's insights and roadmap, help us understand and reach our potential. Western pragmatic approaches, with their structure and rigor—in particular, Ken Wilber's model—spanning the full spectrum of consciousness provide us with further intellectual possibilities. Together, the works of both Wilber and Sri Aurobindo help us navigate the deepest intricacies of our psyches and take on the challenging quest for realization of our highest potential.

Vrinte observes the fundamental differences and complementarities between the works of Wilber and Aurobindo:

Could it be that the difference between Ken Wilber, an intellectual thinker who mysticises, and Sri Aurobindo, an integral yogi who philosophises, lies in the fact that Sri Aurobindo starts from his realisations which he tries to express in the inadequate language of the mind, whereas Ken Wilber starts from his mental abstractions of his vision-logic realisations and tries to reach the essential truths in flashes of mystical vision?[2]

Vrinte also makes clear that mental analysis or even a higher integrated vision-logic is not sufficient to understand Sri Aurobindo's writings. Only through a meditative reading of his works can one begin to understand them more deeply.

SHIFT TO AN INTEGRAL PARADIGM

Sri Aurobindo's approach invites us to go from an ego-centered to a soul-based paradigm, essentially a transformation of consciousness. The ego is composed of body, mind, and emotions, each with their drive to fulfill outer desires in perpetual competition with one another. We till, weed, and cultivate the ego by addressing our issues and avoiding pitfalls. Gradually the ego gives way to the soul. The soul, the highest unifying force of our being, brings light to the dark places and congruence and harmony to the outer self. According to Sri Aurobindo's vision, this transformation in the axis of the individual and eventually the collective consciousness brings about an entirely new level of functioning. Consciousness descends into the material/physical plane, creating a new and vibrant physical body.

The classic Eastern yogic view holds that the root of our disharmonies is within. "You should not be so dependent on outward things; it is this attitude that makes you give so excessive an importance to circumstances. I do not say that circumstances cannot help or hinder but they are circumstances, not the fundamental thing which is in ourselves, and their help or their hindrance ought not to be of primary importance."[3]

What we experience outside is a reflection of our inner state. Some approaches even tell us to disidentify from or transcend the outer situation, feelings, attitudes, thoughts, and behaviors that appear to be the cause of suffering. Other approaches such as the Buddhist mindfulness approach will advise us to sit with whatever we are feeling or thinking and use it as a springboard or a gateway to begin the inner journey to the core.

The integral approach addresses issues both internally and externally, identifying and liberating the root causes. The attitudinal shifts that naturally take place result in behavioral changes that are congruent with the inner shift. We move away from an exclusive, unidisciplinary, unidimensional, "either-or" or "us-them" approach to an inclusive, pluridisciplinary, and multidimensional paradigm.

At the onset of our journey, we set out searching to alleviate our suffering or perhaps an uncomfortable sense that there is something more to life. We begin seeking where this "more" might be. Our consciousness is like a rock in its pure, uncut form. As we explore the rock and chip away what we no longer need, we begin to discover that it is made of alabaster. We are intrigued and yet, sometimes forget, deny, and get distracted from it. At other times, we have a sense that it is the only truth and are drawn into its mysteries and its potential with single-minded focus. We chip away and fine-tune its form. Little by little, as the form begins to emerge, we move away from outward distractions and are increasingly drawn to the mystical form emerging from within. As we chip away at the illusions and distractions, the alabaster becomes smoother and more sublime. As we become totally focused on its emergence, we become aware that beyond the alabaster form lies the Divine, God, Universal Consciousness, like a diamond encased in its outer form. And, just as we walked in the direction of the discovery and then the realization of our soul, we begin to walk toward the Divine until it too becomes our sole aspiration, our sole desire. The summit of this metaphorical or aspirational journey is the gradual identification and final merging with the indwelling divine.

Theoretical and Therapeutic Potential

The ego is like a cat, capricious and devious. Cats seduce us with their green eyes, their taunting challenge, the way they lead us to believe we are finally going to get some love and affection when in fact it is all a ploy for them to fulfill their self-centered desire. Putting our ego at the center of our being, our worldview, and our actions does not result in anything noble. On the other hand, the qualities inherent in soul-consciousness lead us to altogether more righteous, wholesome, and congruent thoughts, words, and actions for the highest good of ourselves, others, and the planet. Consciousness is infinite, and so are the inner and outer implications of making this shift. When it comes to our psycho-spiritual development, the only limitation is the one posed by our own minds.

DEFINING INTEGRAL

Integral, a keyword for our times, reflects man's deepest inner drive, the quest for unity. According to the context, the word integral has different meanings. On a basic level, it can mean whole, as in whole-grain flour. A synonym reflecting its deeper potential is "at the heart of." Wilber defines it as: "to integrate, to bring together, to join, to link, to embrace. Not in the sense of uniformity, and not in the sense of ironing out all the wonderful differences . . . but in the sense of unity-in-diversity."[4] Sri Aurobindo used the Sanskrit word *purna* which means infinite, full, limitless, complete, whole, absolute, reality, and perfect, a fundamental unity holding the diversity in its matrix. For our purpose, we use it to refer to a comprehensively multidimensional and complete view of consciousness and human potential.

Now let's apply this concept to psychology. While Sri Aurobindo doesn't specifically use the term integral psychology but integral yoga, Wilber's approach is more specifically psychological in scope. At the same time, Aurobindo's famous saying, "Yoga is nothing but practical psychology"[5] demonstrates the way his philosophy approaches and bridges the gap between psychology and spirituality.

A theory for integral psychology requires defining elements to lay some foundations, and yet needs to be open and spacious, leaving room for each individual to evolve in their own way. Rather than setting out to define a standard, comprehensive theory, I will instead put forth four pillars that define and distinguish my integral approach. Pillars hold the structure together while leaving space for expansion, exploration, and evolution. Pillars are my edifice of preference insofar as they reach toward both earth and sky.

1. Unity in Diversity

Unity refers to a deep and subtle place in consciousness, the place where there is an underlying oneness of all existence. Wilber states that unity does not mean homogeneity. On the deepest, inner levels of consciousness, we are all one. On the outer level, the level of personality and individual lives, we each have a unique personality, path, and life purpose. Both psychology and history tell us that coercing ourselves or others into homogeneity leads to stifling our material, emotional, intellectual, and spiritual potential. Let's leave the quest for homogeneity for the control freaks.

2. Spiritual Worldview

Spirituality is the path from outer self toward our innermost and highest consciousness, the quest for the inner divine. While spirituality is often used synonymously with religion, I use it to refer to something that is nondenominational or even transreligious:

> Spirituality is an umbrella concept that includes several dimensions of intrapersonal experiences (the inner side of spirituality), interpersonal experiences and person-situation experiences (the outer side of spirituality) and the

connectedness between these types of experiences. At the concrete level, it has to do with attitudes, values, emotions and behaviors related to an inner force in human beings that lead us to self-actualization and happiness.[6]

Spirituality can be sought through ancient, traditional yogic disciplines or modern techniques. It involves perception or realization beyond the mind and the five senses and toward finding and merging with the inner divine light. We may be endowed with or develop spiritual qualities such as openness, love for others, compassion, and joy. The emergence of these qualities is a by-product of our spiritual development but at the same time, only one aspect of it. The innermost expression of spirituality stems from the deepest, inner self.

Many concepts can be included in a definition of spirituality. Ken Wilber offers the following four principles:

> (1) Spirituality involves peak experiences or altered states, which can occur at almost any stage and any age; (2) spirituality involves the highest levels in any of the lines [of development]; (3) spirituality is a separate developmental line itself; (4) spirituality is an attitude (such as openness, trust, or love) that the self may or may not have at any stage.[7]

For Sri Aurobindo, "Spirituality is in its essence an awakening to the inner reality of our being, to our spirit, self, soul which is other than our mind, life and body, an inner aspiration to know, to feel, to be."[8]

A spiritual worldview places soul or spirit at the center of our being and life purpose. At the same time, spirituality is a path, an inner quest, not a concept. It, therefore, implicates a mindset and lifestyle that facilitate that quest. On the theoretical side, many schools of thought, philosophy, and religion give us insights, guidelines, and techniques to help us work our way toward purification and sublimation of our being and consciousness.

3. Multidimensional Grasp of Consciousness and Human Potential

The multidimensional nature of consciousness is not a concept but a reality that is perceptible in varying degrees. It includes the material or physical, the emotional, the mental, and more subtle realms of consciousness beyond these. Sri Aurobindo's model (chapter 4) gives a detailed breakdown of levels of consciousness, but there are many such models, each with varying degrees of detail and unique perspectives. The meaning and perspective they bring translate into a whole new way of perceiving and working with our life challenges.

4. Levels of Truth

Many spiritual schools teach us that the truth is within and that everything outside—body, mind, emotions, senses, society, and the world—is an illusion. Identifying with this illusion distracts us from our spiritual quest. Other religions and mystical schools advocate that there are many levels of truth. As we climb the ladder toward higher levels of consciousness, we reach greater and more subtle truths.

In my early days as a spiritual aspirant, I took on the truth vs illusion construct and applied it to my worldview and lifestyle. You wouldn't have seen me undertake any activities that were not distinctly spiritual, no idle time, no entertainment, everything was oriented toward reaching the goal of enlightenment that I so desired. As a result, I lived in a dualistic world of spiritual vs not spiritual and applied this construct to every thought, word, and action on which my spiritually ambitious ego could get its grip. Yes, I was living exactly according to the spiritual teachings I was following and, yes, I was miserable.

Over time, as my understanding began to shift, I was liberated from the torturous dichotomy of truth vs illusion. I discovered that each perception of truth comes from its own unique perspective, much as the color of sunlight according to the shade of the sunglasses we are wearing reveals particular aspects of the truth while concealing others. The implication is that what it reveals is not essentially unreal (or an illusion), but that it is incomplete and being incomplete is thus likely to be misleading. Rather than illusion, one can use the terms transitional truths or partial truths. By corollary, partial truths require other perspectives to find their proper place and function in the larger scheme of things. The perspective of levels of truth is inclusive rather than divisive and, therefore, fits into the vision of integral psychology.

Having built a basic structure with four pillars, where do we go from here? How can we integrate earth, sky, and everything in between into a psychological model?

WHERE SHOULD PSYCHOLOGY BRING US? WHY NOT SHOOT FOR THE STARS?

A client once asked me, "How long do I need to come for therapy?" I answered, "It depends on what you are seeking." We can aim to resolve an issue, or we can set out on an infinite path of self-knowledge.

Are we merely physiological mechanisms or creatures of habit and conditioning? Are we here in this life to be moral and productive citizens, employees, spouses, and parents? Do we, as conveyed in the East, have a higher purpose beyond these? Our approaches to psychology and psycho-spiritual development are based on our points of reference and worldview. In turn, this determines our therapeutic goals. The West, with its predominantly scientific and pragmatic worldview, has its own particular views and corresponding goals. The East, with its more ancient, traditional, and inherently spiritual worldview, has others.

When we understand the currently existing perspectives, we can move forward and integrate them into a larger, inclusive, and therefore integral perspective. This increases the scope of possibilities and understanding, thereby creating space for our infinite potential. Let us examine some of the common therapeutic goals.

Adjustment and Adaptation

Western psychology typically focuses on the ego level of consciousness, on the outer self, on self-identity, and on bringing out and integrating contents from the subconscious. We examine our beliefs, feelings, and behavior, and make a conscious effort to modify them. This starts with the outer self and goes gradually to the subconscious sources of imbalance and suffering to help us come to terms with them.

In the East, each person has roles and responsibilities, or dharmas, to fulfill based on examples given in the scriptures without further thought. The idea of ego-based adaptation is alien to traditional Indian thought.

Alleviation of Emotional Distress

In the West, much research has been done to understand and help manage or eliminate our emotional distress which is considered to be undesirable or even pathological. Our inability to deal with, contextualize, or constructively express emotions may be considered to be a symptom or a cause, physiologically based, contextual, or systemic depending on the school of thought.

In the East, human nature is seen as being multidimensional, with emotions occurring on the vital plane (Aurobindo). When unmastered, they are forces of commotion and chaos which are obstacles to our spiritual realization. Eastern principles advise us to practice vigilance and detachment with our emotions so they are in service of our spiritual evolution rather than being an unruly and mischievous barrel of monkeys.

Material and Affective Fulfillment

Material, affective, and social fulfillment are the major emphases of popular psychology and culture in the West. We are led to believe that it is our right and duty to achieve emotional fulfillment which is the key to happiness. Many therapies in the West focus on getting to know our emotions and our emotional functioning, as a means of creating and sustaining harmonious relationships with ourselves and others.

In the Vedic tradition, these goals do not exist as an end in themselves. Instead, they translate into a complex system of social responsibilities described in scriptures and parables. The Indian view of *dharma, artha, kama,* and *moksha* lays the foundations and traditionally has a strong influence on how Indians perceive their lives. *Dharma,* inherent in this system, in turn lays the foundation for the three aims of *artha, kama,* and *moksha. Dharma* means correct fulfillment of our various duties, roles, and responsibilities as children, siblings, students, and then, later on, as spouses, citizens, and devotees. *Artha* applies to our pursuit of wealth and abundance and *kama,* to pleasure. Both *artha* and *kama* are our right and duty if we choose a worldly path and have to be pursued in harmony with our *dharma.* Once we have fulfilled these worldly desires, we then retreat in pursuit of *moksha,* or liberation. This system is not desire or ego-based but is designed to guide individuals through their worldly experiences, bringing about balance and fulfillment without getting lost. Ultimately, the goal is to transcend it all and achieve liberation. Traditionally, this perspective defined people's roles and ensured collective harmony on a societal level. However, over time, these principles got codified into rigid and sometimes oppressive aberrations as in the case of the highly controversial caste system.

Elimination of Suffering

Suffering is one of the main motivators for seeking psychological help. Yet, the cause of suffering is defined differently by the ego-based Western approaches and the soul-centered Eastern ones. Equally different are the subsequent beliefs on how to address suffering and whether its absence can be equated with happiness. Suffering is addressed macrocosmically in the West, in relationship to events in the outer world and the outer self. In contrast, in the East, whether or not the apparent stimulus is external or internal, the way out is through looking into the microcosm, the inner sphere which includes our attitudes and inherently spiritual foundations, giving an opportunity for objectivity and meaning.

Peace with Oneself and Self-Acceptance

The ideal of making peace with oneself is more present in the humanistic, transpersonal schools than in the earlier, mechanistic approaches.

In the East, outer peace is considered to be transitory, as this earthly plane is replete with discord and incongruence. True peace is ultimately a state of mind, a state of being independent of external events—a "felt" inner experience. Our inner peace, built on our connection with the Divine, radiates into our outer life and our relationships, creating peace and harmony to the extent that these two qualities are possible in the outer world.

Integration

An important goal of the Western schools, influenced by psychoanalysis, is integrating the unconscious wounds and thoughts that we succumb to, react to, or resist. Through dialogue and introspective and uncovering techniques we bring unconscious, disharmonious material to our conscious awareness and resolve or release it. This results in a greater state of fluidity. As this occurs, it can open up gateways to deeper aspects of our nature. The more holistic schools see integration as the possibility of greater connection and, therefore, congruence between the different aspects of the personality and self that can occur through healing the wounds. In addition, peak experiences and other extraordinary insights cultivate a stronger relationship to the inner self around which the other parts begin to reorganize.

In Eastern thought, integration occurs naturally through right living. Traditional lifestyle in regards to family, dietary hygiene, spiritual rituals, and time spent with realized beings awakens and nourishes the inner self. Aligning our thoughts, words, and actions to our innermost wisdom and our potential brings us continually closer to our inner truth. A harmonious relationship with all parts of ourselves and our environment facilitates the flow of consciousness within our being and opens the gates to higher states of consciousness. In contrast to the Western principle of sin, one of the concepts I love most about Hinduism is that each thought, word, and action either brings us closer and more in harmony with ourselves or alienates us from our true nature. This puts the responsibility in our hands. I am the creator of my existence in the sense that I can bring myself up, or down. The choice is mine. A by-product of taking the upward spiral is ironing out the kinks in our outer nature. In contrast, being at odds or in conflict with ourselves does the opposite and leads to greater disharmony.

Thus far, we have examined the goals of psychotherapy in terms of the East vs the West. This is because, up until here, as we address the outer parts of ourselves, the East and the West have distinctively different perspectives on them. Working from an integral view will keep sight of the most basic, outer-oriented goal of adjustment and adaptation, becoming aware of our emotions, learning how to live with and express them, material and affective fulfillment, elimination of suffering, peace with oneself, and self-acceptance and integration while keeping them in a larger picture of our further potentials. Each goal is part of a whole, larger picture rather than a self-limiting perspective on the issues at hand and our potential.

Spiritual Development, Transcendence, and Transformation

Here we venture into more subtle zones of consciousness and higher aspects of human potential beyond the body, emotions, and mind. This phase of our evolution is sadly neglected, psychologized, or even pathologized by mental health professionals. At its highest limits, exploring the higher reaches of human nature is done by the mainstream schools of psychology, but only conceptually. The goals of psychology in the West are based on a temporal and personal vision of human potential. The description of spiritual approaches to psychotherapy is reduced to the psychology of religion, spirituality, and the dynamics of faith.

Many years ago I had the opportunity of having a lengthy stay in Israel. I was quite young but had already begun my research into inner development through breathwork and meditation. I was thirsty for experiences that unveiled the mystery of inner truth. We went on a trip to Mount Tabor, the place where Jesus was transfigured. Rather than visit the museum, I felt drawn to venture into the forest. I sat down on the earth beneath some trees in a meditative posture. I closed my eyes and began to focus inward, surrendering into the breath as I did every morning in my meditation. As I sat there on the forest floor, I had a most extraordinary sense of seeing 360° around me as if my eyes were open. I felt every aspect of that place, earth, trees, animals, sky, wind. I tasted the richness and multidimensionality of the present moment, which I savored without reserve. I felt fully alive, fully aware, and fully at one with my surroundings. After a time, I naturally came back to my normal, waking state. I got up and limped back to the parking lot on pin-and-needle-filled legs. The first thing I saw on the steps of the museum was a group of French tourists debating about the concept of transfiguration. I smiled to myself as I delighted in the impression left on me by this experience that I can still vividly recall.

We can conceptualize until the cows come home, but only in introspection and silence can we experience transcendence. Reading a book or having a discussion on transcendence might help us understand it, but there is nothing like experiencing it for oneself! Such an experience from a Western perspective would either be labeled as pathological (and diagnosed as a dissociated affective state) or considered to be a new-age fad. In the East, such phenomena are understood and respected.

The inherently spiritual Indian worldview is reflected in various ways according to family tradition, individual choice, and level of understanding and development which range from superstitious, ritualistic, and fundamentalist (rare in Hinduism) to profound yogic interpretations and corresponding life-styles. It is never limited to mere worldly pursuits and aims toward either transcendence or transformation. In both cases, the aspirant starts with the aim of transcending the binds of worldly consciousness and ascending to a perma-nent state of spiritual realization or enlightenment as depicted in the analogy of the alabaster form above. There are various approaches to transcendence. *Grihastha*, or householders, aim to live a dharmic life—being in the world but not of the world. More ascetic schools emphasize an exclusive focus on transcendence—ascension into a higher consciousness and disidentification with all but the Divine.

Sri Aurobindo taught that once we have transcended into higher conscious-ness, we are to bring it down into the material plane and endeavor for its transformation. Sri Aurobindo defines transformation as "a change of con-sciousness radical and complete and of a certain specific kind which is so conceived as to bring about a strong and assured step forward in the spiritual evolution of the consciousness."[9]

The goals of human development reflect our vision of human potential. In the East, the aim is the highest, multidimensional potentials of man. The goals of the West such as psychological development along with other horizontal aims of life are often by-products of our spiritual pursuit but are not an end in themselves.

Psychotherapy should aim to address and work with the full range of human experiences and potential. In addressing our highest potential, we do not stop at incremental steps in our development, but each one of us, in our own way and at our own pace, can make a paradigm shift, changing our axis of consciousness from ego to soul. In this case, psychotherapy is a use-ful and sometimes essential means of freeing ourselves from barriers to our development. Psychotherapy, like spiritual practice, can be a means as well as a preparation for our transcendence. Psychotherapy roots out the block-ages on the human levels and spirituality takes over from there by deepening and expanding our awareness to more subtle zones. The insights gained from transcendent experiences translate into our outer lives, resulting in personal goals and a lifestyle that are more congruent and radiant, reflective of a deeper truth.

Spiritual development is a continual process of identifying, integrating, and transcending our limitations, our small, outer self and unfolding to greater and greater heights, depths, and breadths in our own conscious-ness. While I have greatly elaborated on the limitations of earlier schools of Western psychology, and even pointed out how making a true shift to a greater worldview has to involve a transformation of consciousness, here, the East gets its due. Diving willy-nilly into the soul or the infinite univer-sal consciousness will most likely be accompanied by a fair dose of trials, tribulations, and challenges. Keeping these in mind will hopefully make the journey less perilous.

DANGERS OF SPIRITUALITY AND SPIRITUAL APPROACHES TO PSYCHOTHERAPY

Spiritual teachers and wise psychologists have written many volumes on the trials, tribulations, and dangers of spiritual seeking and spiritual evolution. Integral psychology, through explicitly addressing the spiritual end of the spectrum, has the potential to recognize and help individuals having spiritual issues or imbalances. In addition, spiritual seekers may encounter certain dangers and pitfalls in the course of their spiritual development. Explicit training in identifying and working with both dangers and imbalances in spiritual pursuits can help us to find our way in these troublesome and illusive areas.

Imagine a person who has endeavored to tackle his shadow and climb to great spiritual heights. He begins to have profound insights and powers such as clairvoyance and healing. He may even have a peak experience of oneness with all of existence. Despite having spiritual experiences, it is important not to assume that we have arrived and even more important not to develop a spiritual ego that says: "I am the only one who knows, I am the only one who understands, I am the only one who perceives. I am spiritual, I am right, no one else sees it as broadly and completely as I do. My technique, my school, my philosophy are the right ones, the best ones."

Spiritual ego has many different masks: spiritual perfectionism, spiritual absolutism, spiritual materialism, illusion of being omniscient, and many more. On the spiritual ladder, spiritual ego is the chute. As spirituality brings us to higher heights the risk of falling increases and—in this case—we have further to fall.

The dangers and pitfalls of spiritual development can all be attributed to one culprit, the ego. Vedic epistemology describes four defects found in every human being that hinder our ability to gain knowledge. These defects are the cause of all our errors: *bhrama*, our tendency to be deluded by believing false perceptions to be real; *pramad*, the tendency to make inadvertent mistakes; *vipralipsa*, the propensity to cheat or deceive ourselves and others due to the false understanding of what is important; and *karanapatava*, inability of our senses to perceive truth. We can be certain that one or more of our defects—*bhrama*, *pramad*, *vipralipsa* and *karanapatava*—are at play when we find ourselves in a spiritual bind. Keeping our shortcomings in mind helps us to be more realistic, keep these tendencies in check, and lessen the negative effects of our weaknesses.

Here are some of the ways in which we can get caught up or lost in our spiritual pursuits. Although I have described them as distinct categories, there is often an overlap.

Distraction by Physical, Emotional, Mental, or Astral Phenomenon

The path of spirituality is a knife edge between abysses. On one side is the danger of mere rejection and escape and on the other the danger of mere acceptance and the enjoyment of things which should only be used as instruments or symbols. [10]

On the physical level, we might overly identify with our physical bodies and material aspects of life. Emotions, drama, and therapeutic catharsis, due to their intensity, seem like profound experiences. They may, in fact, be life altering and positive but they mustn't be taken for something they're not. Affective experiences experienced in such activities as ecstatic dance and chanting can also be mistaken for spiritual experience. The intellect is so distracting that an entire period of history mistook it for the highest potential of man! Patanjali and countless other sages and teachers warn us that the lure of subtle phenomenon or the development of our intuition are equally distracting. We may get lost or distracted in any of these experiences and forget that there is a mountain peak toward which we can keep ascending.

Life is the subtle presence and not the dramatic sensation. It is the being which unites, not the form which divides. It can only be known by the pure perception of undivided awareness. [11]

Spiritual Bypass

Spiritual bypass is one of the most common pitfalls of spiritual seekers. We employ various means to escape into spiritual heights or a spiritual alter ego. Spiritual bypass can occur in the form of dissociation, adopting a spiritual persona, escaping into spiritual la-la land, and countless other mutations.

There are obvious problems with rising to the heights while ignoring the lack of foundations or the cracks in the foundations. It may cause nothing more than a roller coaster between the highest heights and the glum reality of our human condition but can also result in more serious imbalances.

Vignette—Spiritual Bypass

I met Sam at a lecture I had given on detachment. He rang me up a few days later to make an appointment for a breathwork session. His speech and body language seemed slow and choppy and he appeared to be zombie-like or drugged. He could certainly talk the talk, but I had the uneasy sense that the detachment he demonstrated was a façade, a defense mechanism. His story was vague and destructured. He said that after a difficult breakup, reading Eckhart Tolle's Power of Now *had helped him to feel better. And yet, it was apparent that the wisdom on letting go of pain conveyed in this book had served as a catalyst for dissociation rather than a true state of detachment. I guessed that he was carrying with him some experiences or attitudes that were easier bypassed than dealt with and that his reading made him jump into the "detached" mindset that was, in reality, dissociation. I felt the best approach to take would be to help him start to address and come to terms with the fragile state he alluded to, that lay hidden behind his outward detachment/dissociation. It didn't take long, endeavoring to create a most delicate and safe space, before he opened up and poured out his deep pain and despair around the early loss of his mother due to alcoholism. As the sobs subsided, he spontaneously blurted out the realization of how he had built a wall around that pain, and this had caused him to build a false sense of self. After that session, he decided to continue working with me toward developing a more realistic and wholesome sense of self.*

There is a fine line between dissociation, a pathological split between our outer self and our emotions, and detachment, the ability to stand back and observe what we are experiencing from a neutral standpoint while still engaging in it. Adopting a spiritual persona and conveying an image of being the perfect congregant or disciple is another form of spiritual bypass. Not a successful strategy for masking poor self-image or escaping our workaday reality.

HUXLEY PLACED MUCH EMPHASIS ON THE PERILS OF IMBALANCED SPIRITUAL DEVELOPMENT

When God is regarded as exclusively immanent, legalism and external practices are abandoned and there is a concentration on the Inner Light. The dangers now are quietism and antinomianism, a partial modification of consciousness that is useless or even harmful, because it is not accompanied by the transformation of character which is the necessary prerequisite of a total, complete and spiritually fruitful transformation of consciousness.[12]

Mystical Judaism or Kabbalah warns about the dangers of premature transcendence. Traditionally, observant Jews believe study of the Kabbalah should not begin before the age of forty. By this time a depth of study and learning, as well as life experience, is achieved to ensure moving into Kabbalah in a balanced way:

> To achieve [higher consciousness], the Kabbalist must observe the working of the *Yesod*, his ordinary mind or ego, so as to see through his own foibles and self-delusions and bring into awareness the unconscious forces that shape his thoughts and actions. To do this, he seeks to reach the level of awareness called *Tiferet*, a state of clarity that is witness or "watcher" of the *Yesod*.[13]

Spiritual bypass often reflects an impulse to avoid ground-level, psychological issues. This is why psychotherapy can be an important, if not sometimes crucial, element of a healthy and successful spiritual life.

Lack of Discernment

Lack of discernment or misinterpreting that which we perceive can occur for various reasons. Our emotions and unmet needs and desires are waiting in the sidelines for the perfect opportunity to overshadow our perception. Discernment helps us navigate both in the world of our inner experiences and in the outer world. In turn, developing objectivity and discernment in regards to our issues helps us apply these same qualities with our clients.

In the same way that ethics has different implications when addressing spiritual matters, the same holds true for discernment. Shadow takes on increasingly subtle and slippery forms at the spiritual levels, both for our inner trajectory and in the outer world.

The wolves in sheep's clothing in the world are one thing, those lurking in the spiritual realms are another. Fortunately, many of these wolves have pretty shoddy disguises revealing their characteristic canines and long snouts, yet others look pretty much like sheep and can be harder to detect. One of the most common errors I've seen is the tendency to pool all subtle phenomena together under the belief that it is spiritual. Unfortunately, all that glitters is not gold.

Whether it is due to ignorance or an impulse to escape into fantasy, no one has perfect discrimination. We all have to work at it through simple self-observation. Simply paying attention and heeding the messages from our sixth sense goes a long way.

New-Age Fads, Pop Psychology, and Pseudo Gurus

Anyone offering us personal and spiritual development is only human. They may themselves be suffering from lack of discernment or, even worse, be outright devious, power seekers. We can inadvertently follow seminars, trainings, and false gurus that tempt us with ego enhancement, development of the material, physical, sexual, sensual, emotional, and intellectual aspects of life disguised as spiritual seeking. Motivated by a thirst for knowledge and oneness, we may fall into the trap of our naiveté or an urge for spiritual bypass. New-age movements and false gurus are renowned for usurping the genuine human urge to transcendence. We must not assume that someone who has subtle powers or who does large-scale social service is necessarily enlightened. Good deeds may mask a variety of hidden motives.

Almighty Syndrome

Helping others is admirable and useful, and yet our desire or motivation to help can come from different places. It can be laced with hidden agendas that feed the ego at different levels. If our spiritual pursuit is influenced by an unaddressed quest for self-esteem, the impulse to avoid pain, vulnerability, or other defense mechanisms, we may fall into the grips of the almighty syndrome.

Vignette—Almighty Syndrome

Amy, a young woman who came to see me, expressed a strong sense of isolation and difficulty creating harmonious relationships with others. She was active in an organization that studies paranormal phenomenon and I quickly sensed that she was suffering from almighty syndrome. As we worked together, in the early phase, she recognized that she had a defensive relationship style, a need to be the authority and had difficulty in allowing a sense of equality to develop between her and her friends. She realized how this was in response to feeling unsafe in her childhood. Over time, she had developed a means of compensating for her feeling of vulnerability. She created a tough persona and a quest to feeling powerful. When she began to delve into the world of spirituality, her quest for power translated into the almighty complex, a need to feel in control and to have an answer for everything. It also caused her to adopt the role of savior to all and sundry who presented difficulties and vulnerabilities. This once again compensated for her unaddressed feeling of vulnerability. Through our work together, I helped Amy to understand that it is in acknowledging and giving space to our wounded inner child and our vulnerabilities that we become truly strong. Here too, we need to distinguish between vulnerability and weakness. The two are often confused but are not in the least bit the same quality. In a sense, one could say that being unable to acknowledge our vulnerability makes us weak, whereas acknowledging our vulnerability makes us whole and strong. We see then that forms of spirituality, without psychological grounding, can serve as defense mechanisms to escape the daunting feeling of vulnerability that is inevitably hidden behind all psychological wounds.

Spirituality brings with it a sense of power or mastery. If the ego is not in its proper place, that promise of power can be used to feed the ego and usurp the soul. The quest for power is but one of many ways in which our unresolved needs and desires can subtly influence our noble desires to evolve and to help others.

Halfway Up the Mountain

> The content of the unconscious [can] burst in unexpectedly. ... This can
> create several scenarios. The first one is of self-exaltation. One becomes
> aware of one's Self and then not realizing the hard and long journey which
> is often necessary before one can actually integrate these qualities into
> oneself, the mistake is made of thinking that one is actually there. ... It is
> important not to mistake what one actually is for what one can be.[14]

As we evolve personally and spiritually, we may have experiences that seem
like a culmination of a journey. We feel in sync with both inner and outer
life and have powerful visions, intuitions, insights, and experiences. We
assume we have reached enlightenment, develop a spiritual persona and the
role of guru or teacher, and convey our half-baked visions to well-meaning
but naïve seekers. Beware! This may be a plateau rather than the summit.
The Buddhist map of consciousness, the *Visuddhimaga*, advises us not to
attach importance to states of awareness reached in meditation, but rather to
transcend them.

Our experiences are ultimately only a step on the path; we should not attach
too much importance or get lost in the experiences we have along the way.
Keeping in mind the larger picture, our higher potential—the complete transformation of our nature and spiritual realization—can safeguard us from this trap.

Insufficient Psychological Maturity

Lack of sufficient psychological balance may lead to difficulty and downfall.
This can be especially troublesome if the pursuit of spiritual practices leads to
powerful experiences of the inner or higher consciousness. Assagioli emphasizes the dangers of insufficient psychological balance in spiritual seekers:

> [If one] lacks the necessary psychological make-up [he may be] unable to resist
> the spiritual force flowing into him and react in a discordant, morbid fashion.
> This can lead to the over-excitement, imbalance and fanaticism we observe in
> some spurious mystics and self-defined enlightened people.[15]

Traditionally, schools with a purely transcendental focus will not take in
disciples before they have a certain amount of stability and psychological
maturity. The study of the Buddhist practice of Vipassana requires that seekers deal with their ground level issues in psychotherapy before undertaking a
meditation practice and seek therapeutic assistance when necessary to address
issues that arise during meditation practice. Other schools do not advocate
psychotherapy but encourage students to pray, ignore feelings of disturbance,
or focus beyond them onto higher pursuits.

I think we can safely say that until every last human being is enlightened, psychologists will still have work.

Spiritual Narcissism

Narcissism or self-centeredness is built on defense mechanisms or by approaches to psychology that place the ego at the center of our being. A narcissist believes their way is the right way. The unhealed narcissist who delves into spiritual pursuits is more at risk of developing a spiritual ego. When reading spiritual books, attending seminars, or pursuing spiritual practice bear their fruits, a spiritual narcissist can build the need to be right and superior into a spiritual persona. Deluded by our spiritual persona, we put ourselves out as teachers. Far from the outer appearance of being wise, well-meaning, and enlightened, we may actually be inflating our sense of self.

Desire First, Truth Later

Fulfillment of our material, affective, and intellectual desires may seem very important and gratifying. We may push aside our spiritual longing and get distracted in a race that never ends. The Buddha taught us that material and affective fulfillment can never be satisfied. As long as we are identified with our limited ego, we will always feel that we lack something because we are missing our larger universal self. Eastern thought teaches us to forego our egoistic desires in order to find and identify with our true universal and transcendent self. This does not mean we should aspire to extreme asceticism unless it is our true calling. It is not about "to have or not to have," but about having with moderation and balance without our desires dominating us and detracting from our deeper calling.

Spiritual Materialism

Spirituality has many facets; there are many roads leading upwards. A basic and universal spiritual precept is that there is a universal life force representing the ultimate potential of man to transcend the binds of his ego and ignorance and realize light, love, and oneness. We surrender our personal ego and desires and ask nothing more than to have this wise and universal force call us home by the most direct route. That sounds wonderful, but some of us want our cake and want to eat it too. We want to attain the highest heights without surrendering our material desires. We read books or become aware of the universal life force and the power of creative thinking and cheekily sneak in a winning lottery ticket or Mercedes for ourselves. We forget that the purpose of our existence is to align to the inner divine and not to harness subtle powers to get what we want.

Reaching for the Low-Hanging Fruit

We live in a society in which so much is available with little or no effort. If we get lazy or lack discernment, rather than holding out for what we really want, we reach for the low-hanging fruit. This distraction can occur in the material, affective, and mental aspects of our lives. Learning to discern and resist temptation builds essential strengths that make our lives easier. This helps us overcome, rather than give in to, the temptation of instant or instinctual gratification, one of the six realms of animal consciousness defined by Buddhism (see chapter 3). The impulse toward instant gratification takes on an even greater importance when it comes to our spiritual search. Unchecked impulses to go for instant gratification have no place in a sincere spiritual search.

Setting out to explore our spirituality, we will certainly come across countless lessons and obstacles, some of which are mentioned here. We will successfully avoid some traps, thanks to our strengths, maturity, and discernment. And yet, we are bound to make some mistakes; or rather, we have some opportunities to learn and evolve.

Often, during meditation retreats I have participated in these past twenty-eight years, I have a moment where I have what appears to be a poignant perception of other people and their egos. "So-and-so is attention seeking. So-and-so thinks they are the Guru." My observation continues like this until, in front of the mirror, while brushing my teeth or somesuch, I see myself and say, "Oh look at her ego, she this and she that ..." I have a good laugh to myself and trade my judgment in for compassion and acceptance. On yet another judgment day, an early morning ego session gave way to another insight. In fact, all spiritual seekers are mad! But, there are two types of mad spiritual seekers—the ones who take themselves seriously and the ones who laugh about it! Wouldn't it be nice if we could take ourselves lightly all the time!

Spiritual Perfectionism and Other Spiritual Neuroses

Sometimes, rather than being inspired to aspire to the heights we read and hear about, we use those lofty descriptions to mentally pummel ourselves, putting pressure on ourselves to "get there." We think, "If only I could sublimate my sexual drive or overcome such-and-such weakness . . . I would be worthy and able to reach enlightenment." I have seen people work themselves into great states of mental agitation and even mental illness by trying to be more spiritual. They do not become more spiritual; they just become more frustrated.

CONCLUSION

The deepest drive of humankind, no matter how we might express it, is a drive toward healing, wholeness, harmony, and oneness. Western psychological models do not often take that into consideration nor do they provide us with a means to achieve it. They address the pull of our unresolved issues; our psychological disorders and imbalances; and our physical, emotional, interpersonal, and mental aspects, but they do not acknowledge or lead us to the highest possibilities of our consciousness. Because they only address a part of who we are, we explore the fragmented parts of ourselves without taking our higher potentials into consideration.

Few of the brilliant Western thinkers and visionaries of our day realize the highest possibilities of our consciousness. They are looking up at them rather than having realized them. And then there are mystics who have an understanding of the subtle realms but do not necessarily translate them into the practical and psychological domains. Furthermore, in our day, in the absence of both a body of knowledge and respect for mystical realms, genuine spiritual phenomena is often mislabelled as pathology. Our efforts to integrate mind, body, soul, and spirit into a consciousness perspective have not succeeded in fully bridging the gap between our psychological and spiritual dimensions.

Likewise, some of the Eastern traditions have dealt with spirituality but do not address psychological issues. The psychological thought has been elaborated by spiritual masters and not by psychologists. This often does not render it intelligible or acceptable to the Western, intellectual mindset. A focus on a disembodied, transcendent spirituality to the exclusion of the body, emotions, and mind will lead us into a fascinating discovery of the peaks and valleys but may not lead us to the summit.

The ultimate goal and potential of each human life is realization of the inner divine, however one might conceive it. An integral approach brings with it the highest and deepest perspective on consciousness at all its levels, from the physical to the spiritual. Sri Aurobindo's integral psychology comes from this all-encompassing perspective and realization.

Almost all mystical traditions emphasize that love, both divine and human, leads to healing and wholeness. The living spiritual tradition in the East makes this truth easily accessible. To find the same in the West, we must navigate through our pragmatic and scientific limitations. "Love is the strongest and most integral of all powers," said the Mother. Love is the force that unites, creates healing and wholeness. It incites us to seek the highest and truest and gives us the courage to do so. Mahatma Gandhi's insight is that "God is Truth and Truth is God . . . the nearest approach to Truth [is] through love."[16] Let us then surrender the steering wheel to this inner force in the forms of love and truth, rather than to any man-made theory. Theory should be enlightened by insight; insight will never be enlightened by theory. It is something beyond theory that will bring us to the point, to the very experience, that can then be channeled back down and bring light into theory. This is what has the potential to result in a psychological theory and approach that leads not only to our healing but also to the realization of our highest potential.

My daughter, build yourself two cells
First, a real cell,
so that you do not run about much and talk,
unless it is needful,
or you can do it out of love for your neighbour.

Next build yourself a spiritual cell,
which you can always take with you,
and that is the cell of true self-knowledge;
you will find there the knowledge of God's goodness to you.

Here, there are really two cells in one,
and if you live in one you must also live in the other;
otherwise the soul will either despair or be presumptuous.

If you dwelt in self-knowledge or God alone,
you would be tempted to presumption.

One must go with the other,
and thus you will reach perfection.

St. Catherine of Siena

NOTES

1. Despite the tendency in major cities to give it less priority, there is a strong—albeit sometimes underlying—presence of spirituality in daily life, thought, and psychology.

2. Joseph Vrinte, *Perennial Quest for a Psychology with a Soul: An inquiry into the Relevance of Sri Aurobindo's metaphysical yoga psychology in the context of Ken Wilber's integral psychology* (2005, Mumbai: Motilal Banarsidass), p. 459.

3. Sri Aurobindo, "Letters on Yoga IV: Transformation of Human Nature in the Integral Yoga," *The Complete Works of Sri Aurobindo* (2014, Pondicherry, India: Sri Aurobindo Ashram Publication Department), Vol. 31, p. 697.

4. Wilber, Ken, *A Theory of Everything* (2000, Boston: Shambhala), p. 2.

5. Yoga, here, is defined as the pathway to the inner divine, or the spiritual path.

6. Sharda S. Nandram and Margot E. Borden, *Spirituality and Business: Exploring Possibilities for a New Management Paradigm* (2009, Heidelberg: Springer), p. 4.

7. Ken Wilber, *The Eye of the Spirit: An Integral Vision for a World Gone Slightly Mad* (2001, Boston: Shambhala), p. 271.

8. Sri Aurobindo, "The Life Divine," *The Complete Works of Sri Aurobindo* (2005, Pondicherry, India: Sri Aurobindo Ashram Trust), Vol. 21–22, pp. 889–890.

9. Sri Aurobindo, "Letters on Himself and the Ashram," *The Complete Works of Sri Aurobindo* (2011, Pondicherry, India: Sri Aurobindo Ashram Trust), Vol. 35, P. 153.

10. Aldous Huxley, *Perennial Philosophy* (1994, London: Flamingo), p. 85.

11. David Frawley, *Beyond the Mind* (1992, Delhi: Sri Satguru Publications Delhi), p. 25.

12. Huxley, 1994, pp. 26–28.

13. Daniel Goleman, *The Varieties of Meditative Experience* (1977, London: Rider), p. 50.

14. Roberto Assagioli, MD, *Transpersonal Development: The Dimension Beyond Psychosynthesis* (1993, London: Aquarian Press), pp. 49–50.

15. Assagioli, 1993, p. 113.

16. M.K. Gandhi, "What Is God?" *The Essence of Hinduism* (1987, Ahmedabad: Navajivan Publishing House), p. 46.

Chapter Seven

The Making of an Integral Psychotherapist

As it is not proper to cure the eyes without the head, nor the head without the body, so neither is it proper to cure the body without the soul.

Socrates

Theory provides an essential framework, meta-structure, and worldview that is inclusive, pluridisciplinary, spacious, and fluid. From here, there is only one place to go; experience. Now is the time to leave behind the separate identities of East and West and begin to cultivate in ourselves the development and understanding necessary to bring an integral perspective into our work as therapists.

Integral is built on the aspiration and ability to journey into one's inner consciousness, to make one's own roadmaps and choose one's own methodologies for evolving along the psycho-spiritual spectrum. It is not a rigid or systematized approach. Working from an integral perspective requires a combination of analytical assessment of the client and theoretical understanding, insight, and intuition. The fruits of our dedicated inner development bring forth our authentic self, the foundations for our work.

A FOUR-LEAF CLOVER

Taking a walk in the field, we spot a rare four-leaf clover. This legendary sprout becomes the symbol for the four essential and interdependent pillars we are going to build in order to become an integral psychotherapist. The rarity of the four-leaf clover speaks to us of the uncommon quest of becoming a helping professional, not an easy, but a noble, endeavor. Leaving superstition aside, the four-leaf clover symbolizes good luck which we will use to acknowledge the grace inherent in the four leaves. The aspect of grace allows room for the fact that no matter how much we know, no matter what discipline, ultimately existence is a wondrous and fathomless mystery.

Each leaf of the clover represents one pillar for our integral development and role as helping professionals. Our psycho-spiritual growth expands and structures our state of being, clearing the way for our authentic self to come through. Ultimately, the fruits of our endeavors come to serve the individuals who seek our help. Life hygiene means taking care of ourselves by keeping our lives on track, in perspective and in balance, physically, emotionally, mentally, and spiritually and in relation to society and our ecosystem. Skills and tools, covered in chapter 9, give us a means to channel the theories into concrete ways of helping our clients. In the present chapter, we will address the other two leaves of the clover, psycho—spiritual development and life hygiene.

Psycho-Spiritual Development

Physician, heal thyself. Luke 4:23

Training and practice of psychotherapy are authenticated by our dedicated psycho-spiritual development. For some of us, psychotherapy is absolutely essential to help us overcome crippling issues. And yet for others, it is simply a commitment to ongoing psychological life hygiene. In some places, it is also a requirement for psychotherapists to be in therapy. As helping professionals and aspiring helping professionals, we have many roles and challenges. We are psycho-spiritual beings on our unique path of development, we are clients, and we are in the role of helper to those wishing to be clients. Without undertaking our own psycho-spiritual development, we can hope for nothing more than becoming rote practitioners analyzing and applying mechanistic techniques to people who will, above all, gain from the presence we can only learn to offer by first developing it in ourselves.

I'm going to take a strong stand here and dispel the common belief that people cannot change. Whether we start out in life relatively functional or "off the map," therapy has potential benefits for anyone who seeks it. Sometimes we just walk through life with the coping mechanisms we have built haphazardly and sometimes consciously. Sometimes it works and sometimes it doesn't and sometimes we come to a point where it all crumbles to pieces. That's when we see what we're really carrying with us. It either breaks us down or we take the time to evaluate: What are the foundations I'm standing on? How do I know myself? What is the relationship I have with myself? Do I take care of myself? Do I listen to myself? Do I respect myself? Do I take time to get to know and to listen to my soul? And, of course, the microcosm, our relationship to ourselves, sets the stage for the macrocosm, our relationship to others, society, and nature.

The importance of self-knowledge is found in every major spiritual tradition and in the more holistic approaches to psychology as well. Ram Dass[1] believes that for those pursuing spiritual growth, psychological growth is as important as spiritual discipline. John Rowan agrees: "It turns out that personal growth work is not an optional extra, it is an essential step on the spiritual path. In the past, people often embarked on the spiritual path without having done this work, and promptly fell prey to demons, devils, elementals and so forth—most of which were projections of their own shadow, their own nastiness."[2] Addressing problems in thinking patterns, strengthening the will, and increasing vigilance complements deep inner spiritual and body-mind work. Uplifting our consciousness and addressing our shadow places us in the best position possible to provide wholesome insights for our clients.

Sri Aurobindo explains that our negative qualities are always looking for an opportunity to express themselves, and great vigilance is required to refuse them this opportunity.[3] If our negative qualities and emotions are stronger than we are, they'll dominate us, but if we become stronger than they are, we master them. Gaining this mastery can be a long and slow path. We must look at what we are carrying with us through meditative awareness and learn to see ourselves the way we are without judgment. Then, with sincerity and determined self-effort, we withdraw our energy from the negative qualities and invest our energy in counterbalancing positive qualities. It is not simply a question of eliminating the negative, but of simultaneously building the positive. When we build strength and are in a positive state, we have more strength for resisting our negative qualities and eventually mastering them. This requires strong will, vigilance, and work. It is easier not to face that challenge, but then our life is reduced to compromise and mediocrity. Inner growth is not easy; it is the greatest and hardest of undertakings, but also the most noble and enriching.

Our exploration is not limited to our psychological self. It spans what I call the psycho-spiritual spectrum. We come face to face with our psychological wounds and limiting beliefs on one end of the spectrum, and on the other end, we may encounter higher states, psychic powers, and other subtle phenomenon. Dürckheim suggests that "[P]eople who have already gone as far as reason will take them are the likeliest, in our day, to see and recognize Being which reason cannot grasp, and to register the qualities in which it first speaks to us." This is not necessarily a linear progression; it unfolds, as it will.

The aspiration to heal and become whole is ultimately a quest for our inner truth. The journey begins by learning to listen in and address what arises in our inner battlefield. In the most renowned scene of the epic Mahabharata,

Arjuna is a passenger in the chariot driven by Lord Krishna in the battlefield at Kurukshetra where he is to lead his four brothers, the Pandavas, to war against his cousins, the Kauravas. On realizing the daunting mission he is faced with, he becomes overwhelmed and falls into a state of despondency. What ensues is an epic dialogue between Arjuna and Krishna with the latter teaching the former of the psychological and esoteric symbolism of the battle he and his brothers are called to fight. The inner meaning is the battle and the triumph over our conflicting weaknesses, forces, desires, and ignorance from within. We aim and aspire to establish ourselves in inner strength and righteousness to attain our ultimate realization. Our presence of mind, well-meaning guidance, and helpers provide the GPS.

GPS: Guru, Psychotherapist, or Self as Guide

Life is a journey of self-discovery. No matter what we aspire to and where we are on the spectrum of psycho-spiritual development, we will come face to face with countless triumphs, challenges, and obstacles. Do we undertake the journey as solo travelers, accompanied by a therapist or guided by a spiritually realized guru?

Going Solo

If one is drawn to go solo, it is possible to walk the psycho-spiritual spectrum on one's own. Ideally, the solo traveler should be endowed with enough maturity, humility, discernment, and a host of other qualities to ensure smooth sailing. If, on the other hand, one attempts a solo journey armed with defensiveness and arrogance it will more likely lead to perpetual suffering and little or no growth. Some honest self-reflection along these lines can put that decision to rest right from the start. Some of the individuals I know who have gone this route felt that they were receiving the guidance they needed from within. Guidance from spiritual books and friends to share or mull over our experiences and questions may be welcome companions for the less solitary of the soloists. We can gain inspiration and guidance from spiritual teachings from the East and West, past and present.

Malka was looking for meaning and heard about Mussar, a Jewish practice focused on enhancing our character traits. She chose a close friend to be her chevruta, study partner. Each month, Malka and her partner read and discuss texts focusing on given qualities such as courage, gratitude, and compassion. At first, it seemed more of an intellectual challenge. Over time, through working together and sharing their respective ponderings, the experience has become an increasingly enriching pillar for their personal and spiritual journeys.

Psychotherapeutic Accompaniment

Whether or not we, as practitioners, are required by law to be in psychotherapy, it is a most healthy and enriching choice. It signifies a commitment to working on ourselves and over time to self-exploration that can span from personal to transpersonal. This leaves us with the necessity of finding the right fit at the right time. There are several factors we can take into consideration when searching for a therapist. The therapist's school of thought is important, but the mindset and our experience with the therapist in terms of safety, understanding, and constructive challenge. Ideally, they should have an open mind and a big enough toolbox to be able to provide us room to grow personally and spiritually without becoming rote or formulaic.

Finding someone who has gone further than we have in our own development is ideal but not always possible or even necessary. It is, however, important for our chosen helper to have the capacity to accept and accompany us without judgment. Approaches to psychology range from the purely secular to the deeply religious, spiritual, and mystical. The therapeutic path can cover the full spectrum of consciousness from unraveling our deep-seated psychological issues, to self-actualization and ultimately spiritual development and self-transcendence. We can medicate, talk, liberate blocked emotions and energy, perceive and balance subtle phenomenon, and clear up issues from past lives. The choice is up to us. The important thing is to make an informed decision and ultimately trust our intuition as to which approach and therapist to choose.

Choosing—or Being Chosen by—a Guru

> *The master tears up the roots we have barely put down, knocks over the things we thought secure, severs the bonds we have contracted and pulls away the ground on which we stand. ... Life exists only as transition—and the master keeps it alive by making transition a never-ending process.*[4]

The guru-disciple or teacher-student relationship has existed in most ancient traditions in various forms as a means of conveying privileged mystical insights and practical guidance to the most devoted and advanced students. A true guide is someone who has smoothed out all the kinks in their nature and permanently established themselves in universal consciousness.

In the West, the tradition of following a spiritual guide in the form of a rabbi or a Christian saint, for example, for many people has been phased out with the onset of the scientific worldview. We might be inspired by speakers, writers, and seminar facilitators but that type of learning does not involve the intimacy and surrender of the traditional teacher-student relationship from ancient spiritual disciplines. We are taught to think and do for ourselves.

This might free us from a sense of confinement that tradition may evoke. However, it also raises the risk of us getting lost in shape-shifting traps laid by our unfulfilled personal desires and the impulse to escape from our personal issues. Humility, surrendering one's ego to the guru, helps avoid many pitfalls of the spiritual path. Unless and until we are fully spiritually realized, we are susceptible to the ego, and the ego makes us susceptible to illusion. Jung recommended that Westerners seeking spiritual development should follow a highly realized teacher because there are too many ways to get lost. I agree.

The guru-disciple tradition is still common in India. The guru, with her inestimable wisdom, is like a trail guide. She sees our shortcomings, potentials, errors, and karma. She helps us to navigate, evolve, and realize our spiritual potential. We learn and evolve not only through the example of their lives and the wisdom of their teachings, but also from the purity and power of their vibration, stemming from their union with universal consciousness. A guru, guided by deep spiritual insight into our strengths, weaknesses, blind spots, and karmic knots, will teach each disciple in the way and at the level he or she is ready to learn.

I have been meditating and following the same teacher for many years. Year in and year out, every morning I wake up and practice the same technique. And yet, there are no two days alike. Each day reveals new challenges and offers new inspirations. Attending retreats with my guru provides an opportunity to leave the world behind, intensify my practice, and deepen my inner connection with the Divine. The spiritual connection I struggle to maintain in my day-to-day life becomes a flood of openness, fluidity, and lessons.

It is said that choosing one's guru or spiritual guide is the most important decision of one's life. Texts describe the characteristics of the guru and emphasize the necessity of discernment before acceptance. The ongoing strength of the guru-disciple tradition in India breeds some exploitation of the reverence traditionally lavished on gurus. False gurus are all-too-ready to exploit well-meaning and vulnerable seekers. I used to be rigid about discerning the purity of anyone we are to call guru. But having witnessed the spiritual supermarket with all-and-sundry being called masters or even avatars, I have gradually come to replace that rigidity with compassion and faith that all roads lead to Rome. When we maintain our center, our own sense of self, even an encounter with a false guru can ultimately lead us to develop discernment and strengthen our weaknesses so that we can grow spiritually.

It's a blessing to have a guru in the bodily form. Yet, a guru is a means and not an end. If at first we need someone there to guide us, reassure us, and represent the voice of wisdom and guidance in our lives, at some point, we eventually have to find all of these things within. An authentic guru will lead us to this place of autonomy and realization.

I personally believe it is useful to have both spiritual and psychological guidance. Psychotherapy helps us on the human end of the spectrum. A spiritual guide, if we feel drawn to seek one and are lucky enough to find a worthy sage, helps us avoid pitfalls and evolve at the spiritual end of the spectrum.

TAKING OUR TURN AS CLIENTS

There is no right way and no wrong way to approach our personal and spiritual development. We may choose and stick to an approach or approaches such as Vipassana meditation combined with occasional psychotherapy throughout our lives. Or we may flit about like butterflies trying many techniques, schools, and philosophies. Most of us are somewhere in between these two. Choosing our approach with discernment, sincerity, perseverance, and a pinch of grace will undoubtedly bear its fruits.

On a didactic level, the experience of being a client gives us first-hand insight into the various approaches and their applications but also the experience of the therapeutic relationship which ranges from ground-level practical interactions to impalpable moments of being. Being a client is an invaluable experience in which we take the time to bring to light our conscious and unconscious issues and disharmonies. We can evolve beyond survival-level functioning and become self-actualizers. Apart from working with obvious psychological issues, we have the enriching opportunity to reevaluate our foundations, our fundamental relationship to ourselves. As we learn about own healing process, we are on the way to becoming skilled and compassionate conduits for ourselves and our clients.

Creating a Safe and Healing Space for Ourselves

If you begin to understand what you are without trying to change it, then what you are undergoes a transformation

J. Krishnamurti

In my early experiences as a client, my therapists and I spent much time and energy trying to find and fix what was wrong. Many years and boxes of tissue later, I realized that using the goal of personal development to pummel myself is a treacherous experience of endless drama and suffering. The idea that we have to push ourselves to get somewhere or that we deserve the ill-treatment we are lavishing upon ourselves is not only wrong; it is counterproductive. There is a more effective way forward.

Imagine a mother and a child. The mother is unpredictable, rash, reactive, and critical. How do you as a child feel and react to this? How does your emotional, social, and mental development unfold? Now leave that image behind. Imagine a mother who is warm, stable, predictable, kind, and yet, at the same time, firm and encouraging. As a child, how do you feel and react to this? Imagine how that affects your emotional, social, and mental development.

While practicing this imagery exercise, it is possible to actually feel the two different scenarios. The contrast is stark and effectively conveys the point to even the most hard-core self-pummelers. Having understood this, we are hopefully ready to leave behind the toxic mother and integrate the kind mother, in ourselves, learning to hold a wholesome space of our own. We can practice this in our quiet time or take a few moments to evoke the imagery of the good-enough mother when we catch ourselves in the act of self-pummeling. Mindful self-observation, covered in chapter 9, further evokes the importance and the means of being kind and gentle with ourselves.

Creating a warm, safe, healing, and nonjudgmental environment has immeasurable positive repercussions. Hopefully, this will be an inherent part of our experience as clients. Ideally, the space we cocreate with our therapists rubs off on us implicitly through osmosis and explicitly through (1) bringing to light the ways and reasons we are unkind to ourselves and (2) learning new ways forward.

Getting to the Core Causes

When we identify a wound or blockage somewhere in ourselves, we may feel inclined to ask ourselves "why?" Focusing on the why and where does not usually lead to "where do I go from here?" When we are able to address the wound, we liberate ourselves from the hold it has on us. In addition, we gain strengths and insights into its meaning that help us continue to grow. When we can put aside the question of "why," we create a space that is conducive to healing.

We could say that our consciousness is like layers of wallpaper attached to the wall. The glue is made of our negative emotions and attachments behind which we ultimately find fear. Psycho-spiritual development is like using one of those steamers and softening the layers of glue, so the wallpaper peels off with ease. As we start to observe all of our mental and emotional functions, habits, attitudes, attachments, thoughts, and feelings about the past and the future, they become well moistened. No matter how many layers of wallpaper are on the wall and how it appears, ultimately the source of our issues goes back to the state of the bare wall and its foundations. That said, for a thin, outer layer, unresolved emotional issues certainly take up a lot of space!

We often start addressing our issues at the storyline. We come in with varying degrees of self-awareness and the ability to listen to the inner signals indicating our disharmonies to us. We may not realize there is something amiss until it reaches crisis level. We eventually develop the ability to detect the triggers setting off our hidden disharmonies, stand back from them, listen to them, and address them as they arise. As we become adept at journeying into the core of our wounds, we can get a sense of them while they are still in a subtle state. At other times, these disharmonies are mirrored back to us by our experience of physical, emotional, mental, or subtle discord.

The process of meeting our depths can be destabilizing. It may instinctively trigger defenses and distractions. A combination of firmness and gentleness helps us create the space we need to sit with our issues as they arise and to gently, in our own time and at our own pace, delve into them. "The size and depth of the shadow give us the measure of the obstacle we face on the path to our true center. It also gives us an idea of the limitless space that opens in front of us once we have mastered it."[5] As we peel away the layers, we discover a pot of gold. We begin to gain mastery over the unconscious forces that once dominated us. Our inner essence or soul can increasingly shine forth. Along the way, we become our own trail guide as we develop the ability to distinguish between the noise of our ego and the voice of the soul.

Control vs Mastery

One can have no smaller or greater mastery than mastery of oneself.

Leonardo da Vinci

Addressed in a larger context of the flow of consciousness in chapter 2, exploring the control and mastery polarity in terms of our inner process unlocks important possibilities for our psycho-spiritual development. Our annoying impulse to control is one of the most common barriers to our growth and happiness. Feeling out of control, at any level or in any aspect of our lives, wakes up in many of us an impulse to reclaim a sense of control. This can come out in the form of impulsive and compensatory actions or words.

We often use the words control and mastery as synonyms. Pink Floyd's song, "*What Do You Want From Me?*"[6] evokes the subtle but important difference between them. Rather than being synonyms, they are two opposite poles on the same axis; control is on one side, mastery is on the other. Our mindset or attitude determines where we are on the continuum.

We often hear the expression that control is an illusion. In fact, our realm of control is sometimes uncomfortably small. The impulse to control stems from the ego, which is in turn, driven by fear. We try to compensate for not feeling in control by contracting our muscles, our hold on others, or reducing our worldview so that it feels more manageable. Mastery is of the soul. When we come to terms with our fundamental angst about not being in control, we can let go, surrender, and open up to the inner flow. When we let go, we give our inner self breathing room and naturally align more closely to our soul.

We are usually somewhere between fear/control and letting go/mastery. When I notice clients struggling with the control mechanism, I have drawn out this roadmap to pave the way for smooth sailing on the fear-letting go or control-mastery continuum. We start by developing awareness of the thoughts or events that trigger our control impulse and those that uplift us toward mastery. When we understand that it is not about being right or wrong, or needing to get to the good side of the spectrum, we can navigate consciously and intentionally. We gently aspire to walk toward mastery.

Vignette—Control, Letting Go, and Mastery

Marie was a highly successful thirty-something professional. She came to me for psychotherapy because her husband's diagnosis of a serious illness was bringing up unmanageable emotions. What struck me first were her striking good looks and an inner sense that at the core she was a profoundly strong and spiritual woman. I noted the contrast between that impression and her physical movement and mind which appeared agitated and jerky. Marie seemed to go back and forth between moments of deep insight, intuition, and feeling deeply spiritually connected, and other moments where she felt fearful, became extremely agitated, and ruminated uncontrollably. When this occurred, she was prone to magical thinking akin to the order of "step on a crack, break your mother's back." The two states were pretty extreme with no middle ground.

We used cognitive work to explore the trigger that set off her control mechanism. The source of this issue was very apparent. In her childhood, her mother had become deeply depressed. The energy in the house felt out of control. Marie developed a tendency toward hypervigilance and hypercontrol. She would dissociate and ruminate. I call this taking refuge in our head. We did some gestalt work to help her complete and let go of this broken record that had dominated so much of her life. This involved visualizing the presence of her mother and the suffering that Marie went through because of her mother's withdrawal into depression. In session, we used gestalt dialogue to help Marie recontact and express the emotions that she could not express as a young adult: her hurt, anger, and difficulty coming to terms with feeling abandoned. When we release the negative emotions that are under pressure it leads to a natural resurgence of life force. This flowed out in the form of forgiveness, love, and acknowledgment of all of the good and positive aspects of the mother-daughter relationship.

Once the pressure from her deep-seated emotions was released, we could start to do more subtle work. We explored the dynamic of control vs mastery and worked on strengthening her healthy aspects, including her spirituality. In each session, as in most sessions, there is time focused on bringing content and deep-seated attitudes to the surface, and time for breathwork to help liberate and reestablish harmony in their place. The breathwork brings out the core of the issues from the subconscious and the deep, emotional, visceral, cellular, and muscular memory, helping them to release. In this part of our sessions, the breath clearly reflected the fragmentation of her psyche as she would struggle to get out of her head and let go into the breath. When she let go, she would gain deep insights that helped her gradually to bring the inner voice of wisdom and balance to the forefront and be less dominated by the fear-driven mental states to which she was prone. In these moments, she experienced the liberating sense of self-mastery and could clearly grasp how the impulse for control and the élan toward mastery are essentially the same drive. But it is experienced very differently on each end of the spectrum. One end is dominated by fear and the other, faith.

Despite Marie's difficult life situation, she steadily and gracefully shifted into a more connected, fluid, and stable way of being. Over the six months in which we did our weekly sessions, Marie gained the mental understanding she needed to better manage her extremes and went a long way in healing the mind-body split by developing a more consistent relationship with her inner, intuitive core. Today, Marie still drops in for a session from time to time, but the period of our intensive work together has come to an end. She remains inwardly stable and connected even when faced with strong challenges and stressors.

LIFE HYGIENE

The fourth leaf of the clover represents life hygiene. I borrowed this expression from the French *hygiène de vie* because it feels more wholesome and complete than "healthy lifestyle," its English equivalent. Where complete life balance might be figured into traditional ashram and village lifestyles in India, balance today is a high-speed juggling act for most of us. I do not want to define life hygiene too closely, but rather put forward a loose idea from which each of us can explore, experiment with, and integrate an evolving approach into our lives. Essentially, we are talking about care of our body, mind, soul, and spirit—fitting into the larger scope of big picture life balance. We may draw inspiration from the works of Wilber's integral life practice or other integral development systems mentioned in chapter 5, or we may innovate or intuit our own method. Here are a few basics that, to me, make sense to consider.

Physical hygiene might involve developing a congruent relationship with the common sense things, taking care of our bodies and the earth.

The foods we eat, the water we drink, the products we use on our bodies—in our living spaces and finally in our farms and cities. The source of our foods and products end up in our inner and outer systems. Making conscious, informed, and proactive choices with respect to all these elements brings congruence to our physical hygiene and supports sustainable ideologies.

It is naturally assumed that we will take into consideration care of our emotional selves, covered at length in this book. On an intellectual level, continuing education and general interest help keep our minds sharp and up-to-date on what is going on in the world. Care of our spiritual aspects is another important aspect of life hygiene. Whether we feel drawn to experimenting with new psycho-spiritual ideologies and practices or follow a long-standing meditation practice, regular spiritual discipline helps us at all levels and in all aspects of our lives.

The question is raised in chapter 5 as to whether we set ourselves a rigorous program or go with the flow. There is no right or wrong answer to this question. It depends upon your nature, your aspirations, and a number of other elements. The ultimate guide in our life hygiene is our inner compass—letting our thoughts, words, and actions be guided by our inner voice.

Waltz or Slam Dance—Taking Care of Our Subtle Bodies

Our physical bodies appear to be separate entities. In fact, apart from Siamese twins, our bodies are the only part of us that are self-contained. Our energetic bodies are in a constant dance with other people, animals, and, today, devices. Depending on our sensitivity, we are more or less aware of this phenomenon. Some interactions leave us feeling on top of the world. Others drag us down or are outright toxic. The same is true for the spaces in which we live and work.

One day in a group supervision session, I asked my colleagues how they dealt with the energetic exchange that takes place in our work. A few replied that it was nothing a glass of wine or two wouldn't fix, another liked to air out her room and take a walk in the park after finishing her sessions for the day, one just turned on the TV and tuned it out. As helping professionals, we are perhaps more intimately involved in the dance of energies that occurs between people. Thus, we understand the importance of purifying and fortifying our energy and the spaces we work in. Some of my favorite practices are

- Salt bath: Put a handful of rock salt in a tub of water or bathtub and then rinse or bathe with it.
- Lemon juice: Rub lemon juice on the bottoms of your feet, lie down, and rest until your feet are completely dry.

- Mantra: Practicing specific mantras for purification and fortification can be very effective. In this case, you may have a spiritual tradition that gives you mantras, or you can experiment with various practices until you find the one that suits you.
- Smudging: Borrowing from a Native American tradition, smudge sticks are bundles of dried sage that can be burned. Smudging ourselves and our healing rooms purifies remnants of energies left behind.
- Himalayan salt lamps: It is said that keeping Himalayan pink salt lamps in healing rooms absorbs negative energies.

There are countless, ancient, traditional, and new techniques for energetic purification using breath, yoga asana, visualization, essential oils, specialized room sprays, prayer, and becoming one with uplifting music. Adopting a daily routine of purification will make a difference to how you feel, your quality of work, and what happens in your healing space.

Just Do It

Talking about ideologies and methods for our development is one thing, but it is surprisingly common for most people to have goals and aspirations that they neglect. We can set ourselves physical goals such as getting fit, going organic, or saving money; emotional goals like being kind to ourselves and others; or a spiritual goal such as meditating, practicing a mantra, or remembering to focus on the breath. Although they are at the top of our list of priorities, in ideal, in practice, they are the last to be taken care of. Putting off our aspirations may be a sign of lack of self-respect, low self-esteem, or fear of success. Where spiritual aspirations are concerned, we may fall into what Robert Desoille called repression of the sublime. This can be due to the fear of loss of control that occurs at the idea of facing the unknown. Barriers aside, our desire and commitment to our psycho-spiritual development is like a fire. The more we fuel the fire, the brighter it burns. Finding a source or several sources of inspiration will be more effective to fueling the fire than giving ourselves guilt trips or pressuring ourselves. Little by little, through perseverance and taking baby steps, we get the fire going. Before we know it, we gain enough momentum to sustain the actions or attitudes we need to realize our goals.

Getting to the Essence: Simply Being Our Authentic Self

Cultivating the four leaves of the clover in our professional and psycho-spiritual development, we have overcome many hurdles. We have cleared away traps and illusions of the ego and developed the humility to continue this journey. What may have started out as patchy and unstable foundations has been transformed into a delicately interwoven tapestry of balance, congruence, wisdom, compassion, clarity, humility, and respect. From this place, our continued development is ideally wholesome, gentle, and smooth. The ego has gone through its healing, becoming fluid, and released its dominance over us, giving way for the soul to come to its rightful place at the center of our being. Our authentic self, the soul, is able to shine forth more freely. If you find yourself needing to prove to yourself or to others that you are being your authentic self, it is a surefire sign that you have not arrived. On the other hand, if you find yourself feeling it from within—a subtle, empowered, aligned, and guided sensation—you are heading in the right direction. The truth is, few of us are there. Most of us are simply on our way. Acknowledging this ensures our humility. It keeps us questioning, learning, growing, and evolving. In truth, I am not the doer. I pave the way for the authentic self to shine forth and bring light into the darkness.

Our work on each of the four leaves of the clover is ready to be extended outward, shaping the space we create for our clients" adventure of self-discovery and healing. We are equipped to create a balanced, safe, healing and wholesome, multidimensional space for our clients.

INTEGRAL ETHOS: PUTTING OUR IDEALS INTO PRACTICE

Placing our four-leaf clover in a vase, let's look at an important quality, some core guidelines, essential knowledge, and skills for creating a space that is conducive for accompanying our clients on their integral adventure.

Humility

Any quality that cultivates self-actualization and altruism enriches our work as helping professionals. Humility is foundational, a building block that holds a wholesome space for who we are, our potentials and limitations. Humility can be cultivated by a combination of sincere self-reflection and detachment.

Face it, no one's perfect. We are all barking up the tree of one illusion or another. Our psycho-spiritual development and search for inner truth become easier if we make no bones about our weaknesses. We ask ourselves, "What are my illusions? How is my ego manifesting in this situation?" This eliminates the endless strife that occurs when we avoid these questions. Judging makes it difficult for us to see ourselves just as we are because if the truth is emotionally charged, we tend to distort our view and fall into the trap of carrying our shadow into our spiritual evolution and work as helping professionals.

Looking at our uncomfortable places with a sense of adventure, rather than defensiveness, creates a safeguard from the spiritual ego. If we neither expect ourselves to be perfect or imperfect, which is a huge investment of time and energy with no returns on investment, it simply ceases to matter.

Humility is inherently inclusive. It helps us not to identify with the fruits of our work but to keep journeying both in our inner work and in the learning space we hold for our clients. It is a recognition that "I am not necessarily the one who knows, and my school is not necessarily the one that is right," but rather allows space for different schools, different techniques, different worldviews. The therapeutic process can then be inclusive for each client with their unique path and worldview and the entire spectrum of their experience. We transcend judgments, the dichotomy of normal or abnormal psychology. We open the floor for seeing, validating, and working with whatever arises in the client's world in the therapeutic process. With proper boundaries and discernment, this is a surefire way to help clients walk toward healing, wholeness, and a meaningful and fulfilling life. The rest is not in our hands.

Discernment: The Crown Jewel

Humility paves the way for discernment, defined in the Viveka Chudamani, the eighth-century scripture written by Adi Shankaracharya, as the ability to distinguish truth from untruth. This quality is essential for navigating our day-to-day experiences more gracefully. Discernment takes on an even greater importance where spiritual development is concerned.

In the previous chapter, we addressed the danger of lack of discrimination. Here we will be exploring its role as a quality. The roots of both discernment and lack of discernment are always in us. Expecting ourselves to have perfect discrimination just puts pressure on us. A more viable and gentle approach is simply to do our best. Paying attention with humility goes a long way.

In the therapy office, discernment first helps us keep ourselves in check. Second, it implies an increasing ability to perceive the client's nature and situation without personal bias. Alternatively, if we have a personal bias, we can identify it, keep it in check, acknowledge it if appropriate, and address it in supervision so as not to hurt or influence our clients with it. Discernment draws on our capacities for objectivity, observation, and analysis, but its most important source is intuition.

Client Autonomy

Respect for clients and the aim to help them develop autonomy is a core principle of most schools of psychology. If we observe power dynamics, either on our behalf or on behalf of our clients, I believe in speaking the unsaid, making the implicit explicit. In this way, we do not succumb or give our power to unconscious and toxic mechanisms that undermine the potential of our work. Maslow, among others, noted that every human being has an inner drive toward self-actualization. That drive is in varying states of dormancy, disrepair, and incongruence in most of us. When provided with the right environment and elements, this drive will naturally awaken and come to the forefront. Therefore, our job as helping professionals is to find the tools, skills, and right atmosphere for each person to awaken to their self-actualizing and self-transcending drives. In some phases of therapy and for some people, this may involve a phase of affective dependency. By paying attention to the signs, we can work with this phase consciously and intentionally.

Vignette—Respect for Client's Worldview and Freedom of Choice

After completing my breathwork training, I lived in New York City for a couple of years and got involved with a HIV support group. It was 1986, the very early days of HIV awareness. During a group sharing I was facilitating, I met Johann, a middle-aged man with HIV. Johann was looking for someone to live in and be there when he needed help and company. I became Johann's care partner. It was not long before I realized that Johann's lifestyle reflected a choice not to fight for his life. He was not attempting to keep himself healthy, including taking what medicines were available at that time. I, being an avid healthy lifestyle advocate, went through a dilemma. I contemplated my discomfort, held back my impulse to intervene, and quickly realized that my role was to accompany Johann, in the best way I could, not to bring him over to my camp. I was able to let him know that I saw and respected his choice and that I would be there beside him until the end. This led to a deep, trusting, and soulful connection that certainly enriched the last weeks and months of his life better than if I had tried to force my beliefs on him. Not an easy lesson but one that has stayed with me to this day.

Bring Our Ethics Up to the Mark

Ethics goes hand in hand with humility and discernment, all of which are essential parts of being effective and having integrity as a psychotherapist. Let's look at it this way: Offering advice on relatively minor issues such as choosing what laundry soap to use carries with it a certain level of ethics. The soap should work and not be harmful. Moving up a notch, working with people on a basic human level, for example, giving life guidance in any way carries with it another level of responsibility. The advice we offer should be wholesome, sound, and free of our personal biases and influence. When working with vulnerable and fragile people, the guidelines and ethics change accordingly. Spiritual issues are increasingly subtle and all the more important. Therefore, when working on a spiritual level, it is important to bring our ethics up to the mark.

The Western mindset is accustomed to having an external set of ethics for life in general and, more specifically, in respect to professional life. In addition to this, listening to our inner voice enables us to sense when our approach and interventions feel appropriate and when they feel off the mark. Inner ethics is simply about consistently choosing the former and disengaging in the latter. Ideally, the clinical code of conduct we learn and apply provides the theoretical guidelines, and our inner sense guides us in the fine-tuning within those guidelines. Humility comes in handy here as it gives us the ability to acknowledge our mistakes when they occur. Our mistakes are nothing more than an opportunity to learn.

Consciousness Is Multidimensional

Modern science explains consciousness from a purely neurological level, but in the perspective of integral thought, all things occur on all levels of consciousness. There are different models of multidimensional consciousness from the simplest, body-mind-soul model to the more elaborate models of the Kabbalah and Sri Aurobindo. Having a theoretical understanding of the model or models of our choice helps us situate our client's experience at the appropriate level and, in turn, work with issues at the level at which they occur. Endowed with openness—and, if we are lucky—advanced empathy and intuition, sharpened by our psycho-spiritual development, we have a reliable rudder to help us navigate. We will have a chance to go deeper into this topic in the next chapter where we will be exploring a multidimensional view on psychological issues. In addition, in chapter 9 we will explore the techniques I use in my clinical practice and what it looks like to apply them from a multidimensional perspective.

Nonjudgmental Understanding of World Spiritual Traditions

As helping professionals, we inevitably encounter clients who share overt and covert experiences, beliefs, phenomena, and crises that have spiritual and religious significance. We may have biases or judgments in respect to our religion of origin. For example, we may have had experiences that didn't sit right with us, been at the receiving end of unethical practices or hypocrisy, or even witnessed the horrors of holy war. In the same way, we may carry prejudices about other peoples' belief systems or religions. Exploring our personal beliefs, influences, and experiences on spirituality and religion helps us develop sensitivity and empathy toward clients' beliefs and experiences. Learning about religion and spirituality in general, and specific religions and spiritual approaches in particular, will help us work with our clients in a nonjudgmental and constructive way. There are many resources covering clinical ethics and guidelines for working with spiritual and religious beliefs in a clinical setting.

Ability to Distinguish Between Healthy and Unhealthy Spiritual/Religious Experience

Religion, spirituality, spiritual seeking, and spiritual experiences take many forms. There is no right or wrong form. However, there are dangers and pathologies with spiritual dimensions and spirituality with pathological aspects. Learning to distinguish between healthy and unhealthy spiritual states and experiences helps us avoid pathologizing and stigmatizing experiences that, if properly accompanied, can become healing and transformational. Whereas, in chapter 6, we explored dangers of spirituality and spiritual approaches to psychotherapy which are, according to the *Textbook of Transpersonal Psychiatry and Psychology*,[7] commonly encountered in the therapeutic setting, here we touch on the topic of healthy and unhealthy spiritual experiences and states.

Healthy development is a continual and nonlinear process. As we grow, we reach the edge or limit of our level of functioning and transition to different levels. This process can be hindered or even derailed due to disharmonies, blockages, and imbalances that can occur at every level.

Spiritual issues, although they may have some of the same manifestations as ordinary psychopathologies described in the *DSM*, are of a more subtle nature. They stem from beyond the ego (in this case, emotions and mind). For example, at the psychic level, there can be spiritual emergencies such as chaotic, spontaneous awakenings and kundalini experiences, structural imbalances due to faulty spiritual practice and dark night of the soul.[8]

The practitioner can learn to distinguish between states and pathologies using a combination of knowledge, patient history, experience, and subtle perception developed through their inner work. An attitude of understanding, establishing trust, and a way to create a positive experience with non emphasis on the idea of disease or sickness will be the most conducive for helping the client. Therapeutic work with spiritual issues can involve creating a support community, bodywork, yoga therapy, and other forms of movement, chanting, psychotherapy, and meditation. Acupuncture, gestalt therapy, and transpersonal psychotherapies such as breathwork may also be helpful to help the individual go through the experience, not inhibit it, and regain their balance for the way forward. Medical examinations can also rule out the possibility of physical pathologies that may disrupt our stability and mental state such as thyroid, hormonal imbalances, and brain tumors.

Healthy spirituality and religion respects our autonomy and our unique purpose. It is uplifting and leads to our realization, our liberation. Learning to distinguish between healthy and pathological spiritual and religious beliefs and experiences gives us the unique opportunity to accompany our clients in the most well-suited ways. Annex I provides useful guidelines for distinguishing healthy from unhealthy spiritual states.

Practice What We Preach

Helping people can uplift us, open us up, and connect us to a greater, universal force. We often gain deep and noteworthy insights while working with clients, which may be useful to ourselves or others. One evening I was winding down and recapitulating the sessions I'd had that day. I realized I'd given a particularly inspiring insight to a client. This inspired me to make a habit of practicing what I preach; review what I tell my clients and be a therapist to myself.

Contribute to Society and Planet

A natural outflowing of our psycho-spiritual development is the desire to contribute to the world around us. Action and advocacy driven by our deepest truth and desire to contribute to planetary transformation have a different impact than ordinary actions. Sri Aurobindo tells us that attitude is just as important as the actions we undertake. For example, imagine the difference between angrily fighting a battle for an environmental cause or fighting that battle from a place of inner peace, love, and centeredness. Even if we do not get the urge to actively contribute to society, cultivating spiritual consciousness spreads "spiritual consciousness" through osmosis. If, however, we find ourselves engaging in incongruent actions that do not reflect love and respect for the planet, we might need to go back to the drawing board and explore what this tells us about ourselves.

Take Off Our Helping Hat

While doing my masters degree in Durham, England, there was a pub down the street from our classroom. After class, we would all head to the pub for a drink. "How are you doing, Margot?" a classmate would ask. "I enjoyed tonight's lecture on psychosynthesis and look forward to exploring its implications in my life and work. It was really interesting, don't you think." "I hear that you found psychosynthesis interesting and are looking forward to exploring it more deeply," parroted my dear classmate with all good intentions. I giggled and made a note to myself. The office is the office; the pub is the pub.

Keep a Flexible Mind

Ideally, a healthy mind and body are supple, movable, and vibrant. We can work on the mind through vigilance, psychotherapy, and meditation and work on the body through yoga, massage, breathwork, or similar practices.

Vignette—The Mind: Gateway or Gatekeeper

Jean-Claude was a foot reflexologist and past-life therapist. He worked with the classic principles of reflexology putting pressure on points in the feet to address imbalances in the body. He felt that harmony and disharmony in the body stemmed from unresolved issues in past lives. The very deep and exquisitely painful (if, like me, you enjoy that kind of pain) reflexology sessions were followed by breathwork sessions similar to the ones I facilitate with my clients. The therapeutic work was very effective in reaching and liberating profound blockages. On the other hand, the sessions would leave me in an overly emotional state tending toward instability. There was another prominent reason that I could not recommend clients to him, and that is what eventually led me to discontinue working with him. Jean-Claude had a habit of coming up with formulaic statements representing his theories that were set in stone and had nothing to do with me, the client. For example, if I had a pain in the shoulder one day, he would say that it was because I had been murdered with a bow and arrow in a past life. He attributed knee issues to amputation in a past life. I took advantage of the benefit of the reflexology and the emotional clearing from the breathwork and wrote off the rest. His commentaries became more and more far-fetched, and I decided to find another therapist.

Supervision

Supervision is an aspect of practicing psychotherapy that is required in some places and not in others. In addition, the interpretation of this helping relationship varies according to school of thought. Supervision styles can range from surveillance and control to a collaborative and cocreated space for exploring the client's process and the therapist's inner experience, learning, and any emotional reactions that may arise in their client work.

Coming from a background in person-centered psychology, my first experiences of supervision were magical. It was a space in which I could share and explore my own process of working with clients. The gentleness, openness, and safety opened up deep learning enriching my work with clients along with my personal development. When I finished my studies and changed countries, I joined a person-centered supervision group. While it was rich,

I struggled with the lack of spiritual worldview and with the lack of personal development of some of my colleagues. Rather than uplifting and inspiring, I found it deep and dark with no way out. I dropped out of the group. I thought it would be ideal to work with a spiritually oriented supervisor since I thought that would match my worldview and way of working better than any other. That search proved to be disappointing. I met a few supervisors with spiritual egos or new-age ideas, but none who understood or respected my Eastern bent. My interest in dreamwork drew me to a psychoanalytically oriented supervisor. Although our worldviews and styles were worlds apart, I decided to take the good with the bad and focus on learning what I could from that experience. Eventually, it began to feel more confining than interesting. Returning to person-centered supervision, I found the right fit and I am enjoying the same magic of deep unfolding as in my first experience.

Supervision provides support, a sense of collaboration, and continual learning and is an important ethical pillar to our roles as helping professionals. Finding the right supervisor and setting regular appointments is an enriching and essential part of the commitment to working with our clients.

CONCLUSION

We now have a foundation for our personal, professional, and spiritual development that is sufficiently structured to make it appealing and accessible. It is also spacious enough to leave ample room for the soul. Feet on the ground, head in the clouds—bringing spirit into mind and, finally, into matter.

They say that an ounce of practice is worth tons of theory. The practice of integral psychotherapy starts with ourselves and then extends into providing a well-adapted ethos for our work with others, the topic of the next chapter.

ANNEX I: HEALTHY VS UNHEALTHY STATES[9]

1. To what extent does a client have control over the state? The degree of control and the response to states where there is little control give us a sense of whether a state is helping or hurting a client.
2. To what extent is the client aware of the environment when in the state? To the extent that a client is not aware of the environment, the state should be supported by a sitter or therapist.
3. Is the client's concentration fixed, fluid, or fragmented or a combination of the latter three in the state?
4. To what extent can the client communicate while in the state?

5. To what extent is the client energized or aroused in the state? The higher the arousal, the more the need for a sitter or therapist. The arousal may be anything from emerging shadow material to ecstatic trance.
6. To what extent does the client experience calm while in the state?
7. What is the dominant affective flavor of the state? Are the dominant emotions pleasurable or painful? The total balance of the experience should be taken into consideration when answering this question. For example, many states designed to bring about catharsis of shadow material may involve some pain as they emerge but can give way to an ecstatic bliss in the best-case scenarios.
8. What is the client's sense of identity during the state?
9. Does the client report any OBEs?
10. Finally, what is the nature of the client's inner experiences during the states in question? Walsh notes three distinctions, including the degree of organization, the sensory modalities employed, and the phenomenological rating of intensity.

NOTES

1. Ram Dass and Paul Gorman, *How Can I Help?* (1985, London: Knopf), p. 22.
2. John Rowan, *Ordinary Ecstasy: Humanistic Psychology in Action* (1976, London, Routledge), p. 149.
3. Sri Aurobindo, *The Mother and A.S. Dalal, Compiler Looking from Within*, (1995, Pondicherry, India: Sri Aurobindo Ashram Press), p. 145.
4. Karlfried Graf Dürckheim, *The Call for the Master: The Meaning of Spiritual Guidance on the Way to the Self* (1975, New York: Dutton/Penguin).
5. Dürckheim, 1975, p. 135.
6. From Pink Floyd, "What Do You Want From Me," in album *The Division Bell*. Song by David Gilmour, Richard Wright, and Polly Samson; Lyrics by Robert Ellis/Orrall Curtis, Wright. 1994.
7. Bruce W. Scotton, et al., *Textbook of Transpersonal Psychiatry and Psychology* (2009, New York: Basic Books), p. 178.
8. Ken Wilber, "The Developmental Spectrum and Psychopathology: Part II Treatment Modalities," *Journal of Transpersonal Psychology* (1984, Vol. 16, No. 2), pp. 75–166. Ken Wilber, "The Developmental Spectrum and Psychopathology: Part I Stages and Types of Pathology," *Journal of Transpersonal Psychology*, (1984), Vol. 16, No. 1, pp. 75–118.
9. Elliot R. Ingersoll and David M. Zeitler, *Integral Psychotherapy: Inside Out/Outside In* (2010, New York: SUNY Series in Integral Theory), pp. 211–212. See also Scotton et al., 2009.

Chapter Eight

Integral Psychotherapy in Practice

Praxis and experience integrate and are an integration of all of the theories covered thus far. Having drawn our map of psycho-spiritual development, equipped with theory, wisdom, compassion, and many other qualities, we are now ready to walk alongside those seeking help from us. Integral consciousness will be the capstone of this exploration. Starting to work with clients is a big step. In addition to the fruits of our self-exploration, it evokes some questions: How do we bring our whole self into our work? What types of clients will we come across? What dynamics might we encounter in our therapeutic relationships? How can we assess and work with our clients from a holistic and multidimensional perspective?

In the thirty years since I began practicing psychotherapy, about every ten years I have taken a year or two off from my practice. Sometimes I felt the need for the structure of an ordinary job which gave me insights into the workaday struggles my clients sometimes bring into therapy. Mostly, I set about on an altogether more solitary and adventurous direction taking long retreats, traveling, and writing.

After completing my masters, equipped with a solid foundation of humanistic theory and practice, trainings in many therapeutic techniques and nearly fifteen years of insights and experiences from breathwork, meditation, and studying Eastern philosophy, I set about to build a full-time psychotherapy practice in Paris. Initially, there was a distinct discomfort as I sensed these different spheres, and how separate they seemed within me. I explored and tried to make meaning from the discomfort while pondering how I could bring these various horizons into my clinical practice. Little by little, they naturally began to integrate into one cohesive and yet fluid way of practicing.

THE JOURNEY OF INTEGRAL CONSCIOUSNESS

In form, an integral approach may resemble any other. There will be dialogue, behavioral interventions, mind-body techniques, and existential soul-searching. The spiritual end of the spectrum may also involve past-life regression, shamanistic experiences, and other esoteric and energy-based approaches. We already understand that an integral approach is not merely eclectic, nor should it be confused with integrative psychology. The primary difference is the consciousness of the therapist and the intent to hold and aspire to an integral perspective, the highest and broadest common denominator which, according to Sri Aurobindo, opens the way to entirely new possibilities.

WHO COMES FOR INTEGRAL PSYCHOTHERAPY?

People are like snowflakes. Each one is truly unique.

Most clients are motivated to come to therapy because something isn't going well or something doesn't feel right. It may be a dull sense of mal-être or an acute crisis that drives the decision. When a client arrives in a crisis, the work may start out more like damage control. Deep work will naturally occur when a client is coming from a relatively stable place and can handle the week-to-week shifting of their foundations. The more pro-active clients come to therapy because they sense they are not living out their potential and seek help and guidance to explore and overcome their blockages and reach toward self-actualization and beyond.

Because of my spiritual orientation and work with spiritual emergency, a fair amount of people find out about me or are referred through yoga schools, meditation groups, and other spiritual organizations. Some clients may be having spiritual experiences that have destabilized them or opened up areas of psychological blockage or wounding that need to be addressed. There is no right or wrong reason to seek help. No matter what state we are in, how long we have been in it, no matter what our age, it is never too late. We will inevitably gain benefit from any effort we invest in our own growth and development. Clients also come from various horizons: doctor referral, word of mouth, and increasingly, the internet.

One day I received a phone call from a young English-speaking woman seeking therapy. When she came for her initial appointment, she told me how she had come across my business card. She had been having a meal in a restaurant with her husband and they had gotten into an argument. In a fit of frustration, she had stormed out of the restaurant into the rain. As she stood there trying to figure out what to do, she looked down on the sidewalk and found my business card. The odd thing is, I had never been to that part of town!

The Therapeutic Relationship Begins

The initial session can be a time for client and therapist to start to get to know each other and see if there is a fit. This can be a time to look at the client's personal history. I always make sure to ask about and note the client's goals, wishes, and desires for their psychotherapy. It is important to be centered on what they are looking for, their truth, their worldview, and their own unique quest.

Most of the time, clients choose to jump right in. At other times, what starts as an initial, "getting to know each other" session, turns directly into a therapy session as the client touches on intimate issues, inviting a therapeutic dynamic to begin. This depends on the urgency of the issues and nature and boundaries of each person. While guidelines and tools exist for conducting an intake interview, I find it works to let things unfold as they will. This invites the relationship to start out with greater presence and intimacy.

In the initial session, as in all sessions, I keep my antennae out and feel the space, the client, the way they position themselves with me and even in the therapy room. I take into account what might be material indicators, such as physical appearance and dress, late or on-time arrival; affective dimensions such as body language, tone of voice, communication style, boundaries; mental aspects, such as their worldview, career pursuits, and position in society; and finally, their energetic predispositions such as groundedness, flow or rigidity, whether it seems they are breathing or holding their breath. I try to get a sense of the overall structure and nature of the client and their spiritual worldview.

Taking all that in, I hand it over to my intuition, a combination of subtle cognition and subtle perception. I believe that the type of intuition I refer to here in describing my assessment of clients is something for which every human being has a propensity. It may be more or less pronounced before we do any personal development work but over time, as we learn to navigate in more and more subtle regions of our being, these capacities develop and can be used in our work with clients.

With this inner sense, I explore the client's energetic and subtle makeup. Where is the center of their energy? On the physical level, is there a liver disorder, thyroid imbalance, mercury poisoning from amalgam fillings, a hormonal imbalance, or a known or unknown illness at play? On the emotional level, I tune into the emotional body to get a sense of where the emotions are flowing or stuck, sense the context and content of their inner conflicts. I map out the individual's emotional makeup, pinpointing strengths, weaknesses, and blockages. On the mental level, I look for such things as cohesiveness of thought processes, irrational beliefs, convictions, conditioned responses, unconscious biases, and self-image. At the spiritual level, it becomes more complex. How is their subtle energy flowing and where is it blocked? The spiritual realm is by far the largest and most subtle insofar as it "envelops and transcends" all of the other aspects of the self. Disturbances remaining from unassimilated life experiences, unconscious family or ancestral baggage or strengths, karma (material accumulated from past actions or lifetimes), and occult phenomenon which can wreak havoc in an otherwise healthy and balanced individual. Sometimes issues can appear to be psychological but, upon deeper examination, reveal themselves to be occult in origin.

Of course, an important part of this type of overview is to take into consideration the full range of the client's strengths. These can be observed behaviors and attitudes, but again occurring on more subtle levels. Our strengths are what give us the courage and resilience to navigate the waters when they become rough.

Creating a Safe and Healing Space for Our Clients

Just as a safe and healing space was provided to help us in our own healing and development, now it is time for us to extend this space to our clients. Such a space invites our clients to gradually and naturally let down their barriers and bare their souls in a most wonderful and healing way.

The therapeutic relationship starts with creating space for the client to speak. Through feeling heard, understood, and acknowledged they begin to experience safety. Surprisingly, for many people, it will be the first time they are getting these basic, human needs met. Dialogue, the healing power of which is not to be underestimated, is the most commonly used tool of most psychotherapies.

Dialogue is the opener, the context setter, and the relationship builder. Listening with our heart, we follow our felt sense with compassion in the presence of the client. Listening with our mind to the storyline, the client's persona, concerns, worldview, analysis, context, and script. Tuning in with our intuition to sense and perceive deeper, more subtle phenomena below the surface that are either causing or part of the client's issues or suffering. This is the beginning, the framework for the therapeutic relationship.

Apart from listening to the language of a client, our empathy and intuition guide us in determining which approach is appropriate. When I work with spiritually oriented people, I do not hide the more intuitive aspects of my work and when appropriate will openly use spiritually oriented interventions. At other times, these are more implicit.

Paying attention to our inner resonance as we explore another person's world and their issues is the key. It becomes possible to sense if an intervention will be received or whether it will bring up resistance and lead the client to shut down or put up their defenses. If this delicate approach backfires, there is no cause for alarm. Even our foibles can be useful. As long as the therapist remains humble and does not insist upon and bulldoze the client with their take on things, it can actually help the client to clarify their perception. I consider that it is part of my role to transparently and respectfully share what I perceive, but I am not obliged to always be right.

From the safe, warm, and healing space we provide, we start to build the therapeutic relationship. The client will, at their pace and in their way, open up and bare their burdens as well as their inherent potential.

Client Dynamics—A Bicycle Built for Two

Each client arrives with a different level of self-awareness. They may perceive their mal-être at an externally oriented level focusing on storylines: what happened to them, what other people said or did, what they want and didn't get, what they don't want, and ended up getting, and so on. Other clients may be equipped with a keen sense of the situation of themselves and emotional self-awareness. The problem may have started long ago but they may not have had the tools or willingness to address it from the start. They only take action when it escalates and blows up in their face in the form of an illness, a breakdown, a relationship crisis, a family problem, or something else. Some clients understand the issue they are facing and how they got there in minute detail. But analysis, being of the mind, is static. In this case the client may find themselves stuck with no visible way forward. Yet other clients will have a great amount of analytical as well as intuitive self-awareness. The initial interview will quickly reveal the client's level of self-awareness and rigidity or fluidity and we can navigate our way forward accordingly.

When looking at different types of dynamic in clients, I use the analogy of Michel Odoul, a renowned body-mind therapist in France. He describes the therapist-client relationship like a tandem bicycle. The therapist is in the front seat of the tandem bicycle representing his responsibility to use his tools and knowledge to create a safe and healing space. Some clients pedal actively with the therapist, discovering their own pace and their own way to identify and work with the issues they present. They recognize they have an unproductive pattern and decide to do something about it before it sabotages their potential.

Then there are the clients who let themselves be pedaled by the therapist. They may or may not have ever done therapy before. Sometimes their doctor, friends, or loved ones advise them to seek help and may even book the initial appointment for them. Fortunately, and depending on the nature of the person, after one or two sessions they begin to engage. Their issues and the underlying causes for them start to come forward, awakening a passion for self-understanding and self-actualization.

Clients who fit into the last category, however they get to therapy, sit on the back seat and pedal backward. They may be suffering from victim consciousness, believing and doing everything possible to ensure that nothing can be done to help them. They are experts at self-sabotage. When working with these types of clients, sometimes all it takes is the bicycle analogy to short-circuit their defenses. At other times, it is useful to point out that whatever we invest our energy in will bear fruit. The irony is just how much energy some people invest in their own failure and yet, do not even succeed at that! Then, of course, I ask the poignant question, what would it be like to simply stop investing in your failure and invest in your realization? Any core issues related to this pattern can obviously be addressed to help the client achieve the turnaround.

To continue the bicycle analogy, some clients have let their bicycles go into a state of disrepair. They jump on the bike and might be pedaling like mad but don't realize the chain is off. Sometimes the gears are so rusted that it takes an extreme amount of effort to even achieve a full rotation. Most of the time, they just keep trying to move forward by whatever means they can find, but these means typically are unproductive or even counter-productive. They are so engaged in their efforts that they do not realize that the efforts are not bringing any fruit. This is a tell-tale sign that they are in the fight or flight response.

In the course of a therapeutic relationship, we will be privy to countless stories, situations, and crises. As we walk alongside the client, they will inevitably discover and process at successively deeper layers. Each issue and challenge a client faces can be journeyed into, revealing a deep underlying cause. The cause will be at any number of levels of consciousness inviting us to identify and address issues at the level of consciousness from which they stem. This is an entirely more illusive and yet, much more effective way of working. It avoids, for example, turning around the hamster wheel of trying to think ourselves out of a habit of rumination.

A MULTIDIMENSIONAL VIEW OF ISSUES/WHAT ISSUE, WHAT LEVEL?

The models of consciousness covered, from the Great Nest of Being to the more elaborate and esoteric model of Sri Aurobindo, give insight into the notion of levels of consciousness. Working from a multidimensional perspective allows us to take into consideration issues presented to us by our clients and unveil their roots at the level of consciousness at which they occur. For example, an emotional wound from childhood can be released at the emotional level through awareness and then emotional release or catharsis, whereas an occult disturbance can be addressed through mantra, adapted rituals, or exorcism. Sometimes the root is apparent from the start and at other times, it will naturally come to reveal itself over a number of sessions. Just as I do not believe in digging in one's past or one's shadow, given the right ambiance, whatever needs to will come to the surface in its own time and its own way. More important than identifying the cause, our first call is to respect the psychic space of the client. Therefore, we address issues at the level at which the client is ready.

Table 8.1 demonstrates, at a theoretical level, the various levels of consciousness at which our issues may lie based on Sri Aurobindo's model. At times clients are aware of the roots of their issues or the root cause will reveal itself through introspection, uncovering techniques, or enacting an inner dialogue with affected areas. Logical deduction and analysis may be sufficient for the therapist to identify root causes at the level of emotions and mind. The causes of physical level issues may sometimes be evident and at other times are subconscious (emotional wounds, cellular, and muscular memory) or inconscient (asymptomatic physical ailments). Subtle issues come to light for the therapist and/or the client through developing the ability to enquire into sensations and journey into the subtle aspects of consciousness. This may seem odd at first. Some people do not trust the messages and images coming from within. However, with experience, they can become very finely tuned and reliable. Nothing is written in stone where consciousness is concerned. Nevertheless, it is useful here to simply convey the concept of issues and their multidimensional causes.

A WORD ON DIAGNOSIS

There are arguments for and against the concept and practice of diagnosis. The practice of diagnosis, if based on the idea of normal vs abnormal or pathological traits and behaviors, is more likely to give labels than ways forward. While humanistic psychology favors accompaniment over diagnosis, knowledge of psychopathology, multidimensional models of imbalances and understandings such as those laid out by Wilber and Aurobindo provide important keys. While it is important not to use diagnosis to stigmatize, enclose or otherwise put people in boxes, if used in a fluid and open-ended framework, we gain the benefit of the basic guidelines they provide. It can

TABLE 8.1   Therapeutic Issues and Techniques According to Level of Consciousness

Issue	*Technique*	*Level of consciousness*
Physiological disorders	Ayurveda, naturopathy, all forms of psychotherapy (to clear and address other dimensions)	Physical, emotion, mind, karma
All issues (lack of vitality, physical and structural ailments, stress, agitation, depression, search for meaning, search for spiritual development ...)	Yoga therapy	All levels (depending on issue)
Habits, self-sabotage, repetition of unconscious patterns	Cognitive dialogue, uncovering techniques	Mind, emotion
Self-image, unresolved issues and emotions from the past, fragmented self, the full range of psychological issues	Person-centered approach	Body (to some extent), emotions, mind
Working with subconscious, unconscious, and dreams	Dreamwork	Subconscious, superconscious
All body/mind and psycho-spiritual issues	Flower and plant essences	Subtle physical, subtle affective, subtle mental, spiritual
Unresolved emotions, undigested events or relationships	Gestalt	Mind (conscious & unconscious)/body (cellular & muscular memory)
Deep emotional blockages, disconnection from any aspect of self	Psychosynthesis	Mind (conscious & subconscious)
Unresolved issues with parts of our self, or people or events from past	Inner dialogue	Mind (conscious & subconscious)
Issues stemming from ancestors	Psychogenealogy, family constellation	Mind (conscious and subconscious)

Issue	Technique	Level of consciousness
Body/mind issues, somatization, energetic or emotional blockages, domination by negative or destructive attitudes, weaknesses, unconscious and subtle disturbances, chronic issues, structural weaknesses.	Jin shin jyutsu	Physical, emotion, mind, soul
Blocked emotions, domination by unconscious patterns, rigidities, well-being, cultivating harmony, openness, deep, inner connection	Breathwork	Body (& cellular & muscular memory), mind (conscious & subconscious), subtle bodies (auras), soul
Issues stemming from perinatal matrices, karmic issues		
Changing habits or habitual ways of thinking, body/mind connection, awareness and integration of issues on all levels	Mindfulness	Mind
All issues	Prayer	Emotion, mind, subtle
Stress, creating a stable base from which to work on delicate issues, spiritual quest	Meditation	Body, mind, soul, spirit—depending on the approach and proficiency of practitioner

help to frame and address recurring cultural, personal, and interpersonal patterns.

There are arguments for and against the very concept of diagnosis. Why not create a new way to diagnose, drawing from the DSM and multidimensional perspective (Wilber, Aurobindo) along with a wide and broad and deep treatment modality. Each system in isolation has its strengths and limitations.

When we find a cohesive way of putting them together, respecting the unique contribution of each one, we can create a truly holistic model for diagnosis.

Physical Level—Medical and Intuitive Assessments

Sri Aurobindo and the Mother tell us that physical disorders begin in the subtlest bodies. When the disturbances are not addressed, they gradually densify and eventually may end up as physical illness. Some physically based issues can wreak havoc in our emotions and mind. Working with the physical can be a case of getting a blood test in case of emotional instability to test for things like hyperthyroidism or other endocrine disorders that can disrupt our emotional stability. It can also be intuited. Either way, it does no harm to call on the physical sciences for verification.

Vignette—Medical and Intuitive Assessments

In the Kolkata practice of Dr. Soumitra Basu where I've regularly collaborated since 2002, I was presented with a client who suffered from poor moods and feeling "blah." Upon looking at this middle-aged, working class man, I picked up a sense of feeling slightly nauseated. In my inner consciousness, I enquired into the cause and immediately got a sense of liver swelling and congestion. Whether this was the core cause or not, my consciousness indicated to me that this was the first issue to be dealt with. Back in Dr. Basu's office, I shared my findings. Dr. Basu asked the client to lie down on the examination table and palpated his liver which was indeed swollen and congested. Had I been given further opportunity to follow up with this patient, I would have examined diet, alcohol intake, the possibility of infestation by parasites, but also attitude, emotional factors and lifestyle.

No matter where we experience disturbance and where the root cause lies, it is said that everything exists at all levels. The questions then are, where does the root of the issue lie and is that place accessible or do we need to loosen up the soil around the issue until the root can easily be addressed? Addressing the issue at its physical level will already help the client feel better and may even clear up the issue at the other levels of consciousness.

Emotional Level

Most of us experience our issues at the emotional level. No matter where they stem from, when they manifest in the discomfort or outbursts characteristic of the emotions, they become too unpleasant not to notice. Whether we like it or not, when our emotions are out of check, they wreak havoc. We may experience minor distress or extreme states that drive us off the map. When we do not acknowledge our emotions, we make messes in our lives by projecting them onto our near and dear ones and by tinting our perception of virtually everything.

Vignette—Emotional Healing

Alexandra came to see me because she was having a hard time establishing herself as an adult in her personal and professional life. At thirty-something years old, she still had a little girl's voice, an indicator that part of her was stuck in childhood.

In our first session, she talked about her childhood which she felt was the source of her difficulty. Her parents had had an intense love affair and were the envy of all those who knew them, representing an ideal couple. They married and had Alexandra in this period of intense bliss. And yet, over time relationship issues began to come to the surface and neither her mother nor her father were equipped to deal with their emotional turmoil, expectations, disappointments and the conflicts that arose. When Alexandra was three, her mother decided to leave her father. She packed up all their things. At the last moment, when they were about to leave, her mother had doubts about her decision. She turned to her three-year-old daughter and asked her if it was the right decision to leave her husband, Alexandra's father. When faced with threats to our vital space, a child will try to protect it in any way possible. She was torn between needing to preserve her survival, wanting to protect her parents' marriage and needing her mother's approval. In this pivotal moment Alexandra inadvertently stepped out of her place as a child and took on a responsibility that was not hers. She stepped into the role of adult and caregiver to her mother, agreeing with her mother's decision and they moved out. She was left burdened with guilt for causing her parents' breakup and her father's pain. These emotions were still stuck inside of her. Part of her was blocked in childhood and having difficulty fully becoming an adult.

Our work occurred in phases over a period of four or five years. Alexandra would feel it was time to do some work on herself and come for two to three months of work together on a weekly basis. The first cycle dealt with her story in raw form with accompanying powerful emotions. In the second cycle, we noticed that while we touched on the same themes, the material and emotions that surfaced were more subtle and that she was working with the material as an adult seeking to heal rather than as an "inner child" in crisis. A year or so later, she contacted me again. She was at a place in her life where she was having to overcome limitations and move forward both in her personal and professional life. It is often at times like this that our issues get triggered again and come up from the depths. This time the issues were coming up in increasingly subtle ways and required some more of our time. Rather than doing breathwork, working with the material in raw, precognitive or noncognitive form, it seemed appropriate to work in a sitting position using a mindfulness-based approach. We revisited the event that triggered her suffering, this time, in the form of a visualization and dialogue with each of her parents. She realized it was time to stop feeling responsible for their happiness and stop blaming herself for causing

*her parents' divorce. This series of sessions took on a distinctly different quality.
Alexandra, rather than as a distressed, inner child was in the position of adult,
working toward wholeness. It felt like I was there to hold the space, but that she
was self-guiding, from within, visiting and dialoguing, through inner awareness and words, with the places that still needed addressing. After a couple
of months, Alexandra felt like the weight was lifted. She spontaneously began
positioning herself differently in the face of her new responsibilities, decisions
and also her life partner. We both felt that this series was complete and with
warmth and humor, we looked at the pattern of how life brings up core issues
from time to time. As we said goodbye, I suggested that she was better equipped
to give space to her issues when they arise rather than to spiral into distress, but
that my door remains open should she wish to work together again in the future.*

The Emotional Body Is Like a Minefield

Just as we have a physical body, metaphorically speaking we have an emotional body. The untilled emotional body is like a minefield. The mines, that
we all have to one extent or another, are made up of all of the unresolved
emotional wounds. We learn to walk gingerly in the wild hope that our inner
and outer detonators do not get triggered. Our thoughts, beliefs or elements
of our self-image that we feel sensitive, protective, and rigid about are the
detonators. We encounter an external situation, interpret and then react to it.
A little explosion or, occasionally, the big one blows up in our face. Our near
and dear ones receive the fallout. Not liking parts of ourselves, fear of aban-
donment, fear of being disrespected, mistreated or criticized trigger a deeper
fear of not being lovable, fear of being vulnerable, fear of not being good
enough. If that isn't treacherous enough, we also have inner triggers that we
set off all by ourselves, through mostly unconscious trains of thought.

We can make efforts to avoid the mines. This approach might lead to fewer
explosions, but it is a compromise as it leads us to live our lives defensively
rather than fully. Needless to say, all the energy involved to avoid setting off
mines is ineffective because walking on a minefield is never a good bet. The
good news is that there's another way forward. Each explosion is actually a
gateway, an opportunity to learn more and accept something in ourselves if
we know how to harness it. As we begin to examine each of the ways we get
triggered and set off these bombs, we find that each one that gets triggered on
the surface of our day-to-day lives is, in fact, part of a larger network. There
are layers in this network and there is one core or central mine behind all of
the triggers—our bottom line negative belief and the emotional wound it was
built around. The surface issues are generally created as defenses or reactions
to our core wound or vulnerability: the Big One. For example, on the ground
level we think, "Why didn't so and so ring me today?" That leads down one

level deeper to, "So and so, is upset with me or doesn't love me." Further down the network, "Nobody loves me." And finally, "I'm unlovable, I'm unwanted." The ironic thing is that no one on this entire planet is unlovable and in the ultimate scheme of things, no one is unwanted. Although, if we believe we are unwanted, a concerted effort can sometimes actually turn this into a reality. A therapeutic journey down and into our minefield gradually diffuses the triggers and eventually the mine.

Over time, when our core issues are no longer under pressure because they have been brought to light in a most gentle and healing way, we develop the ability to take a step back. We disengage from the drama, none of which is ultimately true, and instead set out to understand, love and accept ourselves as we are. Ultimately, through introspection and making peace with what arises, the minefield turns into a field of green grass and flowers.

The Mind

Ideally, our thoughts, words, and actions are aligned or congruent with our deeper self. From birth onwards our ideas, beliefs, attitudes, and values are formed in response to internal and external stimuli. The positive side is that the right set of cognitive beliefs can make our lives a breeze. The negative side is that when we inadvertently take on baggage that limits, sabotages, or blocks us in any way, it makes our life difficult. Cognitive self-observation and evaluation is aimed at bringing these inconsistencies to our awareness. This may enable us to choose different attitudes and corresponding behaviors. However, if the core cause of our mental short-circuits occurs at more unconscious or subtler levels, working at this level only, may not be powerful enough. For example, our disharmonious behavior may be caused by a deep-seated and maybe even unconscious resentment. Until we address this cause at the emotional level, our efforts to change the mindset and behavior may be ineffective.

Subtle Mind

Until now, the types of issues we have covered are addressed by classical therapeutic approaches. If this level of working were systematically effective, we would need to look no further. My observation is that working at the physical, emotional, and mental levels of consciousness is like looking at the outermost levels of the self. Some of our issues do stem from these levels. Yet, where do we go when this isn't the case?

Before entering specifically into something we could call transpersonal or beyond the outer self, Sri Aurobindo describes a level called the cosmic mind or cosmic consciousness. At this level, we can address issues stemming from the perinatal matrices, the time from conception to birth and family and ancestral subconscious. It is said that we carry memories from the seven generations that preceded us. My observation is that with each generation, that memory becomes increasingly subtle and harder to place unless we happen to know the stories. Nevertheless, its influence is still there.

Vignette—Family Secrets

Jane was a sixty-eight-year-old woman suffering from anxiety and emotional instability. She had a strong tendency to make situations into dramas and didn't have the self-awareness to stop herself. She appeared to have a lot of bodily tension and was high strung. We began the session by dialoguing about her life and her inability to stop dramatizing things in her day-to-day life. Nothing extraordinary came out of the dialogue. Jane had tried many healing techniques over the years and had recently begun practicing meditation which she felt was helping.

Jane wanted to try a breathwork session to see if we could make some headway in unblocking her issue and helping her to relax and stay in the present. Her breathing was erratic. She felt tension in her solar plexus. I guided her to gently breathe into the solar plexus, penetrating with her breath and consciousness into the blockage. Her breath became even more erratic. She could not stay focused on the blockage and over the next twenty minutes, acted out various forms of distraction: erratic breath, scratching, moving about, getting sleepy and forgetting to breathe. These indicated a strong and apparently impenetrable defense mechanism. It was like trying to put two like poles of a magnet together, the minute we'd get close to the blockage, her consciousness would bring her away from it. I inquired into the blockage and sensed she was carrying an ancestral taboo. I asked her whether she had a feeling of taboo around the blockage, as if she weren't allowed to go there or even question. That struck home. She had a realization that her grandmother had had an affair in their village which resulted in the birth of an illegitimate child, one of her uncles. The family knew about it and Jane had heard the story, but until then she hadn't realized the shame that had been carried down from her grandmother, to her mother and then passed down to her. The problem with the shame was that it was around a taboo topic. This is what had formed the resistance around it, making it impenetrable until now. She was able to get through the taboo, breathe through the shame and liberate the blockage in her solar plexus. Her habitual tension and bodily rigidity were visibly alleviated after this session and Jane felt more in tune with herself.

Where the subconscious is the memory of everything we've experienced in this lifetime, Sri Aurobindo placed the memory of all of our lifetimes in the cosmic consciousness. This is where we encounter personal, family, ancestral, and other collective karmas.

Religious, Spiritual, and Subtle Issues

We are entering now into a different realm, one where the concepts that give us a roadmap can only be drawn from our inner journeys. Subtle realms of consciousness function differently from body, emotions, and mind. The body functions according to physical laws. Emotions also have their logic. Just as emotions sometimes appear to be irrational, upon learning to explore them more deeply, it becomes obvious this is not at all true. The mind too has its own way of functioning. Sri Aurobindo said when our mind is well-ordered, informed, and open, it is the gateway between our experience, our perspective on it and our ability to convey it to the world. Where spirituality is concerned, we are dealing with increasingly subtle phenomenon. Subtle realm material is trans-rational. Although spiritual theories can be helpful, without direct experience to bring them to life, they will not have the same resonance or vitality and will be more likely to fall into empty rituals or dogma.

Spirituality is an inner, personal relationship to our essence. Yet, on a psychological level, we interpret and assimilate our spiritual experiences according to our culture and level of development and integration. Religious background, even if we have fully or partially turned our back on it, may influence the way we contextualize our spiritual experiences and insights.

Spiritual experiences may be overpowering or subtle, positive or troublesome. Positive spiritual experiences range from a simple transcendent moment of oneness or extraordinary insight, conversion experiences, shamanic awakenings, premonitions and premonitory dreams, bursts of altruism, moments of insight that lead to life change, and transformation to profound and lasting states of oneness, light, and harmony.

Beyond the psychological realm, spirituality opens up a vast and infinite pool of consciousness. Spiritual experiences are not always easy to understand or manage. They can unleash inherent weaknesses in our structure or bring unaddressed wounds to the surface.[1] Spiritual crises, due to their subtle and seemingly abstract nature, may be difficult to identify and put into words. Even positive spiritual experiences can be difficult to integrate. They can lead to postexperience drop, a feeling of void, disappointment at arriving back at one's ordinary state, and loneliness due to the inability to share it with others.

Spiritual issues and insights may be identified at a psychological level or, phenomenally, as a manifest or subtle experience. Having a safe and nonjudgmental place to discuss them is an inherent part of the healing process that psychotherapy can offer. Western psychology's traditional rejection of religion, or relegation to clerics, may result in clients missing out on inherent opportunities by withholding their spiritual experiences from their therapist for fear of misunderstanding or stigmatization. Indeed, sharing them may result in being judged, trivialized, or even pathologized. In addition, traditional psychiatry might systematically single out symptoms, such as hearing voices, as psychoses or bipolar disorder, not taking into consideration the possibility of it being a chaotic spiritual experience. However, having a context in which we can share positive experiences can be extremely beneficial. It can help us to assimilate the content and provide insights. With proper care, we can turn a breakdown into breakthrough.

Vignette—Spiritual Emergency

While on a meditation retreat, one of the organizers approached me and asked if I could look in on Daniela. We found her curled up on the floor of the meditation hall, rocking herself. She had a troubled look on her face. In the first ten minutes of our time together, Daniela had laughed, cried and expressed venomous anger. I could gather by the disjointed content of her words that she was reliving vivid scenes of childhood abuse.

My first course of action was to try to reassure her and help her feel safe with me. I explained that I was a psychotherapist and I could help her. Somewhere in the whirlwind of her emotions, I could see that she registered my words and seemed to understand. I suggested we find a quiet place in the garden and spend some time together. She was in a great state of confusion, blurting out scenes that seemed to be going on in her mind.

I had seen Daniela on one or two retreats in the past, but did not know her very well. I sensed that the intensive meditation practice had somehow touched on a vast ocean of painful unresolved emotions. This crisis was an opportunity to heal.

When we settled down in the garden, I decided to take a direct approach.

"Who hurt you?"

She seemed not to understand. She was lost in an inner chaos. After a moment she replied. She blurted out a disjointed story, flitting between mumbling, talking, crying and laughing. Her father had taken a job abroad due to financial difficulty. She was left alone at home with her three brothers while her mother held two jobs. Her brothers had ganged up on her and engaged in severe, cruel and prolonged physical and psychological abuse. They swore her to secrecy. She had had no place to turn. As her story unfolded, she began to engage with me. It was doing her good to get her story out. She started to calm down and seemed tired. I gave her Bach Flower Rescue Remedy and suggested she take a rest. We moved her into a room where she slept for fourteen hours.

We contacted her husband to explain the situation. I asked him to come to the center and spend time with her until she stabilized enough to return home. In the meantime, he gave me more perspective on her background. Daniela was emotionally hypersensitive, but had never shown signs of psychosis. She had occasionally done psychotherapy with someone in her city. I asked him to have

*her therapist phone to make sure Daniela would receive proper care upon her
arrival back home.*

*I have seen a quite a few such cases while on meditation intensives. Knowing
that Daniela did not have a background of mental illness reassured me that the
purging of unassimilated emotional trauma was brought on by the intense practice of meditation. She was having a spiritual emergency.*

*After she returned home, I stayed in touch with Daniela, her husband and her
therapist. After three months of intensive gestalt therapy, Tai Chi and nurturing, she started to become more stable and wholesome. She was on the path to
healing.*

Karma

Karma is our experience in the present and future based on the collective
results of all of our past actions and attitudes. It is not a punitive concept
but a view that opens up opportunities for understanding, acceptance and
working with our experiences and perceptions. In the theory of karma and
reincarnation, the only reason we incarnate is because through births, deaths,
and rebirths, our trajectory toward enlightenment, we still have karma to
address. We can identify karmic issues either intuitively or through deduction.
It is possible that if we encounter a blockage that has not been cleared up
by housecleaning at the level of ordinary psychology, we may find a karmic
blockage is the culprit. Touching and working with karmic issues can occur in
the form of past life recall when the consciousness is fluid and allows ready
access to the more subtle layers. It can also occur spontaneously in apparently
random ways. Working with past life recall can be a bit tricky. Sometimes
material that appears to be from past lives can surface. Yet, these can actually be displaced or dissociated parts of ourselves rather than past life recall.
My feeling is this doesn't matter. Whether or not what we encounter is truly
a story from a past life or a fragment of our consciousness that comes up in
the form of a story or an archetypal imagery, the most important thing is to
take the opportunity to work with these experiences, to integrate the material
and emotions, wounds and beliefs associated with them. I have worked with
karmic blockages using visualization, inner dialogue, breathwork, and past-
life regression therapy.

Vignette—Past Life Recall

*In chapter 3, we explored how Hermione began having spontaneous past life
recall during her breathwork sessions. When the recall experiences arose,
I used various angles of introspective questioning with her while she was in an
expanded state of awareness, to help her identify and complete the issues that
got blocked in these lifetimes.*

Hermione: "I see myself on an island in Ancient Greece. I am with someone who is dying, holding their hand. I sense that I am going to be left alone. Inside, I am frozen, unable to connect to the loss of, I think, my husband. I am feeling terribly guilty about not fully being present for him in his final moments. In anticipation and out of self-preservation, I abandoned him before he abandoned me but then I got stuck there. I still am."

M: "Okay, stay there with him, holding his hand. Let yourself fully reconnect to how you felt. Let that be okay. You are frozen with fear, right?"

H: "Yes, I am terrified."

M: "Look at your husband, in his eyes, if they are open. Let yourself see him, fully. Who is he? Does he look familiar? Does his look remind you of someone you know?"

H: "Yes, he is my brother in this lifetime. Due to our circumstances, we could never really connect in this lifetime. I have always felt guilty, like I abandoned him, failed him as a sister."

M: "I understand. Now make space in yourself to fully engage with this process, feel the feelings. Tell him everything you need to say."

Hermione pours out her heart and soul to her dying husband releasing the energy that had gotten blocked by her shutting down. I ask her if there is anything left to say or do while sitting with her dying husband. With tears of relief, she says that she feels much lighter. When her husband departs, they feel deeply connected. Hermione feels sad and alone, but at peace.

Our work, prior to her recall, was like loosening the soil around her rigidity and guilt but it persisted. Hermione experienced four different scenes from different lifetimes related to these core issues. Following each session, Hermione experienced major breakthroughs toward releasing her blockages, opening up and accepting herself.

Past life issues are part of our karma, the accumulated impressions from our thoughts, attitudes, and actions from this and all of our past lives. Each individual has their own karma. In addition, there are various forms of collective karma such as the country, family, ancestry, and religion into which we are born.[2] According to some, all issues are karmic. Any blockages we liberate also free us from their binds at one or all levels, including the karmic levels. It is useful to be able to work with karmic issues when they manifest. The ability to work in these subtle regions can be developed in specific trainings, and implicitly, from one's own personal development. Enquiring into our perceptions, we can develop our ability to discern and validate this and other subtle phenomena and distinguish between the different types of psychological experiences.

External Disturbances

In addition to disharmonies that can arise from within ourselves, outer influences and disturbances can also be at play. According to ancient world traditions, the stars and planets influence our positioning in life as well as the unfolding of life events. In India, some astrologers are equipped to detect this type of blockage that can be released with help from local healers and Brahmin priests who advise addressing them with mantras, amulets, and pilgrimages.

Working with external disturbances is a highly specialized field. It opens up further possibilities for identifying the causes and corresponding means of clearing the issues we face. At the same time, this view may raise many an eyebrow and requires discernment on the part of the seeker. The current tendency in mental health is to pool all unexplainable experiences together and label them as pathologies. Rather than stigmatizing our clients with such labels, being able to identify subtle phenomenon, or at least acknowledge their existence, gives us possibilities for accompanying our clients or referring them for outside help, in some cases. Further external influences from the subtle realms are occult disturbance and possession.

Occult Disturbance

Occult disturbance has two manifestations in psychotherapy. On one hand, clients can bring in beliefs and related fears of subtle or occult disturbance. On the other hand, there are actual phenomenal experiences. Subtle disturbance, occult interference, and possession may manifest perceptibly by creating chaotic or irrational experiences and behaviors. Although it is not uncommon to be affected by subtle disturbances from time to time, most people may only perceive chaos or destabilization. Their awareness may not be finely tuned enough for them to perceive what is actually going on. In other cases, the disturbance may be so great that it turns their life upside down. In either case, when the origin of a disturbance is occult-based, it is important to know how to identify and work with it. As in the case of spiritual emergency, the ability to distinguish between subtle phenomenon and mental illness is important so that we can appropriately work with the issues.

Vignette—Occult Disturbance

Aysha, a strikingly beautiful young woman, of North African origin came to see me seeking help from disturbing and distressing feelings. We began our work together with a brief exploration of her current life and history. She had a troubled childhood, suffering from persecution by a disturbed mother. She married early to an African immigrant and had a son. Abuse and neglect caused her to leave the marriage quite early on. The necessity of raising their son required

Aysha to maintain cordial but distant contact with her ex-husband. Although he was often out of line, she seemed to have everything in perspective and dealt with it as constructively as possible. What struck me about Aysha was the lucidity of her thoughts and awareness. Despite her difficult past, it did not seem like the experiences she was having were due to any psychological cause. I sensed that somehow, her energy field was being penetrated by unwanted energies that were wreaking havoc.

This type of phenomenon can be looked at in two ways. The first is to understand that if we are hosting unwanted energies, there is something in us that has invited or at least let them enter into our energy field. Aysha was highly sensitive to the subtle world, which indicated an openness to these realms. If the ego is not sufficiently balanced and structured, such an opening can lead to psychosis. One can distinguish the difference between healthy and unhealthy subtle opening to these realms by determining the lucidity and congruence of thoughts. Intuition is also a big help in working with this type of issue. Aysha did not show signs of psychological pathology, as she had enough clarity and congruency of thought to keep her feet on the ground.

The second aspect of hosting unwanted energies is the possibility of external causes such as occult attacks, possession or other subtle influences. In Aysha's case, I suggested that the cause of her suffering was not psychological. It appeared to be due to subtle adverse forces. I referred her to an exorcist I knew of, a priest from the Greek Orthodox Church.

Aysha underwent two sessions with him during which he perceived two different sources of hostile energies, one coming from her mother's ill will and one from her ex-husband whom, the exorcist said, had hired occultists to stop her in her tracks. She felt the priest was not only powerful, but kind and human. He took the time to explain to her what he perceived and made sure she felt safe and comfortable with the experience of exorcism. The two sessions were effective and her problems promptly ceased. She now undertakes a daily practice of spiritual reinforcement and purification to keep any further occult attacks at bay.

Volumes can and have been written on the many types of subtle disturbances that can we can encounter, some of which have been addressed above. Those who are drawn to work at these levels and who can find reliable sources and teachers will set out on a very interesting adventure. If we do not feel comfortable working in these regions, we should at least be able to distinguish them and develop a reliable referral network.

CONCLUSION

When we hang our shingle, who will come to see us? From what horizons will they be coming? What types of people will they be? What issues will they bring? My answer to all of these is to cultivate our personal development, develop understanding of the various theories we are drawn to and build an understanding of a multidimensional framework. Then, put it all neatly aside and bring forth your authentic and skilled presence.

NOTES

1. See chapter 2: Transpersonal Psychology and chapter 7: Ability to Distinguish Between Healthy and Unhealthy Spiritual/Religious Experience.
2. See chapter 5: Vignette—Collective Healing.

Chapter Nine

Techniques

An Integral Therapy Toolbox

Since the beginning of time, countless tools have been developed by sages, healers, scientists, and psychologists to address our imbalances and challenges and help us evolve. Tools provide the means to translate our intuition, perceptions, and theories into hands-on action for healing and transformation.

Over the years, I have trained in many different techniques and integrated them into my holistic approach. Each technique was chosen in response to a need, curiosity, or a deep inner resonance. I have always been attracted to the most holistic approaches aimed at working with our clients as whole beings. A broad range of tools and perspectives are helpful for navigating the obstacle course of our unfolding. Any approach that contributes to raising awareness, liberating blockages, and building qualities that lead to our self-actualization and self-transcendence fits under the inclusive umbrella of integral psychotherapy.

As practitioners we are each unique and practice according to our training, nature, and level of development. It is the "depth and breadth of knowledge and awareness that the clinician brings to the session. The therapist provides the parameters within which clients' experiences are facilitated and which, to a large extent, clients make meaning out of their therapeutic experience."[1] The key is not to navigate from mechanistic or formulaic places. A blend of theory and techniques, but most importantly worldview and consciousness of the therapist, will lead individuals to a cul-de-sac, a finite development or path of healing, structuring, transformation, and liberation. An open mind and heart inspired by the inner flow of consciousness coming from our intuition is the ultimate navigator.

DEVELOPMENT OF A TRI-FOLD APPROACH

My initial training focused on diving headlong into the unconscious via the breath, an uncovering technique to bring out and relieve the pressure and liberate us from the domination of our emotional wounds. With emotional issues demanding less airtime, the mind and body respond by reorganizing around the more harmonious inner core. Working this way was like a breath of fresh air. Yet when the honeymoon phase was over, I was left with the familiar sense of discomfort. Something was missing. We can heal our emotional wounds, but what is to stop us from creating more of them? I began to explore ways of integrating cognitive work to develop a more well-rounded approach.

Cognitive and behavioral interventions filled that gap by providing a structured means of evaluating and developing congruence at the level of our ideas, beliefs, attitudes, and behaviors. Working with the unconscious through breathwork and the conscious mind through cognitive work proved to be powerful. They complement each other and wake up our will, empowerment, and sense of responsibility. We actively engage in our own process of healing, developing self-esteem and waking up our drive toward autonomy, another step on an upward spiral toward realizing our potential.

After this triumphant step forward, I again discovered a limitation to my approach. I found that even when the core wound is liberated and the defense mechanisms are at bay, sometimes habits, self-sabotage, or self-destructive behaviors persist. My process of discovery, or navigating in the dark, continued. I experimented with mindfulness. Mindfulness, by helping us develop objectivity, empowers us to consciously choose our thoughts, words, and actions. We free ourselves from the hold of inner and outer triggers, old habits, and instinctive reactions. Mindfulness was the missing link I was looking for. My approach, although it continues to evolve along with me, felt complete.

Art is the marriage of structural theory and creative flow. Integral psychology is no exception. Structure and theory on their own are dry and disconnected from life energy or the flow. The flow stems from the fruit of our inner work, our ability to let go and let our inner consciousness come forth. Deep connection to our intuition brings forth an inherent structure that can seem quite abstract and difficult to convey. Just as mastery of painting or music is a delicate interweaving of theory and flow, so is integral psychology.

Some of the tools I use are concrete and can be taught. Other tools are intuited on the spot. Every human being has their own unique nature and issues. Just as I would have a hard time believing that any one approach is sufficient for every single therapeutic challenge, the same holds true for techniques.

Any therapeutic technique that helps us move in the direction of our greater potential has its niche in an integral toolbox.

PERSON-CENTERED DIALOGUE

My strong resonance with the healing power of gentleness and presence has led me to adopt person-centeredness as one of my core principles—walking alongside the client in their world, their life path, their time frame. The core conditions of congruence, unconditional positive regard, and accurate empathic understanding create an environment in which the client's drive toward self-actualization and autonomy awakens and comes to the forefront. For me, this translates to the single-most important element of the therapy session, simply being present with the ears, heart, mind, and more. This sounds simple and it is simple, but it's also complex and powerful.

Dialogue can occur at different levels from the external storyline and narrative level to the deepest I-Thou moment. All become a gateway to deeper, nonverbal, subtle places in ourselves. Some clients are comfortable and adept at delving beyond the surface story and into the root of the matter. With other clients, it is a long, hard way there.

Vignette—Person-Centered Dialogue

Angelika, a 19-year-old student, was referred to me for counseling by her university. We worked solely using person-centered dialogue to explore her social anxieties stemming from her low self-esteem. Although she was committed to her therapy, it sometimes seemed like our weekly sessions revolved around the same content and issues and was not evolving. Toward the middle of our third year of working together, she had to face the imminent death of a family member. This painful challenge brought her strengths to the forefront. She was sad and anxious, but had also gained the ability to manage her emotions with gentleness, wisdom, and perspective. Through our years of person-centered dialogue she had indeed been growing stronger and developing useful skills for navigating life's challenges.

Listening and dialogue help to identify what is not okay, what is blocking, what is in disharmony. Feeling heard and safe helps us open up to deeper levels of self-discovery. Expressing experiences that have had a strong emotional impact on us helps us to digest and integrate at some levels. This is one of the reasons it is the most common form of therapy and counseling.

Although our issues manifest in our outer lives, most of the time the roots lie deep within and not at the level at which we perceive them. Dialogue is limited in scope and often not enough to "get the job done." Issues may need to be addressed by other means.

BREATHWORK

*Our life exists by the breath alone. The Therapist takes care of this breath
that gives life to the body. All healing of the Being is done through "liberating the breath." The breath allows us to become aware of the tensions
blockages and resistances that prevent it from circulating freely. It is the
path of fulfilling the soul in the body and opening ourselves to Creative
Intelligence.*[2]

Philo of Alexandria

I love breathwork for its simplicity and multidimensional effectiveness. It is
the single-most effective technique I have come across for developing awareness of our core issues, bringing them to the surface, releasing whatever got
stuck, and connecting us with our center. Used in a structured and responsible
framework drawing on humanistic, transpersonal, and integral philosophies,
it stands at the core of my work.

Understanding of the multidimensional significance of breath was prominent in many ancient wisdom traditions. In ancient India, the concept of
prana signified breath, air, and "the sacred essence of life," the vital energy
that drives us. The yogis of India, since ancient times, have mastered this science of *pranayama* (breath) and identified forty-nine types of breath. Each
one corresponds to a state of mind, such as anger, excitement, and stress. The
fiftieth type of breath is called *nirvikalpa samadhi*, a meditative state which
is so deep, it is beyond breath, pulse, and heartbeat.

Chinese philosophy denotes *chi* as the cosmic or vital essence related to
our physical, emotional, and spiritual being. In Japan, breath plays a central
role in spiritual disciplines and martial arts.

In ancient Greece, *pneuma* referred to air, breath, the spirit, and life essence.
The Greek word *phren* refers both to the mind and the diaphragm, which
happens to be the largest muscle involved in breathing. The ancient Greeks
understood that disturbances or imbalances in the breath both reflected and
were the cause of physical and emotional illness.

The ancient Hebraic tradition used the term *ruach* to denote both the creative spirit and breath. Both the Essenes and the ancient yogis of India taught
that the gateway to the heavens was between the inhale and the exhale. Moses
said, "And the Lord God made man, having taken clay from the earth, and
he breathed into his face the breath of life, and man became a living soul."[3]

Modern Perspectives on the Breath

Despite this rich and universal heritage, our current scientific paradigm strips
away the traditional sacred notions and reduces breath to nothing more than

a physiological function. In fact, the prana or vital energy absorbed through the air we breathe nourishes our material and immaterial aspects, our vitality and creativity.

The West, drawing on ancient wisdom traditions, innovated new ways of working with the breath. Holotropic breathwork and rebirthing are the most well-known breathwork-based approaches. Each, in their own way, aims to harness the healing and therapeutic power of the breath. They purify the physical and subtle bodies of accumulated psychological issues and ultimately lead to deep integration and expansion of consciousness. Breathwork is no longer Eastern or Western; it is universal.

Rebirthing was discovered in the 1970s when Leonard Orr and friends were spending long periods of time in a hot tub in northern California. Something in the womb-like ambiance and the extended exposure to hot water caused them to spontaneously deepen the breath. They experienced expanded states of awareness including reliving birth memories. Complex psychological blockages were liberated, resulting in greater well-being.

Breathwork is not rational and linear; it is experiential. Although breathwork is more transformational than working at a purely cognitive level, the intangible nature of the experience and process lead to its lack of credibility in the psychology community. Holotropic breathwork, due to Stanislav Grof's rigor, research, and trainings, enjoys popularity with the transpersonal psychology and personal development movements. Rebirthing has remained marginal and is more prominent in new age circles. The "everything goes" philosophy, accompanying the otherwise effective breathing technique, lacks discernment and common sense. Misuse of the term to represent other techniques further adds to its lack of credibility in the therapeutic community. Reframing the rebirthing technique in a structured and responsible way results in a powerful, safe, and balanced approach.

Physical Benefits of Breathwork

> *The mere function of breathing into and out of the lungs is only the most sensible, outward and seizable movement of the Prana, the Breath of Life in our physical system. The Prana has according to Yogic science a five-fold movement pervading all the nervous system and the whole material body and determining all its functionings.*[4]

> Sri Aurobindo

Seventy percent of the breathing function is to eliminate toxins. Sixty percent of our metabolic and toxic waste is released from the breath in the form of carbon dioxide, twenty percent from sweat, and ten percent from each of our eliminatory organs. Once our eliminatory functions have been met, the surplus oxygen goes to the brain, enhancing its functioning. The Indian healing tradition of Ayurveda defines the root cause of all illness as an accumulation of toxins or debris. The physical toxins are treated with diet and herbs while the toxins of the psyche are treated with the breath.

The HeartMath Institute has shown the power of the breath for harmonizing the sympathetic and parasympathetic nervous systems that make stress more manageable. By simply breathing deeply and slowly for 5–10 minutes, focusing on the inhale and exhale and breathing into the heart is effective for reducing many types of stress—whether it comes from internal stimuli such as depression or negative emotional states or external stimuli such as overwork or trauma. Cardiac coherence is a state where the heartbeat becomes more rhythmic due to slow and deep breathing. When a person's nervous system is in harmony, their production of cortisol, a hormone associated with stress, decreases.

Emotional Benefits

The roots of our emotional issues are more closely linked to the subconscious mind than the conscious mind. From the subconscious mind, they manifest in the form of felt sensations in the body such as tensions, feelings of blockage, heat, or uneasiness in the chest. When we do not recognize and deal with our emotional disharmonies, they may get somatized or repressed in the body in the form of deeper, underlying tensions in the muscles or internal organs. Breathwork is effective because it gives us access to the roots of our emotions not accessible in our ordinary waking state. Most of our negative and limiting beliefs and attitudes are caused by past experiences, some of which occurred before our cognitive brain was even developed. Breath is any easy means to go beyond the surface to access and heal the core wounds. This can occur in the form of subtle realizations and shifts during the breathwork session or in the form of emotional catharsis.

On a physiological level, the excess oxygen from deep breathing hyper oxygenates the brain, bringing up unresolved emotions, disharmonious beliefs, and attitudes from the subconscious. The general medical view is that this is some form of pathology. What the medical profession doesn't realize is that when we learn how to bring out and reach completion with what arises, it results in defragmentation, healing, and harmonization of the psyche.

When they hear about my unorthodox way of working, sometimes fellow psychotherapists cut off my description and exclaim, "Oh, you teach relaxation." Taking a deep breath, I explain that relaxation is a by-product of dealing with the core issues that get addressed in the breathwork. Breathwork is much more than a relaxation technique.

From the perspective of yogic philosophy, when we inhale we bring in life energy and with the exhalation, we release negative sensory, emotional, and mental experiences. As Philo of Alexandria pointed out, the state of our psyche is mirrored in the quality of our breath. Liberating our breath means liberating our lives.

Healing Cellular Memory

Cellular memories are confining patterns stored in the consciousness of our cells. We react to stressful or traumatic incidents by tensing up in our bodies. When we do not resolve or integrate these experiences, this tension can get stored in the body in the form of very obvious muscular impact. At other times, the impact is more subtle and can get recorded in the form of cellular impressions. While most people are not aware of the subtle disharmonies stored in the muscles and cells, they can come to our awareness and be released during breathwork sessions. In this case, the effect is a sense of lightness, liberation, openness, and harmony.

Breathwork brings to our awareness and releases not only subconscious memory but also cellular memory. Through clearing all these sources of limitation and blockage in our subconscious, we experience healing of psychosomatic and stress-related illnesses.

Mental Effects of the Breath

Distinguishing between emotional and mind issues can only be done on a theoretical level to convey a certain understanding. Disharmonies exist at all levels of our being. They are usually interrelated. Although they may impact many aspects of our lives, they inevitably have a root cause. Breathwork brings to our awareness disharmonious or incongruent thoughts, attitudes, and beliefs and the insight into how they lead to estrangement from our soul. This incites and empowers us to clear up our unconstructive attitudes and beliefs and navigate more sustainably with ourselves and others. Awareness of our cognitive disconnects stemming from spontaneous insight is generally a strong motivator for implementing positive changes in our lives.

Spiritual Dimensions of the Breath

Breath is the royal road from ego to soul.[5]

Cultivating awareness of our breath and our relationship to it gradually gives us access to more and more subtle awareness of the flow of consciousness in our body, mind, and soul. As it clears away the accumulated dross at our physical, energetic, and emotional levels, the breath starts to take on its most spiritual function, opening the way and bringing us into deep connection with ourselves.

Deep and dynamic breath works on our denser levels of consciousness: body, mind, and emotions. As the breath becomes more subtle, we journey into correspondingly subtle parts of our consciousness. At this phase in the breathwork session, it is common to gain deep insights into ourselves and our life experiences, leading to integration and acceptance. Expansive states of oneness and universal love leave us feeling vibrant, fully alive, and joyous.

WHAT HAPPENS IN A BREATHWORK SESSION?

Every session begins with a dialogue. The dialogue stimulates the conscious and subconscious mind around our problematic issues like loosening the soil around a weed. Sometimes the client comes with an issue they'd like to work on and at other times, an issue will come to the forefront through our dialogue. The client lies down in a comfortable position and I begin to guide them in the breathing process. Often the issue discussed at the beginning of the session will unfold and become profoundly clear. The client can tap into unresolved emotional states. By learning to surrender and breathe into whatever arises, each experience becomes a possibility for healing and a gateway into something deeper.

Vignette—Liberating the Root Cause

Zoe observed that certain situations seemed to trigger an uncomfortable stress response and she wanted to explore its significance and work on it in session. She had been analyzing and working on it in various ways for a few years, but it persisted. We explored it through dialogue while she held her attention on the uncomfortable feelings in the body. As she mindfully explored the uncomfortable state, she could see it was related to shame. She began her breathwork, breathing into and holding her awareness on the shame and related discomfort. She spontaneously went into a deep state of consciousness and had a vision, a plant being lifted from the floor of the ocean with all of its roots. She intuitively knew that she had reached and liberated the roots of the issue. Upon returning to her normal, waking state, a thought crossed her mind that would have typically set off her shame and stress response. She experienced only peace. In the days and weeks following the session, this occurred many more times and the stress response never returned.

During a breathwork session, we can experience physical and emotional sensations and more subtle states of awareness. For example, old physical symptoms may temporarily surface as the related emotional patterns come to our awareness and are released. We may remember specific scenes that were not properly integrated. We can become aware of self-sabotaging thoughts or behaviors and experience desires and means to change them. In the thousands of sessions I've accompanied, I have never seen two sessions alike.

Vignette—Breathwork

Garrett, a young and highly successful executive, was referred to me by a colleague. Garrett reported extreme panic attacks each time he tried to enter his office building. The attacks had come on suddenly with no apparent reason, leaving him incapable of going to work. We began by dialoguing about his recent life events. He was in the process of an amicable divorce. Despite the obvious assumptions that this was the cause of his problem, he felt it was going well and would end in a lifelong friendship. We talked about his work a little. He liked his job, enjoyed the challenge, got on well with his colleagues and superiors, and could not understand why going to work had set off his attacks. Nothing in his story gave off alarm bells as to the possible cause of his attacks and yet, as he spoke, I was struck by a sense that beneath his outwardly easygoing and likeable nature, he had a deep need to please and to gain approval from others. Even though this is something most people have to some degree, I felt that this was the direction to explore. It was my only clue as to what was going on behind the scenes. I asked him about it, "I get a sense that there is something inside of you that feels a need for reassurance and approval from others, you might experience it as a need to be liked."

"Yes, I noticed that but never really paid much attention to it." The five-minute dialogue that ensued revealed the fact that he had always noticed a sense of pressure inside, as if he needed to be liked in order to exonerate himself and prove himself worthy. I felt that just bringing that realization to the surface would provide sufficient stimulus for the breathwork and suggested we move into the next phase of our session.

Everyone breathes differently and their way of breathing reflects their innermost attitudes toward themselves and life. From the beginning of the session, Garrett breathed fully, giving himself completely into the breath, no holds barred, the sign of someone who plunges into his experiences in life, full on, with no reserves. Other than his extraordinarily dynamic breath, nothing remarkable happened for about fifteen minutes. All of a sudden, Garrett was in a total catharsis, consumed with violent sobbing that seemed to be coming out of every pore in his body. Normally, I try to provide some gentle reassurance in moments of vulnerability, but in this session, Garrett was apparently so fully in the experience that he was oblivious to the outside. The convulsive sobbing went on for perhaps five or ten minutes and gradually gave way to intermittent spaces of quiet breathing and catharsis. Gradually, the catharsis subsided and Garrett settled back down on his back, continuing the deep breath. Tears of what looked like joy, gratitude, and relief were flowing down his face as he experienced a different catharsis, the experience of opening up after releasing a blocked emotion. His face beamed with radiance and openness as he continued to breathe.

*Gradually, his awareness naturally came back into the room as he reached the
end of the natural breathing cycle. He opened his eyes and was clearly eager
to share his experience.*

*During the breathing, he spontaneously recalled and relived a traumatic inci-
dent from when he was four years old. He had been in the garden shed playing
with matches. His baby brother was there recovering from a corrective surgery
on his legs. Both of his legs were bound by bandages, leaving him completely
immobilized. In his carelessness, Garrett set the shed on fire. He panicked and
ran out of the shed. He was able to call his parents' attention to the situation
and, in the nick of time, they were able to rescue his brother and bring the fire
under control.*

*The only emotions that were expressed in his family were the relief at having
saved his brother. Garrett's parents did not reprimand him or talk about his
mischief in any way. This left Garrett unconsciously feeling incomplete about
his wrongdoing. He realized that, at that point, he had taken on a sense of
being guilty and wrong. Because it did not get addressed, it developed in him a
compensatory mechanism in the form of seeking to escape from guilt and gain
approval.*

*In the session, he realized how he had unconsciously carried his guilt and
shame into every single relationship he had ever had. He experienced deep relief
as he realized he could move on and no longer carry on this dynamic that had
subtly put a false note in his relationships.*

*The pattern, which up to now had been largely subconscious, was triggered
by Garrett's divorce and its repercussions came to the surface in the form of
panic attacks. Somehow reexperiencing this event helped him to reach a gestalt,
come full circle, and finally complete it. He felt liberated and experienced waves
of relief and gratitude.*

*After any powerful, opening, and consciousness-expanding experience,
I always advise clients to give the experience time to integrate and not to make
any life changing decisions in the 7–10 days following the session. This time is
necessary to integrate the experience itself and the associated inner structural
changes and/or adjustments. I suggested Garrett ring me back for a follow-up
if he wanted after 7–10 days. Two weeks later, Garrett rang me back to thank
me for the life-changing session. He felt he had addressed the core issue and
was now able to move forward in life much more in harmony with himself. He
had been able to return to work with no repercussions and did not feel it was
necessary to do any further work together. While there is always potential in
doing further breathwork to release other issues or to follow the lifelong path of
fine-tuning our relationship to ourselves and our surroundings, I felt that in this
case my client had made the right decision.*

The cases have not always been easy. Although most of the time clients do
experience improvement, sometimes the going is not quite so straightforward
as it was with Garrett. The factor that holds the most power in determining
how quickly and deeply breathwork will progress depends on how fluid the

client's consciousness is, in other words, their ability to let go. The more open clients will get results in a shorter time and even reach their therapeutic goals more quickly. Those who have rigidity and resistance, whose consciousness is not in the flow of life, have a harder time with breathwork because the basic principle is that it helps us through helping us to let go.

Through a series of breathwork sessions, we become aware of issues at multiple levels of our being, resulting in release of negative thoughts and attitudes; healing of psychosomatic and stress-related illnesses; more harmonious relationships with ourselves and others; increased vitality; and improved self-knowledge, self-esteem, and self-image. With this greater awareness and integration we experience greater well-being, relaxation, and harmony. Breathwork leads us to deeper experiences than most of us have ever had. At the spiritual level, when we open to the flow of life energy in our being, we become clear on who we are and what we want out of life. We find and align to a deeper sense of purpose.

MINDFULNESS

My work with breath and catharsis helped me to see that plunging into our pain and going through it takes the pressure off us and liberates our minds and energy to pursue our lives less encumbered. My approach was like a pickaxe. This can be liberating, but it can also trigger reactions, resistance, and instability without leading to sustainable change. When I discovered the mindfulness perspective I realized that working more gently with ourselves and our emotions not only releases the pressure but builds us into stronger, more functional individuals. Mindfulness-based psychotherapy quickly became one of the foundations of my practice.

Mindfulness in Psychotherapy

Originally practiced as a part of Buddhism, mindfulness has highly developed psychological teachings. There are hundreds of books on the psychological teachings from both Western and Eastern Buddhist masters and the scientific study of its benefits, embodying approaches taught by John Welwood, Jon Kabat-Zinn, and many others. Leaving its Buddhist origins of monasteries, retreats, and the meditation cushion, there are a few ways I like to bring mindfulness into my psychotherapy sessions.

In practice, it can be as simple as focusing on the breath. Observing what "is" and gently breathing into it. It is not aimed at negating and transcending our experience in the here and now, but rather sitting with it, watching it, while not engaging or identifying with it. This creates a stable base for us to begin unraveling from surface issues and delve inwards.

Welwood teaches a way of practicing mindfulness to help clients develop awareness of the roots of their emotions in the body. Tightness, knots, discomfort, or other visceral feelings are the way our emotions are expressed through the body. Sometimes we have become so accustomed to blocking out these signals that we do not even know they are there. Yet, if we bring our attention inward, depending on our level of awareness, we may notice slight sensations in the body indicating an emotional response. When this arises in session, I gently guide the client into an exploration of that sensation. Some of us have cut ourselves off from our emotions to the extent that we have dissociated from the feeling roots in our bodies. When this is the case, the bridge first has to be built. Simply placing our attention on what we experience at any given moment, even when there is no particular perception at all, allows our awareness to develop over time. A common misunderstanding here is for ambition and the pressure to get somewhere or change something, to get the better of us rather than simply sitting with or giving space to what we are experiencing. When we listen in to our body, it is like an antenna, giving us a moment-to-moment update on how we are feeling. When we feel tension or disharmony, we may find an inner reaction to outer stimuli or a reaction to our own inner dialogue. Either way, by holding this disharmony in our awareness with nonjudgment, we can walk through it rather than being with it and escalating to the point where we have an outburst, breakdown, or just a plain old bad day.

Simply being present with our emotions as they arise with no judgment, no resistance, turns—to use Ram Dass's analogy—great, huge monsters into tiny, powerless rascals. Through mindfully placing our attention on our experience and spending time with it, simply holding a space for whatever is, we disengage from the downward spiral of reaction. Creating space for what we experience turns it into a gateway inward, to more wholesome parts of ourselves. This leads to insights into our own functioning and attitudes. This kind of mindful enquiry is useful for building the body–mind connection, for helping identify and open up emotional blockages in the body. Eventually it leads inward to a deep sense of centeredness and peace as the blockages unravel.

Mindfulness is a great tool for working with our feelings on a day-to-day basis. It helps us develop emotional mastery, the objectivity and empowerment to address and express our emotions consciously and intentionally. It helps to steady the mind, making it easier to deal with difficult emotions such as anxiety, anger, and depression.

Mindfulness, because it helps us to develop a neutral way of observing ourselves, makes it possible to find a way to safely bring up old and traumatic memories in order to help us release the emotional pressure they carry and move on. Practicing mindfulness in the context of psychotherapy can actually help to bring to the surface memories that have been suppressed but whose effects are influencing us from behind the scenes in negative ways. When avoidance, coping, or any other forms of resistance arise, we can simply watch them too, without identifying or engaging with them. We can start to deal with what is disturbing us at the root, rather than our reactions, defenses, and resistance to it. By doing this, we are able to work through the issues that arise and move on.

Accept It

Mindfulness goes hand in hand with the notion of acceptance. This may have negative connotations for some.

Many years ago, I was neurotically fussing about some now forgotten aspect of my life and a dear friend said to me, "Just accept it." "What!? And let it run my life?" An hour later, after a soul-searching dialogue, I understood that acceptance does not mean submission to passivity or despondency. It means embracing, making space for the bothersome issue rather than resisting it. Acceptance is an attitude that allows us to delve into our discomfort rather than react to it. We give our power to whatever we resist. This subtle difference in attitude opens up the way to empowerment. We come back into our center and out of reactivity. Once we have owned our reactions and emotions, it liberates us to take action from a centered, empowered, and nonreactive place. This positively impacts the results of our action.

Acceptance is a positive quality related to equanimity, having an equal heart. It is also closely related to detachment, which is yet another concept that is misunderstood in our modern go-getter mentality. Acceptance requires strength and courage, but it does not preclude action. Where action is not possible we may simply need to come to terms with life's events in our own heart. Acceptance gives us the possibility to transcend and integrate our experiences.

Vignette—Embodied Mindfulness

Adam was a 33-year-old musician. He was experiencing difficulty with his breathing. He said that when singing or playing wind instruments he would reach a certain level and then experience a distinct impression that something was blocking his lung capacity and diaphragm. His music teacher felt the problem stemmed from an emotional blockage and referred him to me because of my specialty in working with the breath. In our first session, we explored his life history with a particular focus on any areas that could be related to his symptoms. We quickly identified a probable cause. Adam's father was very introverted, leaving Adam unable to get a sense of bearings with him. What place did he have in his father's life and heart? This created a deep, inner tension that had no immediate means to be resolved. In response, Adam was destabilized and went into a fight-or-flight response. He retreated into his head and, with great inner tension, played a constant guessing game about where he stood with his father. He out-wardly sought love and acknowledgement, which was unproductive. Inwardly, he felt scared, isolated, and enraged. In an effort to come to terms with his father's noncommunicativeness, Adam put his father on a pedestal, telling himself that his father's introversion was a reflection of a very deep and spiritual man. It never became clear as to whether this was true or not or if it was just a means of learning to live with the situation. In response to this painful conundrum, Adam locked away his feelings and self-expression. Ironically, his own survival mechanism mirrored that of his father. He, too, could not express his emotions and they remained bottled up inside. Most of the time, Adam appeared to be stoic. But when he reached breaking point, his emotions would explode in the form of a messy outburst, leaving him feeling shameful and his family shell-shocked.

We began working on contacting and freeing the emotions Adam had so care-fully locked inside of himself for most of his life. He realized how much pressure was created in his chest and diaphragm by habitually holding in his emotions.

As the core emotional issues came to the forefront, our work turned increas-ingly to mindfulness as a means for him to create and maintain a safe, inner space to learn how to live with and express his emotions constructively. I tried to help Adam be more kind and gentle to himself. The beauty of being mindful of our emotions is that by not resisting or judging them, they become less extreme and more manageable.

A: I feel angry, it's not fair that I should have to go through this suffering. What did I do? Why does it have to happen to me?

M: I can understand your reasoning and your anger. As you talk about it, I won-der how you feel inside?

A: I feel angry and agitated.

M: Do you have a sense of where the anger and agitation is in your body?

A: I feel it in my chest.

M: Would you be willing just to hold your attention there and allow yourself to feel that sensation?

A: (closes his eyes, focuses inward for a time) The pressure is releasing, it feels a little better. I just feel so helpless.

M: Let's just sit with that feeling of helplessness for some time.

A: It's just not fair.

M: I understand that this is a reaction to something deeper. Can we sit with that for a moment?

In this way, I kept guiding Adam to be present with and give space to whatever he was experiencing, keeping him present with his emotions rather than his reactions.

A: It's just not fair. Why have I gone through life not being able to express myself? How many people have I hurt? How much have I hurt myself?

M: Hmm, how does it feel to express that? What's the feeling associated with it?

A: Anger. I'm angry with myself for causing myself to be emotionally blocked and angry with life for doing this to me.

M: Would you be willing to sit with that anger, acknowledging it, holding your attention on it? Remember, we are not trying to do anything or get anywhere . . . simply acknowledge the anger.

A: I just feel so helpless.

M: Okay, would you be willing to just sit with that helplessness?

A: It feels hot, in my chest, there's anxiety around my helplessness.

M: Okay, would you like to sit with that heat and that helplessness in your chest?

A: I guess underneath it all, I'm just afraid.

M: I wonder what would it be like just to acknowledge that fear rather than build so many reactions and defenses to it? Let's try that.

A: Yes, I'm just afraid and because I don't want to listen to my fear, I react to it with anger and resist it, which makes me feel anxious. Actually, when I acknowledge the fear, as the source of the suffering, it feels much more simple, much lighter, and more manageable. Something is opening up. There's a feeling of warmth in my heart, like something opened up and is flowing again. I feel a sense of relief, like coming home to myself. My heart and my chest feel full, warmth, openness.

Over time, Adam realized that he could engage in his inner healing: his attitudes, self-love, and self-acceptance. Adam was eventually able to give more space to his deep emotions and spend less time in reactions and protective mechanisms. He developed an uncanny ability to go deep within and explore his blockages and fears on a very subtle level. As his awareness became subtler, his outer life became more smooth and manageable. The blockage in his chest was released over time, opening up his lung capacity and his ability to master the breath. His musical expression flourished. Adam learned to open up more and share his emotions with his loved ones. He began being able to let people into his life by joining a men's support group and learning to express himself more with his family.

Mindfulness helps us to calm the mind and live more peacefully and meaningfully with our inner and outer difficulties. This creates space for nonjudgmental exploration of weaknesses and vulnerabilities that make up our emotional minefield. The objectivity and emotional mastery we develop give us power to overcome unconstructive habits.

Mindfulness does not have the spiritual focus of many yogic-based techniques and can therefore be adapted to psychotherapy as well as other contexts, such as coaching and business.[6] It gives us the autonomy and the means to process our life experiences and is a bridge between outer self and inner, transcendent self.

With person-centered dialogue, breathwork, and mindfulness as the bricks and mortar of my work, I like to keep a host of other tools in my toolbox in order to be able to help clients effectively address whatever arises.

COGNITIVE AND BEHAVIORAL INTERVENTIONS

When there are self-sabotage mechanisms and short circuits in a client's inner scripts, attitudes, beliefs, and ideas, cognitive dialogue is an effective way of bringing them to light, reevaluating and updating them. Our cognitive short circuits are formed in two ways: we pick them up through osmosis or we adopt them as survival mechanisms to compensate for emotional wounds, poor sense of self, and lack of strong and stable affective foundations. While self-observation and self-analysis can pinpoint cognitive short circuits, we inevitably have blind spots. These occur around the most highly emotionally charged areas, emotional wounds, and unmet core needs. Even when we have identified them, we do not necessarily know what to do. Our cognitive beliefs influence our behaviors.

Once we have caught ourselves red-handed in an incongruent cognitive script and experienced the benefit of eliminating it through the empowering experience of modifying our thoughts, beliefs, and behaviors, we will keep this phenomenon in our awareness and adopt a proactive stance. We make a habit of identifying and addressing issues as we become aware of them. By freeing up energy and opening the way to connect to our deeper self, we can awaken our self-actualizing drives.

Working at the cognitive and behavioral levels is a long shot when the emotional roots of the issue are stronger than the demons to be overcome. This is why, try as we may, some of our behaviors are hard to change. The reason is simple: cognitive incongruencies are generally a symptom, not the cause. We can change the wallpaper, but if the wall and foundations are not structurally sound, the problems will recur. In the end, addressing and working with our issues at the level at which they exist is the most effective way to change. To uncover and work with core issues behind cognitive short circuits, we usually need to do deeper work.

JOURNALING

Therapy is a process of self-discovery, healing, individuation and evolving in consciousness. It is important for the client to engage in their own way and at their own pace. It is not limited to the time spent in the therapist's office. The therapist plays a part but it is the client who, through their commitment to attend sessions and engage in self-development in between sessions, wakes up their will and takes responsibility for their own development. Some clients may spontaneously journal their experiences and insights from their sessions. This allows us to recall the wonderful, and sometimes painful, steps in our process and helps us develop greater self-awareness and integrate changes into our lives.

Journaling as an Intervention

I find it useful to give clients material for reflection, self-observation, or exploring creative ways to address issues and innovate the way forward in their lives. Journaling enables us to reflect and process out our thoughts, experiences, and feelings. Inviting clients to do journaling exercises develops their will to engage in their process of healing and transformation. When, in session, it becomes apparent that a client lacks awareness in a particular area of their lives and is therefore being dominated by unconscious patterns, journaling is particularly useful. I might ask a client to note down their feelings, reactions, and behaviors without self-judgment. If a client has artistic tendencies or a desire to develop their creativity, they may like to create collages, images, or write poems or songs in regards to their process. I might ask a client to describe their goals, desires, and aspirations. Exploring these journal entries in session reveals the underlying process taking place in the client. It also enables identifying, setting, and working toward achieving their goals. Journaling techniques vary widely and I generally bring them into my work as a spontaneous idea rather than a set technique as a tool for building self-awareness and insights for personal growth.

EMDR

EMDR is an information processing therapy using an eight-phase approach to address the experiential contributors of a wide range of pathologies including trauma and PTSD. It attends to the past experiences that have set the groundwork for pathology; the current situations that trigger dysfunctional emotions, beliefs, and sensations; and the positive experience needed to enhance future adaptive behaviors and mental health.

During treatment various procedures and protocols are used to address the entire clinical picture. One of the procedural elements is "dual stimulation" using either bilateral eye movements, tones, or taps. During the reprocessing phases the client attends momentarily to past memories, present triggers, or anticipated future experiences while simultaneously focusing on a set of external stimulus. This leads to insights, changes in memories, or new associations.[7]

Vignette—Post-Traumatic Stress Disorder

Priyanka was referred to me during some work I did on-site following a natural disaster. Since the disaster had happened a week before, she had been unable to sleep. She experienced repetitive thinking and was reliving scenes from the disaster as well as apprehending further scenes. The most mysterious of her symptoms was that she had begun wondering whether she was being punished for a childish and perfectly innocent misdeed she had done when she was six years old, telling a fib to her parents. I didn't have to probe too far to determine that Priyanka had a classic case of PTSD. I explained to her that I was going to help her express her experience while moving my finger from left to right in front of her eyes and that, she was to let her eyes follow my fingers as she told her story. She had gone through a harrowing and terrifying moment during the natural disaster in which she could have lost her life. As she relived the tension and anguish but also the sense of powerlessness and a poignant fear of abandoning her three-year-old baby, should she not survive, this brought up several waves of emotion during her recall. The session was helped by the fact that Priyanka was able to quickly let go and let her emotions out. Each wave of emotion, fear, anguish, grief, sadness, and powerlessness subsided as quickly as it had come up. After awhile, Priyanka's facial expression shifted from suffering to relief. We continued talking until I could see that she had stabilized. I made sure she understood that she was not ill but that her nervous system had taken a shock. When it does that, the anguish has nowhere to go and can turn inward, against ourselves in the form of the shame of her childhood fib, but also outward, making us project danger onto our lives, even when the source of danger has passed. As Priyanka and I said goodbye, I could see by her face and especially her eyes that she felt reassured. She expressed a renewed sense of hope. I made sure the team knew to set up two follow-up sessions as per the protocol for EMDR treatment for PTSD. I took a deep breath, had a glass of water and welcomed in the next client.

In her subsequent sessions, Priyanka was fairly stable. There was some fine-tuning to do in terms of helping her come to terms with both her experience during the disaster and her brief episode with PTSD.

DREAMWORK

Dreams have been used for understanding our psyches, our experiences, and our spirit since time immemorial. Insights into the content of dreams may differ widely according to epoch and culture. My favorite takeaway from working with dreams is the insight into the psyche and soul.

Ordinary dreams are a means of working out and integrating the contents of our subconscious, vital-level experiences, "created by one's thoughts and feelings during the waking state . . . come back in sleep in the form of dreams. . . . Subconscious dreams are useful for understanding our present state of consciousness."[8]

In addition to ordinary subconscious dreams, Sri Aurobindo talks about three types of dream experience: astral, premonitory, and divine intervention. Through the practice of meditation, paying attention to our dreams and even developing the capacity for lucid dreaming, we can start to distinguish between the different types of dream experiences. This enhances our therapeutic healing process and spiritual development.

The meaning of dreams can be grasped through analysis—introspecting on the various elements of the dream, inquiring into the emotions associated with the people, things, and occurrences in the dream—and intuition. Rather than using any particular technique, I draw on what I've learned through my personal dreamwork, training, and research to work with each person and each dream in a unique way. Sometimes I find it useful to just sit with the material and let the meaning arise. When working with clients' dreams, I enquire into the nature of the experience to try to determine, if possible, what type of experience it is and then work with the material accordingly.

The hypnagogic or alpha state, the state between waking and sleeping, opens up interesting therapeutic possibilities. Accessed through yogic *shavasan* (the corpse pose), breathwork, and deep meditation, this state allows us to engage in conscious dreaming that leads to self-knowledge, profound introspection, and deep healing.

Vignette—Dreamwork

Cécilia, a twenty-four-year-old woman, came to me because she felt unable to deal with her relationship with her mother whose invasive relationship style made it difficult for her to establish healthy boundaries. This pattern was making Cécilia's adult life uncomfortable and difficult.

Cécilia had a very subtle and well-developed mental understanding of herself with a high level of spiritual congruence (sense of the soul, sense of her own potential), but very little integration of emotions or body. She had dissociated from the traumatic incidents of her past and took refuge in her mind where she had a sense of having some control and well-being. Her wisdom was disembodied.

In her second session, Cécilia brought a dream in which a country was divided in two by a lake (she is torn between her parents or two different parts of herself). The bottom of the lake was full of very dangerous monsters. This can be interpreted as a feeling that the shadow side is dangerous. She is with a little girl (her inner child) who has been touched by a monster and is condemned to die. She is desperately looking for a way to help her (she is seeking to heal her inner child). The little girl refuses to accept help (she does not believe she has the right to integrate her past and become whole). She questions whether she has the right to trust the light, or does she deserve to stay in the shadow? She makes her way to the opposite end of the lake and finds a nurse (me?) to whom she entrusts the little girl. She then sacrifices herself to the monsters at the bottom of the lake.

This dream tells of great inner darkness, despair, and hopelessness. Cécilia does not believe anything can be done. Either her or her inner child will have to be sacrificed to the shadow (monsters). She is currently dominated by shadow (she sacrificed herself to the monsters) and does not believe she can trust the light and overcome her shadow. This dream tells me that part of her healing could involve learning to accept the help (the nurse) that is available to her. Through gaining the understanding that there are both shadow and light and that life is a mix of both, Cécilia would be able to see that we do not have to succumb to the shadow but only accept that it is a part of our lives along with light. She is both dominated by and terrified of her shadow. Ironically, she is afraid to delve into her shadow while on the other hand she resides in her shadow.

Our work on this dream was an invitation to explore the world of her shadow in which there were boundary issues with women along with a dark impression of women and being a woman herself. Women were dangerous as they could swallow her up and humiliate her. Lack of sense of self, both hers and theirs, is the root of the issue. Her impression was, "Women do not know how to hold their own ground and do not assert themselves. To make up for this, they have to be coquette, manipulative, and invasive to get their needs met and to exist." We explored an alternative image of womanhood in which women become empowered and strong by owning their own fragility and therefore are not dominated by it. A real woman has inner (feminine) strength and self-confidence that allow her to be authentic. This image felt healthy to her and we worked on transforming her relationship to other women and to herself as a woman. In some ways, I was aware that I was to play the role of the healthy mother with her. I represented to her the image of the empowered and healthy woman and we explored what it might be like for her to become the type of woman she respects, admires, and feels safe with.

Cécilia's dream, at the start of our work together, was an invitation to work with her shadow and explore a more wholesome way forward. Over the weeks, we were able to work with and integrate the emotions and beliefs around the life events that had left the strongest marks on her: the ones she was carrying with her and that were causing her to sabotage her dreams and potential. Little by little, Cécilia felt safer experiencing her vulnerability and her emotions and also began developing a more congruent connection to her body.

GESTALT ROLE-PLAY

When dealing with unresolved issues and conflict with another person, especially where anger is involved, I call on the famous role-playing technique from gestalt therapy. Visualizing someone with whom we harbor conflict and engaging in a dialogue with the other person is an effective way to release stuck energy. Unsaid words and unresolved inter-personal conflicts are the cause of much disharmony, disconnect, and consequent suffering. Expressing them in a role-playing or visualized dialogue helps us move past blockages that stop us from expressing ourselves and, finally, helps us build new ways of communicating in difficult situations.

INNER DIALOGUE AND PSYCHOSYNTHESIS

Whereas gestalt dialogue is used to work with interpersonal issues, the inner exploration and dialogues evoked by images and sensations arising from within can be worked with using inner dialogue or psychosynthesis.

Inner dialogue is not a technique in itself but rather a direction or an invitation to journey into sensation or image that arises in session through opening an exploratory dialogue with it. One can ask it what it is doing there, does it have a message for us, and does it need something from us. The questions I will put to the client, as they sit and allow themselves to be in contact with what they are experiencing, can be simply logical or can arise from intuition. This can lead to unlocking blocked emotions, developing self-awareness, and learning to live and work peacefully with the contents of our psyche.

Certain cues lead me to take the client into a psychosynthesis-based guided imagery work. Inner imagery helps integrate dissociated or stuck parts in a person's psyche. The imagery and meaning inherent in the sensations that arise in session can become gateways into the subconscious, bringing about deeper understanding, integration, and connection to oneself. Psychosynthesis is more of a mindset than a technique.

"I feel tightness in my chest."

"Yes, I understand that [x or y situation] would bring up such a sensation. How would you describe the blockage? Where is it? Does it have a shape? Does it have a consistency? A color? Would you like to give it a name? . . . Allow yourself to explore the black, heavy, amorphous blob in your chest and enquire into it. . . . What is it doing there?. What does it want to say? What does it need from you? What would you like to do with it?"

The guidance is spontaneous and situational, never scripted. Ultimately, the sensation will reveal its message which we can then integrate. Like embodied mindfulness and gestalt role-playing, inner dialogue and psychosynthesis are yet other means of liberating blocked energy and helping us open up to the natural flow that arises from our deep, inner self.

FLOWER AND PLANT ESSENCES

I discovered Bach Flower Remedies when I was a teenager. My mother took the family to see a naturopathic physician who had us fasting, modifying our diets, and addressing emotional and personality imbalances with this gentle yet powerful system. The flower remedies appealed to my truth-seeking nature and are helpful in times when I am seeking answers or encountering challenges.

Bach Flower Remedies were developed in the 1930s by Dr. Edward Bach. Disillusioned with Western allopathic medicine due to its focus on illness rather than on people, he moved to the English and Welsh countryside in search of a plant-based healing method. His system, working with disharmonious emotional states and personality characteristics, was developed through both intuition and empirical observation. They help bring about greater harmony and well-being.

In recent years, a comprehensive system of Australian Bush Flower Essences was developed by Ian White, with over sixty plants and flowers, none of which overlap with Bach Flower Remedies. I have also experimented with Findhorn Flower Essences, Auroville Flower Essences, and others.

Each of the flower essence types provides descriptions of the flowers and the issues they help address. This makes it easy for self-diagnosis, diagnosis from any mental health practitioner, or referral to a flower remedy expert. Most schools offer trainings providing a more in-depth understanding and first-hand experience of their remedies. This will afford the deepest and most effective use of these wonderful and gentle helpers.

Flower essences work on an energetic level at all levels of consciousness from the physical to the most subtle. We can identify the outer and innermost disharmonies from which we are suffering through dialogue, uncovering techniques and intuition. Then we choose the corresponding remedy or combination of remedies. Flower essences have no side effects and can be used on a day-to-day basis to work with our emotional and mental states. I particularly like to call on them when faced with the most tenacious and difficult challenges.

Some of the techniques in this chapter require active engagement, will, and effort on the part of the client, yet others such as Jin Shin Jyutsu and flower remedies are wonderful for many things. They are particularly useful in cases where a client's challenge is stronger than their will and objectivity.

JIN SHIN JYUTSU

Jin Shin Jyutsu (JSJ is a holistic body-mind technique that originated in Japan. It effectively and gently releases blocked energy from one or more of the twenty-six energy locks on either side of the body. It can be used to address issues at all levels of the spectrum. One can train in JSJ for self-help or to become a professional and treat others. When clients are experiencing difficulty with disturbing emotional states, I use a quick, effective, and easy-to-practice JSJ technique called *attitudes*. Unlike many techniques that require self-effort or know-how, attitudes can be practiced on our own and with no training. The basic principle is that when we experience surface disturbance, if we are able to delve within no matter what negative state we are experiencing at the time, we will inevitably find that the root of our emotion is fear. Fear is harmonized by holding either of the index fingers. On the other hand, when we do not identify, work with, and resolve this fear, it turns to anxiety (thumb). Again, when we do not acknowledge, work with, or resolve our anxiety, it escalates into anger (middle finger . . . go figure!). Anger is a big and tricky emotion. As our vital space feels violated, either by an outer intrusion or through our own inner disorder, it often wakes up a reaction of anger. Inherent in anger is power. When we can identify and use that power constructively, it is nothing other than an expression of a need to regain control of our own selves or of our vital space or boundaries. . . . "Stop!" To continue on, when our anger doesn't get addressed or resolved, it escalates into sadness, depression (anger turned inward against ourselves), or despondency (ring finger). In turn, when we do not address or resolve our sadness, we can fall into the game of pretending everything's fine when it's not—false pretention. We can play this game with ourselves and in the face of others (little finger, i.e., think of the image of holding a tea cup with the little finger in the air). Each finger is not only related to a family of emotions but also to one of the six depths at which disharmonies exist. JSJ is a gentle, very pleasant, and comprehensive approach.

Energetically this technique is related to the twelve minor and major meridians and their associated emotions. Each finger has an ascending and descending meridian and by holding the finger, we help harmonize the corresponding emotion. This technique does not eliminate the emotion but lessens the emotional charge and enables us to more calmly and lucidly work with it.

Vignette—JSJ "Attitudes"

Charles came to me suffering from acute anxiety and unhappiness. The picture of a bourgeois Parisian, he arrived for our first appointment wearing a very expensive suit and perfectly polished shoes and carrying a designer briefcase. As he spoke of his life, it felt like what he said was more about giving off a perfect image of himself than pouring out his woes. I felt like the hidden message shouting out behind Charles' story was, "I am a successful, upper crust man." As I listened to him, I said, "Charles, I'm very interested in your story and I'd like to hear more of it. May I ask you to hold your little finger while you are telling it?" Charles obliged, and, holding his little finger, continued his story. Less than a minute later he blurted out, "Why am I always pretending to be something I'm not?." I couldn't have imagined how effective and quick holding the little finger would be. This was the perfect cue for me, as the therapist. It opened up the way for us to explore Charles's dysfunctional childhood. The dynamic in his family was extremely chaotic and dysfunctional. And yet, his parents went to tremendous lengths and indebtedness to present the ultimate picture of material success and happiness to the outside world. Realizing that he was still living with the constant pressure of holding up that unrealistic image was liberating for Charles. Over time, we were able to liberate the real person imprisoned behind the image.

The attitudes exercise of JSJ helps work with strong emotions when they arise while in session or in ordinary life. JSJ has many more dimensions and techniques for unlocking and harmonizing physical, emotional, and energetic blockages. If it feels appropriate, I will place my hands on the appropriate energy locks during the client's breathwork session. Touch can be an inherent part of some therapeutic approaches. In others, and with certain types of clients, it is out of bounds. When touch seems inappropriate for any reason, I simply instruct the client to place their own hands on the various energy locks. JSJ can be used with very little prior knowledge for a quick fix in a moment of difficulty, or it can be a lifelong learning and practice for our psycho-spiritual development.

YOGA THERAPY

Although there are many forms of yoga and many meanings of the word, the core meaning is "the path that leads toward inward realization of the divine." Yoga draws upon physical, philosophical, psychological, and spiritual approaches to help clients address issues occurring at all levels of their being. Yoga therapy can provide an effective means of working with and healing physical, and psychological/somatic issues and developing greater peace with ourselves and our lives. While meditation, as described earlier, works purely through the psyche, yoga therapy incorporates physical asanas where applicable to help strengthen, balance, and energize the physical body; to open up the flow of energy in the energy channels; and to strengthen and purify particular organs. Yoga therapy can also be aimed at unblocking deep-seated emotions through methods involving either or both the body and the mind. While I have read a lot about yoga and Ayurveda, I have not integrated any techniques or practices in these areas. My basic knowledge helps me identify people and situations that can benefit from yoga therapy and refer out to a colleague.

PSYCHOGENEALOGY

Disharmonies can exist at every level of our being from the physical, emotional, mental, and subliminal. When the root cause of an issue does not become apparent or work itself out through more psychological level approaches, it becomes necessary to start delving deeper, into less tangible and more subtle aspects of our being. When working with issues not directly related to our story in this lifetime, I like to explore psychogenealogy. It is said that we carry with us the traces of the seven generations that preceded us. This can be a tremendous source of wealth but also, alas, a source of disharmony. Psychogenealogy can be explored by inquiring into the client's parents, grandparents, and ancestors and simply letting arise the various traumas, uprootings, and other events that would have left a mark on our for bearers. The stories, and sometimes even the emotions or images, spontaneously arise in the dialogue. Once they have been explored, I like to use breathwork to bring out and harmonize the roots of the issues. In this case, I might guide the breathwork session in a particular way to focus it in this direction.

The stories behind our psychogenealogical inheritances and their associated blockages in our lives can be more or less easy to identify and work with. It depends on the client and their level of fluidity. In cases where there were family secrets, it can be difficult to root out the blockages. One of the ways I identify a family secret is when an issue comes up in therapy and the client makes a sharp disconnect. It is like two magnets being put together on their positive poles; there is a repellent effect. This repellent, when it is not related to a client's own resistance or blind spot, can simply be noted straight out, "Is it possible there has been a family secret somewhere along the way?" Bringing the resistance to the forefront can open the way for working with even the most deeply buried issues, as demonstrated in the vignette on my work with Jane in chapter 8.

FAMILY CONSTELLATION

When I get the sense that a client is carrying a heavy burden of family issues, unsaid words, built up negativity, and unhealthy dynamics, I will invite them to consider doing one or more sessions of this work. Due to the context in which it is practiced, a full ninety- minute session, it is not something I can evoke spontaneously like I do with the other techniques I use.

Inspired by a combination of the dysfunctional family system from John Bradshaw's 1988 book and television series *On the Family* and Bert Hellinger's family constellations, I developed a way to work with individuals on their family and ancestral issues.

A family is a system and when one family member is out of balance, each of the family members adapt, in their own way, in an effort to maintain survival of the family as a cohesive unit or broken vessel, as the case may be. The goal of family constellation work, as with any approach involving visualized or role-played dialogue with significant figures in our lives, is to bring out the unresolved material, the things that did not get expressed or resolved and that we are still carrying with us.

The first thing I do when using this technique is to remind the client that the goal is healing and harmony. With this goal in mind, we may have negativity and blocked energy in regards to our family members. In order to liberate that energy, we need to express it at a gut level and allow it to come out in any way, shape, and form it needs to, without censuring or judging ourselves for it. We may have some things to say that are not pleasant. This does not mean we wish ill on anyone or that we are lesser people for expressing negative emotions. There is a big difference between raging, venting, and releasing stuck energy. With that said, I invite the client to close their eyes and invite their parents to appear in front of them as if they were hanging from a mobile. Their positioning, body language, facial expressions, and any other particularities speak to us of the energy in those particular relationships: their relationships to each other and to the client doing the exercise.

After exploring the significance and the resonance of these manifestations, I may evoke gestalt role-play. I invite the client to speak to the visualized images of their parents and family, straight from the heart. Sometimes a client starts out with an adult narrative, saying what they think and what they observe rather than what they feel. They may instinctually want to protect their parents and teach them about good parenting rather than heal their own emotional wounds. Since the roots of our unresolved issues are more on a feeling level, I try to help the client get in touch with and express themselves on an emotional/feeling level throughout the exercise. Usually what happens is that after expressing all of the pent up negativity, saying all the things we needed our parents to hear and acknowledge is that deep love, gratitude and other positive emotions come gushing forth. This is the same dynamic we come across in other techniques; we release the stuck energy and open the way for our deep, loving, and congruent selves. During the process, I check in with the client from time to time to see how the image of their parents appears to them, to see if they have they shifted their positioning, their expression, their appearance in any other way.

When the images appear in a positive light and the dynamic is harmonious, we are ready to move on and invite the siblings to participate in the same process. Similarly, in a family constellation workshop, we can also bring in the grandparents, ancestors, and current family. In most cases, I find that one or at most two ninety sessions are enough for working in these areas, especially since there is an overlap with the other techniques I use.

PRAYER

When working with clients who are spiritually oriented or visibly seeking a more spiritual life, I sometimes suggest the use of prayer or mantra. Prayer is a common spiritual intervention in psychotherapy. It can help clients gain strength to face difficult issues and passages in their lives. Prayer has many forms ranging from asking for help with a specific issue, area of our lives, or goal to asking for personal or spiritual guidance, upliftment, and liberation.

Psychologically, prayer helps to focus the mind in a positive or constructive direction; it reminds us to be humble and rekindles hope. Prayer is often only considered to be a psychological phenomenon and its multidimensional aspects are ignored on a more subtle level. Prayer and mantra strengthen and purify the energy field and align us to higher forces or parts of ourselves. Through prayer, we open our being for receiving strength, courage, clarity, vision, or help with inner or outer life challenges.

Spiritual interventions are not always appropriate and there are ethical concerns to be taken into consideration. I will only propose it when a client has an explicitly spiritual worldview or speaks of prayer, letting me know that it is already part of their lives. The bottom line on the ethics of spiritual interventions is that they must unequivocally respect and reflect the client's worldview, not ours.

Vignette—Prayer

David was struggling with mentally beating himself up and incriminating himself. We had explored the cause, the self-destructiveness of this habit and other dynamics around David's issue which was paralyzing him in every aspect of his life, his work, relationships, and even taking care of himself physically. The constant inner dialogue stopped him from doing anything that was fully good for himself. His life was a constant struggle. We explored what life would be like without the constant nagging of his own mind. He said he would feel free and peaceful.

I knew implicitly that David was very active in his synagogue and had a personal relationship with his rabbi. As he settled in for his breathing session, I suggested he pray for help in releasing his self-criticism and becoming deeply free and peaceful. Taking it to a deeper level, as he closed his eyes, I suggested that he pray with all his heart for help. Prayer from the heart is an act of humility and sincerity that can help us make big shifts. I suggested he begin breathing deeply, openly, and fully into his desire to become free and peaceful. Focusing on the positive intent is always more productive than on eliminating

the negative. Survival mode or damage control is eternally self-propagating.
Self-actualizing or thriving is like putting your foot on the accelerator with
no need for brakes. The session was very rich in content. David went through
some deep realizations about family dynamics that had anchored him in his self-
criticism. Most importantly, at the end of the session, he had a breakthrough
and a commitment arose from deep inside him: the conviction that he had to
become his own ally and move forward with his life. I suggested that David
continue his practice of prayer to support him in integrating the changes into
his attitude and actions.

MEDITATION

My growth seems to parallel my meditation practice. After twelve years of
therapy and eight years of meditation practice, I have gone from being a
distressed, fearful and unhappy person to finding peace. I had to go down
each hellish avenue, learning to embrace and make peace with the experi-
ence. I had to reenact the level of intensity and struggle I'd known as a
child in order to finally break through. That took a lot of trust and safety
in myself and my healing process. That trust came through the silence and
stable relationship to myself that slowly emerged from my daily meditation
practice.[9]

Any psychology that is to address the full spectrum of human experience
and potential would not be complete without a look at the importance and
role of meditation as well as the states it leads us to. A consistent practice of
meditation, using effective, established methods, can be a great help in our
psycho-spiritual development.

Whether from the ancient practices of the East, mystical traditions of the
West, and emerging, high-tech techniques, when practiced regularly it contributes toward our evolution. No matter what approach one decides upon, the
keys to successful meditation practice are sincerity and consistency.

Meditation is the simplest and yet the most challenging undertaking. The
practitioner may begin to access transcendent states at the very onset of their
practice, or they may progressively move in that direction over time. We
may start out with wonderful insights and enthusiasm to match. But is it not
uncommon, as one's meditation practice continues, for the results to become
increasingly subtle and take longer to become apparent. Meditators may get
discouraged and give up, just when they are on the edge of a breakthrough.
Maintaining a meditation practice requires both commitment and detachment
from the fruits of our actions. The Mother says that we require unlimited
amounts of perseverance for our inner development. We have to

above all never lose patience or courage. If necessary, repeat the same thing a thousand times, knowing that perhaps the thousandth time you will realise the result.[10]

This attitude is a fruit of wisdom essential for our inner development as well as for our path of psychological growth. We will undoubtedly encounter challenges and obstacles along the way, but the shift to an inner focus which comes from regular meditation practice will eventually lead us to greater self-awareness, compassion, and emergence of many more qualities and a higher, more subtle consciousness.

Meditation incites many people to make changes in their lives as they seek to transform and align to the insights and qualities that naturally emerge from their sustained practice.

> Just as fasting from food helps detoxify the body, so fasting from impressions detoxifies the mind. Once the intake of impressions ceases, consciousness, whose nature is space, will naturally empty itself out. Its contents will come up to the level of the intelligence which can then digest them properly. This requires deep thinking, inquiry and meditation. When the outer mind and senses are calm and quiet, our inner thoughts arise. Deep-seated habits and memories float to the surface. If we learn to observe and understand them, we can let them go, but this requires that we are willing to be free from them.[11]

Meditation is an experience beyond words, beyond the physical and personal realities. Meditation helps us develop detachment and puts things into perspective through bringing about insight into aspects of reality not normally accessible in daily life. Meditation focuses on going beyond the self. As Urbanowski notes,

> A common focus of meditation practice is to transcend the ego, a state of ego-lessness. For an individual with a solid ego structure this can be a liberating experience with associated bliss, a feeling of oneness with the entire universe, and the perception of a profound spiritual experience in which they may feel a deep emptiness and disintegration of whatever fragment of a self had existed.[12]

Mindfulness Meditation

Mindfulness is the most popular type of meditation technique in the West. This is the case for many reasons. Stemming from Buddhism, mindfulness is the practice of cultivating continual awareness of the present moment. It can be taught and practiced in a religiously or spiritually neutral context.

Many forms of meditation seek to dissociate from our negative emotions and traumatic experiences, whereas mindfulness seeks to help us associate with and walk through the causes of our suffering. It helps to build fearlessness and inner stability that can help us face and work through our suffering. Mindfulness is particularly effective in giving us the ability for compassionate self-observation.

Meditation as a Therapeutic Tool

A true meditation technique strips one of what is no longer useful in order to enrich the essential, it brings problems to life.[13]

Meditation, by providing us with a stable base and objectivity, helps us to work with difficult and emotionally charged issues. It can bring out material from the subconscious and give us the means to process it in the therapeutic setting. Overall, it helps us overcome disturbances or difficulties and find balance, greater insight, and mastery over our emotions, weaknesses, and impulses.

In a therapeutic context, it is useful to know about the various meditation techniques in order to understand what may be helping or hurting our clients and what techniques may be used to complement their psychotherapy. Suggesting any spiritual activity to clients is delicate. When clients express an interest in taking up a meditation practice, I try to provide an impartial view and help them discover a range of techniques, making sure they are given information and feel free to choose what seems best suited to their search.

A Word of Caution

In clients presenting pathologies occurring at the most basic levels of development, meditation is not advised and can even be dangerous because the sense of self is not well-defined enough to handle any technique that leads to subtle awareness or transcendence. As we begin to deal with pathologies occurring at the level of mind, advising simple meditative techniques such as watching the breath or focusing in the *hara* to develop grounding can build objectivity that can help clients stabilize their emotions, move away from negative self-talk, and reexamine and modify destructive attitudes and their corresponding behaviors. As we move up into higher levels of mind development, we can start to work with many forms of meditation while making sure to have adequate safeguard against cultic identification.

When dealing with matters of the higher mind, where the higher awareness is intact but there are developmental gaps in the lower centers (a heightened state of mental awareness with lack of development at the emotional and body levels), meditation can be used, but with caution. In these cases, it is best to do some bodywork and work on core emotions before moving into more subtle ways of working, such as meditation.

Meditation can bring to the surface inherent weaknesses and psychological issues but not provide support for dealing with them. This can lead to spiritual difficulties such as spiritual emergency and spiritual bypass. Meditation, in order to be balanced, must address all levels of life. It is not enough to just escape into an inner bliss, leaving relationships and finances in a bind. The meditative path conveyed in Patanjali's Yoga Sutras begins with a path of purification, balancing, and strengthening of the outer life and the body; it then moves inward and finally upward into the higher spiritual consciousness. This implies that even though the ultimate goal and potential of meditation is transcendence, we do not start there. We must first prepare the terrain.

It is only when we get to the level of the intuitive mind, where the client has a good level of integration and awareness, that we can start to employ more advanced meditation techniques. It may also be good practice, at this point, to continue working toward integrating early life experiences and deep-seated attitudes, emotions, and beliefs through uncovering techniques such as contemplation and breathwork. While a daily practice of somewhere between fifteen minutes to one hour of meditation can be beneficial in clients with psychopathologies, longer periods can actually reinforce the imbalances by increasing the concentration when the self is not sufficiently structured or balanced. In other words, improving the concentration accentuates whatever is going on in our psyche. If that is negative, intensive meditation practice can increase our suffering and pathologies.

Meditation is immeasurably enriching for both psychological and spiritual development. Its benefits are the topics of many studies, including scientific research on the effects on the brain, mental health, concentration, lifestyle improvement, and spiritual development of regular, long-term meditators. It is both the most simple and complex undertaking leading to self-understanding, development of higher qualities, deep insights, and finally, a transformation of consciousness—a shift in the axis of consciousness at our core.

WHICH TYPE OF TECHNIQUE OR INTERVENTION AND WHEN?

With all of these techniques in my toolbox, how do I choose which one to use and when? My approach consists of tools, an experience of the workaday world, and the insights and intuition that are the fruits of my psycho-spiritual explorations.

Over time, I have been able to develop a fluid and seamless approach that includes the techniques shared in this chapter with an underlying aspiration to address the whole person in all of their experiences and dimensions. The first and foremost decision-makers are the client's cues. The choice of technique is not technical. It is about taking in multiple factors such as the client's nature and worldview, their relationship to themselves in terms of self-knowledge, self-acceptance, how developed the relationship with the client is, and the blockage or issue they are presenting with. After nearly thirty years of experience accompanying people in therapy, there is undoubtedly a strong cognitive element in the decision of how to accompany and work with the issues being presented in session. At the same time, intuition plays a strong part. The difference is simple. Intuition provides content and information that is not accessible by normal means.

Having been blessed with a strong capacity for empathy, over these incredibly rich years, my intuition developed into something quite finely tuned. Where intuition or any spiritual power is concerned, humility is essential for keeping us on track. I always express what I sense and never insist that I am right. In addition, for many years, I consistently cross-checked my intuitive insights with the people concerned and intuitive friends in order to learn to distinguish between intuition and the various ideas and images that can cross our minds that are nothing more than wishful thinking or delirium. In fact, when one is willing to listen in, it becomes possible to cross-check with oneself and with our clients until it becomes a finely tuned instrument. Intuition should always be expressed gently and respectfully. I am careful not to tell clients, "I intuitively feel that . . . " because this could override their own belief or experience. With time and with practice, intuition becomes a most wonderful guide for helping others. Intuition is nothing more than the ability to tune into subtle messages. These cannot be perceived by the outer senses but occur with increasing frequency and clarity through clearing up the excess baggage in our psyche and by paying attention and learning to distinguish and interpret it accurately. Intuition is accessible to everyone. Intuition knows no boundaries. It is very useful in the online consultations which I have been increasingly conducting. It also helps in seeing past all of the outer aspects of our clients and in seeing the core issues and the best means to address them.

Each of us has our own unique set of gifts, cognitive abilities, instinct, compassion, patience, empathy, and more subtle faculties of clair-resentience, clairaudience, and clairvoyance. Whatever we are equipped with, if we are sincere and keep our minds and hearts open, I am certain it will lead to beautifully enriching and healing relationships with our clients and our continual development and evolution in consciousness as psychotherapists.

CONCLUSION

Ever since I first came across Sri Aurobindo's work, my lifelong quest for universality has been fulfilled. It's been like having a map for my inner growth but also for my work as a psychotherapist. I have had opportunities to work with countless people, teach courses, facilitate seminars, and even apply Sri Aurobindo's theory toward designing a market research methodology.[14] I have transitioned from my long-time base in Paris to an international practice where I meet my clients on Skype and in person in India, the United States, and Europe.

The journey is immeasurably enriching both personally and professionally. It is a journey of continual discovery and unfolding in integral consciousness. The fruit of this journey fills my heart and soul with wonder, passion, and a desire to convey to my colleagues in the field of mental health, and to all seekers, a sense of our greater potential and the means and possibilities for our own personal growth that are unique to each of us and directly within our reach.

I hope that by inviting you, the reader, to share this wonderful journey of discovery with me, I can help you gain insights into your deepest inner nature and potential and a roadmap for your own personal evolution. I am convinced that through our psycho-spiritual development we can each find our way to walk toward and eventually merge with a greater consciousness, a greater way of being and perceiving that, in turn, enlightens our every thought, word, and action.

NOTES

1. Elliot R. Ingersoll and David M. Zeitler, *Integral Psychotherapy: Inside Out/ Outside In* (2010, NY: SUNY Series in Integral Theory), p. 218.

2. Jean-Yves Leloup, *Prendre Soin de l'Etre* (1999, Paris: Albin Michel, Kindle edition), p. 600 (author's translation and interpretation).

3. C.D. Yonge, *The Works of Philo, Complete and Unabridged* (1993, MA: Hendrickson Publishers), XLVI 134, p. 38.

4. Sri Aurobindo, "The Synthesis of Yoga," *The Complete Works of Sri Aurobindo* (1999, Pondicherry, India: Sri Aurobindo Ashram Press), Vols. 23–24, pp. 534–535.

5. Age-old yogic saying.

6. See, for example, Margot Borden and Prahalad Shekhawat, "Buddhism and Management" in *Spirituality and Business: Exploring Possibilities for a New Management Paradigm* (2009, Heidelberg, Germany: Springer).

7. http://www.emdr.com/general-information/what-is-emdr.html.

8. A.S. Dalal, *The Yoga of Sleep and Dreams* (2004, Pondicherry, India: Sri Aurobindo Ashram Press), p. xx.

9. Taken from researchee interview in Borden, M., "Counselling and Spirituality as Complementary Paths," Master's Thesis, University of Durham, UK (1997, unpublished).

10. The Mother, "Questions and Answers 1950–1951," *Collected Works of the Mother, 2nd ed.* (2003, Pondicherry: Sri Aurobindo Ashram Trust), Vol. 4, p. 95.

11. David Frawley, *Ayurveda and the Mind, The Healing of Consciousness* (1997, Wisconsin: Lotus Press), p. 175.

12. Ferris B. Urbanowski and John J. Miller, "Trauma, Psychotherapy and Meditation," *Journal of Transpersonal Psychology*. Vol. 28, No. 1 (1996), p. 44.

13. Bernard Fillaire, *Le Grand Décervelage: Enquete Pour Combattre Les Sectes* (1993, Paris: Plon) (author's translation with permission from publisher), p. 112.

14. Margot E. Borden, "Applying an Integral Perspective to Business Strategy: A Case Study," in S.S. Nandram and M.E. Borden, eds, Spirituality and Business: *Exploring Possibilities for a New Management Paradigm* (2009, Heidelberg, Germany: Springer), pp. 141–161.

References

Airault, Régis, *Les Fous de l'Inde, Délires d'Occidentaux et Sentiment Océanique*, (2002, Paris: Petite Edition Payot).

Akarta, Aki, "Nonduality and Western Seekers: Delights and Pitfalls of the Advaitic Path," *Gnosis*, (1996, Spring No. 39), pp. 16–24.

Assagioli, Roberto, *Transpersonal Development: The Dimension Beyond Psychosynthesis*, (2007, Forres: Inner Way Productions).

Assagioli, Roberto, *Transpersonal Development: The Dimension Beyond Psychosynthesis*, (1993, London: Aquarian Press).

Assagioli, Roberto, *The Act of Will: Self Actualization Through Psychosynthesis*, (1981, London: Aquarian Press).

Atalay, Bulent and Wamsley, Keith, *Leonardo's Universe: The Renaissance World of Leonardo da Vinci*, (2008, Washington: National Geographic).

Bahman, Shirazi, "Integral Psychology Metaphors and Processes of Personal Integration," in Cornelissen, Matthijs, Ed., *Consciousness and Its Transformation*, (2001, Pondicherry, India: SAICE).

Bhagavad Gita, Chapter VI, verse 47.

Bolle, Kees W., "Animism and Animatism", in Eliade, M., *The Encyclopedia of Religion*, (1987, New York: Macmillan, Vol. 1).

Borden, M.E., *Counselling and Spirituality as Complementary Paths*, (1997, unpublished Masters Thesis, University of Durham, UK).

Borden, M.E., and Shekhawat, P.S., "Buddhist Practice and Principles and their Place in Organization," in S.S. Nandram and M.E. Borden, eds., *Spirituality and Business: Exploring Possibilities for A New Management Paradigm*, (2009, Heidelberg, Germany: Springer).

Borden, M.E., Applying an Integral Perspective to Business Strategy: A Case Study in S.S. Nandram and M.E. Borden, eds., *Spirituality and Business: Exploring Possibilities for a New Management Paradigm*, (2009, Heidelberg, Germany: Springer)

Bragdon, Emma Ph.D., *The Call of Spiritual Emergency: From Personal Crisis to Personal Transformation*, (1990, San Francisco: Harper & Row).

Brown, Molly Young, *Unfolding Self: The Practice of Psychosynthesis*, (2004, New York: Allworth Press).

Burmeister, Alice, *A Touch of Healing*, Energizing Body, Mind and Spirit with Jin Shin Jyutsu, (1997, USA: Bantam).

Caplan, Mariana, *Halfway Up The Mountain: The Error of Premature Claims to Enlightenment*, (2014, Hohm Press, Kindle edition).

Carrière, Jean-Claude, *Dictionnaire Amoureux de l'Inde*, (2001, Paris: Editions Plon).

Chogyam, Trungpa, *The Sanity We Are Born With: A Buddhist Approach to Psychology*, (2005, Boston: Shambhala).

Cleary, Tom S. and Shapiro, Sam I., "The Plateau Experience and the Post-Mortem Life: Abraham H. Maslow's Unfinished Theory," *The Journal of Transpersonal Psychology*, (1995, Vol. 27, No.1), pp. 1–24.

Cornelissen Matthijs ed., *Consciousness and its Transformation*, (2000, Pondicherry, India: SAICE).

Cornelissen, Matthijs, "The Integration of Psychological Knowledge from the Spiritual Traditions into the Psychology Curriculum," *Journal of the Consciousness and Experiential Psychology*, (2000, Vol. 4).

Cortright, Brant, *Integral Psychology: Yoga, Growth, and Opening the Heart*, (2007, New York: Suny Series in Transpersonal and Humanistic Psychology).

Cortright, Brant, *Psychotherapy and Spirit: Theory and Practice in Transpersonal Psychotherapy*, (1997, New York: SUNY Press).

Dalai Lama, *In My Own Words*, (2009, New Delhi: Hay House).

Dalal, A.S., compiled, *The Psychic Being: It's Nature, Mission And Evolution*, (2010, Pondicherry, India: Sri Aurobindo Ashram Publications).

Dalal, A.S., compiled, *The Yoga Of Sleep And Dreams: The Night-School of Sadhana*, (2008, Pondicherry, India: Sri Aurobindo Ashram Publications).

Dalal, A.S., compiled, *Emergence of the Psychic*, (2003, Pondicherry, India: Sri Aurobindo Ashram Publications).

Dalal, A.S., compiled, *A Greater Psychology: An Introduction to the Psychological Thought of Sri Aurobindo*, (2001, Pondicherry, India: Sri Aurobindo Ashram Press).

Dalal, A.S., compiled, *The Powers Within*, (1999, Pondicherry, India: Sri Aurobindo Ashram Publications).

Dalal, A.S., compiled, *Psychology, Mental Health and Yoga: Essays on Sri Aurobindo's Psychological Thought, Implications of Yoga for Mental Health*, (2012, Pondicherry, India: Auroshakti Foundation for the Institute of Integral Yoga Psychology).

Dalal, A.S., compiled, *Psychology, Mental Health and Yoga*, (1996, Pondicherry, India: Sri Aurobindo Ashram Publications).

Dalal, A.S., compiled, *Growing Within: The Psychology of Inner Development*, (1995, Pondicherry, India: Sri Aurobindo Ashram Publications).

Dalal, A.S., compiled, *Looking from Within*, (1995, Pondicherry, India: Sri Aurobindo Ashram Publications).

Dalal, A.S., compiled, *Living Within: The Yoga Approach to Psychological Health and Growth*, (1994, Pondicherry, India: Sri Aurobindo Ashram Publications).

Dürckheim, Karlfried Graf, *The Call for the Master: The Meaning of Spiritual Guidance on the Way to the Self*, (1975, New York: Dutton/Penguin).

Edwin, Bryant, *The Yoga Sutras of Patañjali: A New Edition, Translation, and Commentary* (2015, New York: North Point Press).

Eliade, Mircea, *Shamanism: Archaic Techniques of Ecstasy*, (1951, New Jersey: Princeton Press).

Ellis, Albert, *Overcoming Destructive Beliefs, Feelings and Behaviors: New Directions for Rational Emotive Therapy*, (2001, Amherst: Prometheus Books).

Fadul, Jose, A., General Editor, *Encyclopedia of Theory & Practice in Psychotherapy & Counseling*, (2015, London: Lulu Press).

Ferrer, Jorge N., "Integral Transformative Practice: A Participatory Perspective," The *Journal of Transpersonal Psychology*, (2003, Vol. 35, No. 1).

Feuerstein, Georg, *The Yoga-Sutra of Patañjali: A New Translation and Commentary* (1989, Vermont: Inner Traditions).

Fillaire, Bernard, *Le Grand Décervelage: Enquete Pour Combattre Les Sectes*, (1993, Paris: Plon).

Forman, Mark, *A Guide to Integral Psychotherapy: Complexity, Integration, and Spirituality in Practice*, (2010, New York: SUNY Press).

Frawley, David, *Beyond the Mind*, (1992, Delhi: Sri Satguru Publications).

Frawley, David, *Ayurveda and the Mind, The Healing of Consciousness*, (1997, Wisconsin, USA: Lotus Press).

Freud, S., *The Future of an Illusion*, (1927c), (2011, Create Space Independent Publishing Platform).

From Pink Floyd, (1994) "What do you Want From Me." Song by: David Gilmour/ Richard Wright/Polly Samson; Lyrics by Orrall, Robert Ellis/Wright, Curtis. 1994.

Gandhi, M.K., "What is God?" in *The Essence of Hinduism*, (1987, Ahmedabad: Navajivan Publishing House).

Gifford-May, Derek and Thompson, Norman L., "Deep States of Meditation: Phenomenological Reports of Experience," *The Journal of Transpersonal Psychology*, (1994, Vol. 2, No. 26), pp. 117–139.

Giorgi, Amedeo, *Phenomenology and Psychological Research*, (1985, Pittsburgh: Duquesne University).

Goleman, Daniel, *The Varieties of Meditative Experience*, (1977, London: Rider and Company).

Grof, Christina and Grof, Stanislav, "Forms of Spiritual Emergency" in *Spiritual Emergency Network Newsletter*, (1985).

Grof, Stanislav, *The Cosmic Game: Explorations of the Frontiers of Human Consciousness*, (1998, New York: SUNY Press).

Grof, Stanislav, "Physical Manifestations of Emotional Disorders Observations from the Study of Non-Ordinary States of Consciousness," *The Inner Door*, 9(2) 1, 7–9, 12, May 1997, Copyright c 2003 by Association for Holotropic Breathwork International from Taylor, K. [Ed.] *Exploring Holotropic Breathwork: Selected Articles for a Decade of The Inner Door,* in *The Healing Breath, A Journal of Breathwork Practice, Psychology and Spirituality*, (Vol. 5, No. 1), pp. 257–278.

Grof, Stanislav, M.D., *The Adventure of Self-Discovery*, (1988, New York: SUNY Press).

Halevi, Z'Ev Ben Shimon, *Psychology and Kabbalah*. (1992, New York: Samuel Weiser).

Heisig, J., "Psychology of Religion" in Eliade, M. *Encyclopedia of Religion*, (1987, New York: Macmillan, Vol. 12).

Howard, Louise, *Buddhism for Sheep*, (1996, London: Ebury Press).

Hsu, Dr. Francis, *Clan, Caste, and Club: A Comparative Study of Chinese, Hindu, and American Ways of Life*, (1963, Princeton, New Jersey: Van Nostrand).

http://www.emdr.com/general-information/what-is-emdr.html

Hussain, Akbar, *Spirituality: The Hidden Dimensions Discovered*, (2002, New Delhi: PR Books).

Huxley, Aldous, *Perennial Philosophy*, (1994, London: Flamingo).

Ingersoll, Elliot R. and Zeitler David M., *Integral Psychotherapy: Inside Out/Outside In*, (2010, New York: Suny Series in Integral Theory).

Ingersoll, Elliot, "An Integral Approach for Teaching and Practicing Diagnosis," *Journal of Transpersonal Psychology*, (2002, Vol. 34, No. 2), pp. 115–127.

Jain, Girilal, "Assessing India's Progress," *The Times of India, Bombay* (15 August 1986) in Gandhi, M.K., ed., *The Essence of Hinduism*, (1987, Ahmedabad: Navajivan Publishing House).

James, William, *The Principles of Psychology*. (1983, Cambridge, MA: Harvard University Press).

James, William, *Varieties of Religious Experience*, (1982, USA: Penguin).

Jung, Carl G., "Jung and Eastern Thought," in Jung, C.G. (1948) The Concept of Libido, in *Symbols of Transformation*, Complete Works, (2000, New Jersey: Princeton University Press, Vol. 5).

Jung, Carl G., *The Psychology of Kundalini Yoga*, in Sonu Shamdasani, ed. Notes of the seminar given in 1932 by C.G. Jung, (1996, Bollingen Series, Princeton University Press, New Jersey).

Karen Horney, *The Problem of Feminine Masochism*, Psychoanalytic. Review, (July 1935, Vol. xxii).

Kirkland, Russel, *Taoism: The Enduring Tradition*, (2004, New York: Routledge).

Krishna, Gopi, *The Awakening of Kundalini*, (1975, New York: Dutton).

Lao Tzu, trans. D.C. Lau, *Tao Te Ching*, (1963, New York: Penguin Books).

Leloup, Jean-Yves, *Prendre Soin de l'Être*, (1999, Paris: Albin Michel).

Lesko, Leonard H., "Egyptian Religion: An Overview in Eliade," M., *The Encyclopedia of Religion*, (1987, New York: Macmillan, Vol. 5).

Maharishi Mahesh Yogi, *The Science of Being and the Art of Living*, (1969, Los Angeles: SRM Publications).

Maslow, Abraham H., *The Farther Reaches of Human Nature*, (1976, London: Penguin).

Maslow, Abraham H., *Religions, Values and Peak Experiences*, (1970, New York: Viking Penguin).

May, Rollo, *Love and Will*, (1969, New York: Norton & Co.).

May, Rollo, *The Meaning of Anxiety*, (1967, New York: Norton & Co.).

Michel Odoul, *Dis-moi Où tu as Mal, Je te Dirai Pourquoi*, (2002, Paris: Albin Michel).

Miller, J., "The Unveiling of Traumatic Memories and Emotions Through Mindfulness and Concentration Meditation: Clinical Implications and three case reports," *The Journal of Transpersonal Psychology*, (1993, Vol. 25), pp. 169–180.

Miovic, M., "Sri Aurobindo and Transpersonal Psychology," *The Journal of Transpersonal Psychology*, (2004, Vol. 36, No. 2), pp. 111–133.

Moustakas, Clark, *Phenomenological Research Methods*, (1994, London: Sage).

Murphy, George and Murphy Lois, *Asian Psychology*, (1968, New York: Basic Books).

Nandram, S. & Borden, M.E., *Spirituality and Business: Exploring Possibilities for a New Management Paradigm*, (2009, Heidelberg: Springer).

Naranjo, Claudio and Ornstein, Robert E., *On the Psychology of Meditation*, (1971, New York: Viking).

Nation, Ihla F., "Face to Face: Confronting the Guru-Disciple Relationship," *Gnosis*, (1996, Spring, No. 39), pp. 27–32.

Orr, Leonard, *Rebirthing in the New Age*, (1980, California: Celestial Arts).

Ouspensky, P.D., *The Psychology of Man's Possible Evolution*, (1950, New York: Hedgehog Press).

Paramahamsa Hariharananda, *Nectar Drops*, Swami Prajnanananda Giri, compiled, (1996, Vienna: Kriya Yoga Press).

Paramahansa Yogananda, *Autobiography of a Yogi*, 11th ed., (1971, Los Angeles: Self-Realization Fellowship).

Pedersen, Paul B., Draguns, Juris G., Lonner, Walter J., and Trimble, Joseph E., eds, 4th ed., *Counseling Across Cultures*, (1995, Thousand Oaks: Sage Publishing).

Ram Dass and Gorman, Paul, *How Can I Help?* (1985, London: Knopf).

Ram Dass and Goleman, Daniel, "Truth and Transformation in Psychological and Spiritual Paths," *Journal of Transpersonal Psychology*, (1985, Vol. 17, No. 2), pp. 183–214.

Reddy, V. Madhusudhan, *Values and Value Theories in the Light of Sri Aurobindo*. (1973, Hyderabad, India: Institute of Human Study).

Rogers, Carl R., *On Becoming a Person: A Psychotherapist's View of Psychotherapy*, (1961, Boston: Houghton Mifflin).

Rogers, Carl R., *A Way of Being*, (1980, Boston: Houghton Mifflin).

Rowan, John, *The Transpersonal: Psychotherapy and Counselling*, (1993, London: Routledge).

Rowan, John, *Ordinary Ecstasy: Humanistic Psychology in Action*, (1976, London: Routledge).

Rangaswami, Sudhakshina, *The Roots of Vedanta: Selections from Sankara's Writings*, (2012, India: Penguin, kindle edition).

Sardesai, D.R., *India: The Definitive History*, (2008, USA: Westview).

Scotton, Bruce W., Chinen, Allen B., and Battista, John R., *Textbook of Transpersonal Psychiatry and Psychology*, (2009, New York: Basic Books).

Sen, Indra, *Integral Psychology: The Psychological System of Sri Aurobindo*. (1986, Pondicherry, India: Sri Aurobindo Ashram Trust).

Sen, Indra, "The Indian Approach to Psychology," in Chaudhuri, H. and Spiegelberg, F. (Eds.), *The Integral Philosophy of Sri Aurobindo*, (1960, San Francisco: Cultural Integration Fellowship).

Shirazi, Bahman, "Integral psychology, metaphors and processes of personal integration," Cornelissen, Matthijs ed. *Consciousness and Its Transformation*, (2001, Pondicherry: Papers Presented at the Second International Conference on Integral Psychology).

Shunryu, Suzuki, *Zen Mind, Beginner's Mind*, (2011, Boston: Shambhala).

Sinha, Jadunath, *Indian Psychology Volume I: Cognition*, (1958, Delhi: Motilal Banarsidas).

Sinha, Jadunath, *Indian Psychology Volume II: Emotion and Will*, (1961, Delhi: Motilal Banarsidas).

Sinha, Jadunath, *Indian Psychology Volume III: Epistomology of Perception*, (1969, Delhi: Motilal Banarsidas).

Smith, John E., "Philosophy and Religion," Eliade, M. *The Encyclopedia of Religion*, (1987, New York: Macmillan, Vol. 11).

Sri Aurobindo, "Letters on Yoga IV: Transformation of Human Nature in the Integral Yoga," *The Complete Works of Sri Aurobindo*, (2014, Pondicherry, India: Sri Aurobindo Ashram Publication Department, Vol. 31).

Sri Aurobindo, "Letters on Yoga I," *The Complete Works of Sri Aurobindo*, (2013, Pondicherry, India: Sri Aurobindo Ashram Press), Vol. 28.

Sri Aurobindo, "Hymns to the Mystic Fire," *The Complete Works of Sri Aurobindo*, (2013, Pondicherry, India: Sri Aurobindo Ashram Press), Vol. 16.

Sri Aurobindo, "Letters on Himself and the Ashram," *The Complete Works of Sri Aurobindo*, (2011, Pondicherry, India: Sri Aurobindo Ashram Trust), Vol. 35.

Sri Aurobindo, "Kena and Other Upanishads," *The Complete Works of Sri Aurobindo*, (2001, Pondicherry, India: Sri Aurobindo Ashram Trust), Vol. 18.

Sri Aurobindo, "Synthesis of Yoga," *The Complete Works of Sri Aurobindo*, (1999, Pondicherry, India: Sri Aurobindo Ashram Trust,) Vol. 23–24.

Sri Aurobindo, "The Secret of the Veda," *The Complete Works of Sri Aurobindo*, (1998, Pondicherry, India: Sri Aurobindo Ashram Press) Vol. 15.

Sri Aurobindo, *Essays on the Gita*, The Complete Works of Sri Aurobindo, (1997, Pondicherry, India: Sri Aurobindo Ashram Publication Department).

Sri Aurobindo, *The Life Divine*, (1982, Pondicherry, India: Sri Aurobindo Ashram Press).

Sri Aurobindo, *Letters on Yoga*, (1972, Pondicherry, India: Sri Aurobindo Ashram Press).

Sri Aurobindo, *The Upanishads*, Sri Aurobindo Birth Centenary Library, (1972, Pondicherry, India: Sri Aurobindo Ashram, Vol. 12).

Sri Aurobindo, *Secret of the Veda*, (1971, Pondicherry, India: Sri Aurobindo Ashram Press).

Sri Aurobindo, *Hymns to the Mystic Fire*, (1971, Pondicherry, India: Sri Aurobindo Ashram).

Sri Aurobindo, *Essays on the Gita*, (1970, Pondicherry, India: Sri Aurobindo Ashram Press).

Svoboda, Robert, *The Greatness of Saturn: A Therapeutic Myth*, (1997, Wisconsin, USA: Lotus Press).

Tart, Charles Ph.D. *Open Mind, Discriminating Mind: Reflections on Human Possibilities*, (1989, New York: Harper & Row).

Thapar, Romila, *The Penguin Early History of India: From the Origins to AD 1300*, (2002, Penguin, Kindle ed.).

The Mother, "Questions and Answers 1950–1951," *Collected Works of the Mother*, *2nd ed.* (2003, Pondicherry: Sri Aurobindo Ashram Trust, Vol. 4), p. 95.

The Mother, *Collected Works of the Mother*, (1997, Pondicherry, India: Sri Aurobindo Ashram).

Tobert, Natalie, *Spiritual Psychiatries*, (2014, Kindle ed.).

Trungpa, Chogyam, *The Sanity We Are Born With: A Buddhist Approach to Psychology*, (2005, Boston: Shambhala).

Tyberg, Judith, "The Drama of Integral Self-Realization; The Spiritual Message of Savitri," in Chaudhuri, Haridas and Spiegelberg, Frederic eds., *The Integral Philosophy of Sri Aurobindo: A Commemorative Symposium*, (1960, London: George Allen & Unwin).

Urbanowski, Ferris B. and Miller, John J. "Trauma, Psychotherapy and Meditation," *The Journal of Transpersonal Psychology*, (1996, Vol. 28, No. 1), pp. 31–48.

VanderKooi, Lois, "Buddhist Teachers' Experience with Extreme Mental States in Western Meditators," *Journal of Transpersonal Psychology*, (1997, Vol. 29, No. 1), pp. 31–46.

Vaughan, Frances, "Healing and Wholeness: Transpersonal Psychotherapy." In Walsh, R., and Vaughan, F., *Paths Beyond Ego*, (1993, New York: Tarcher/Putnam).

Vaughan, Frances, "Spiritual Issues in Psychotherapy," *The Journal of Transpersonal Psychology*, (1991, Vol. 23, No. 2), pp. 105–119.

Vaughan, Frances, *The Inward Arc: Healing and Wholeness in Psychotherapy and Spirituality*, (1986, Boston: Shambhala).

Vigne, Jacques, "Psychological Mechanisms of Meditation: Meditation and Mental Health," *Indian Journal of Clinical Psychology*, (1997, Vol. 24, No. 1), pp. 46–51.

Vigne, Jacques, "Guru and Psychotherapist: Comparisons from the Hindu Tradition", *The Journal of Transpersonal Psychology*, (1991, Vol. 23, No.2), pp. 121–138.

Vrinte, Joseph, *Perennial Quest for a Psychology with a Soul: An Inquiry into the Relevance of Sri Aurobindo's Metaphysical Yoga Psychology in the Context of Ken Wilber's Integral Psychology*, (2005, Mumbai: Motilal Banarsidass).

Weiss, Brian, *Many Lives, Many Masters*, (1988, Ontario, Canada: Fireside).

Welwood, John, *Journey of the Heart: The Path of Conscious Love*, (1996, New York: Harper Perennial).

Welwood, John, *Perfect Love, Imperfect Relationships: Healing the Wound of the Heart* (2007, South Africa: Trumpeter).

Whitmore, Diana, *Psychosynthesis Counselling in Action*, (1991, London: Sage).

Wilber, Ken, Patten, Terry, Leonard, Adam and Morelli, Marco, *Integral Life Practice: A 21st-Century Blueprint for Physical Health, Emotional Balance, Mental Clarity, and Spiritual Awakening*, (2008, Boston: Integral Books).

Wilber, Ken, *A Theory of Everything*, (2000, Boston: Shambhala)

Wilber, Ken, *Integral Psychology: Consciousness, Spirit, Psychology, Therapy*, (2000, Boston: Shambhala).

Wilber, Ken, *The Eye of the Spirit: An Integral Vision for a World Gone Slightly Mad*, (2001, Boston: Shambhala).

Wilber, Ken, "The Developmental Spectrum and Psychopathology: Part I Stages and Types of Pathology," *The Journal of Transpersonal Psychology*, (1984, Vol. 16, No. 1), pp. 75–118.

Wilber, Ken, "The Developmental Spectrum and Psychopathology: Part II Treatment Modalities", *The Journal of Transpersonal Psychology*, (1984, Vol. 16, No. 2), pp. 75–166.

Wilber, Ken, *The Spectrum of Consciousness*, (1993, Wheaton, IL: Theosophical Publishing House).

Wilber, Ken, *Grace and Grit*, (1991, Boston: Shambhala).

Wilber, Ken, *Eye to Eye: The Quest for the New Paradigm*, (1990, Dorset: Shambhala).

Wilber, Ken, Engler, Jack, and Brown, Daniel, *Transformations of Consciousness: Conventional and Contemplative Perspectives on Development*, (1986, Boston: Shambhala).

Wilhelm, R., trans., *The I Ching, or Book of Changes*, transl. Richard Wilhelm, 2nd ed. (1966, New York: Bollingen Foundation), p. liii.

Wilson, Colin, *New Pathways in Psychology: Maslow and the Post Freudian Revolution*, (1972, New York, Toplinger).

Wittine, Bryan, "Book Review: Sex, Ecology and Spirituality: The Spirit of Evolution," *The Journal of Transpersonal Psychology*, (January, 1996).

www.integralnaked.org

Index

abreaction (*see* catharsis)

abuse 107, (in vignette, 79, 200, 203), (of power, 113), (substance, 73), (toward oneself, 81)

acceptance 53, 140, 152, 158, 201, 214, (self-acceptance, 147, 148, 221, 238), (mindfulness, 218), (person-centered approach, 29)

acupuncture 180

addiction 52, 106, 107

Adi Shankara/Adi Shankaracharya xxx, 66, 139, 177

Adler, Alfred 10–11, 15, 34

adverse forces 108, (possession, 109), (vignette, 204)

ahamkara 67

almighty syndrome 155, (vignette, 155)

American Psychological Association (APA) 7

analytical psychology 9, 14

anger 210, (gestalt therapy, 226), (Jin Shin Jyutsu, 229), (mindfulness, 218), (Taoism, 85), (Tibetan Buddhism, 80), (Sri Aurobindo, 99, 106, 109), (vignettes, 28, 38, 172, 220–221)

animatism xxix, 2

animism xxix, 2, 7

antidepressants 23, (vignette, 21), (and treatment of PTSD, 23)

anxiety (Aurobindo, 105), (Buddhism, 78), Jin Shin Jyutsu, 228–229), (medical model, 20–21), (mindfulness, 218), (Rollo May, 29, 33–34), (vignettes, 19, 37, 198, 209, 221, 229)

anxiolytics 23

AQAL model (all quadrants-all levels) 121–122, 126, 127, 128, 131

archetypes 9–10, 48, 201

Aristotle xxx, 4, 118

Assagioli, Roberto 42, 47–50, 156

Association for Humanistic Psychology 41

Association for Transpersonal Psychology 41, 52

Atman 50, 67, 69, 76

attention deficit disorder (ADD, ADHD) 22

authenticity 53, 81, 163, 164, (authentic self, 175–176), (vignette, 29, 226)

autonomy 168, 177, 181, 208, 209, 222, (medical model, 20), (vignette, 21, 30, 178)

ayurveda xxix, 73, 192, 212, 230

Bacon, Roger 6

Bahá'í xxxi

Bandura, Albert 17

Basu, Dr. Soumitra 108, 112, 194
Beck, Aaron xxxi, 17
Beck, Don 120, 131
behaviorism xxxi, 16, 19–20, 33,
    37, 39, 56, 57, 74, 133, 186, 208,
    (interventions, 186, 208, 222),
    (limitations of, 17–19)
bellybuttonism (self-centeredness) 40
Bhagavad Gita xxx, 61, 62, 68–69, 71,
    95, 100
bhakti xxx, (devotion, 60, 62, 68, 71,
    95, 103, 140), (yoga, 62, 68, 95,
    99–100)
bodywork 50, 180, 237
boundaries 99, 177, 187, 229, (vignette,
    225–226)
buddhi 67, 69
bulimia (in vignette) 37
breathwork xxii, xxiii, xxiv, 1, 50,
    51, 53, 54, 149, 180, 182, 185,
    193, 201, 208, 210–217, 222, 225,
    230, 231, 237, (in vignettes, 14,
    28–30, 79, 85, 127–128, 152–153,
    172–173, 178, 182, 194, 200, 214,
    215–216)
Buddhism xxx, 22, 60, 63, 76–82, 82,
    119, 141, 156, 158, 217, 235
Buddhist philosophy (*see* Buddhism)

California Institute of Integral Studies
    (CIIS) 111
catharsis xxiii, 152, 184, 191, 212, 217,
    (in vignette, 28, 214)
cellular/muscular memory
    (*see* samskara)
Chardin, Teilhard de 131
Chaudhari, Haridas 111–112
chi 210
chitta 67, 71, 71
Christianity xxx, 3, 6, 61, 75, 119
cognitive-behavioral therapy (CBT)
    xxxi, 20, 138, (limitations,
    17–19), (interventions, 222), (in
    vignette, 29)
collective unconscious 9, 48–50

compassion xxii, 43, 53, 76, 80, 81,
    84, 108, 144, 158, 168, 176,
    185, 188, 235, 236, 238, (in
    vignette, 30, 167)
Confucianism 78, 82, 83–84
congruence (state) xv, 5, 37, 49,
    57, 124, 132, 133, 134, 135, 141,
    142, 147, 148, 150, 173–174,
    176, 181, 197, 208, 209, 232,
    (in vignette, 28, 200, 204),
    (incongruence, 108, 147, 178, 181,
    213, 222)
consciousness—altered state, evolution
    in 53, 54, 126, 133
Coomaraswamy, Rama 68
Cortright, Dr. Brant 9, 42, 111, 112
Cowan, Chris 120

Dalai Lama 81
Dalal, A.S. 14, 105, 112, 113
dark night of the soul 180
da Vinci, Leonardo 6, 171
defense mechanisms 86, 105, 155,
    157, 171, 189, 190, 196, 208, 219,
    (Aurobindo, 105), (Freud, 8, 14),
    (May, 36)
depression 74, 192, 212, (behaviorism,
    17), (Jung, 10), (Jin Shin Jyutsu,
    229), (medical model, 7, 20, 21, 23),
    (mindfulness, 218), (Sri Aurobindo,
    105–106), (in vignette, 19, 21,
    28–29, 172)
depth psychology 10, 14
detachment 11, 37, 146, 152–153,
    176, 219, (meditation, 234–235), (in
    vignette, 152–143)
developmental psychology 15, 92, 95,
    122, (and integral psychotherapy,
    122–124)
devotion (*see* bhakti yoga)
dharma 62, 63, 78, 146, 147
diagnosis 20, 39, 43, 51, 72, 139, 149,
    191, 228, (Sri Aurobindo, 104–108),
    (Wilber, 130), (in vignette, 109–110,
    194–204)

discernment xxiii, 67, 68, 113, 132, 154, 158, 166, 168, 168, 177, 178, 202, 203, 211, (lack of, 154, 157, 211)

discrimination (*see* discernment)

dissociation 14, 127, 149, 152, 201, 227, (in vignette, 14, 26, 152–153, 172, 225)

dreamwork xxiv, 8, 9, 10, 50, 53, 93, 183, 192, 224–226, (in vignette, 225–226)

DSM xxxi, 13, 20, 39, 52, 180, 193

Dürckheim, Karlfried Graf 165

Eliade, Mircea 2, 44, 74

Ellis, Albert 17

empathy 37, 179, 188, 209, 238, (in vignette, 25–27)

empowerment 20, 35, 38, 86, 130, 176, 208, 213, 218, 222, (in vignette, 226)

EMDR 23, 223–224, (in vignette, 224)

Essenes xxx, 5, 210

ethics 83, 87, 121, 154, 178, 179–180, 183, 233, (in vignette, 28–230)

expansionism/expansionist xxiv, 20, 25, 33, 35, 42, 47, 56, 138

family constellation 192, 231–232

fear 11, 13, 37, 56, 70, 81, 85, 99, 106, 109, 127, 170, 172, 175, 196, 200, 203, 229, (in vignette, 14, 28, 35, 38, 39, 124–125, 172–173, 221, 224, 235)

feminism 10, 11, 15

Ferrer, Jorge 127

Findhorn flower essences (*see* flower and plant essences)

Findhorn Foundation xxii–xxiii

flower and plant essences 73, 192, 228, (Auroville flower essences, 228), (Bach Flower Remedies, 228, (in vignette, 200–201), (Australian Bush Remedies, 228)

Forman, Mark 123–127, 131

fragmentation (defragmentation, 212), (of the psyche, 173)

Freud, Sigmund xxvii, xxxi, 8–9, 10, 11, 12, 13, 14, 15, 45, 47, (in vignette, 27)

Galen (Claudius Galenus) 5

Galileo 6

Gebser, Jean 131

gestalt therapy 53, 180, 192, 226–227, 232, (in vignette, 28–30, 172, 200)

Gnostics xxx, 5

Graves, Clare 120

great chain of being (*see* great nest of being)

great nest of being 118–119, 120, 190

Griffiths, Bede 127

grihastha 150

Grof, Stanislav 41, 50–52, 54, 211, (perinatal matrices, 50)

grounding 7, 51, 94, 127, 187, 236, (in vignette, 109–110, 204)

guided imagery 170, 226–227

guru 47, 73, 96, 100, (guru-disciple relationship, 63, 167–168), (false or pseudo, 154, 168)

Guru Nanak xxx

Harappan civilization xxix, 61

HeartMath Institute 212

Hermeticism xxx, 120

Hinduism xxix, xxx, 3, 59, 60–63, 71, 74–75, 76, 119, 148, 150, (in the West, 74–75)

Hippocrates 5

hoarding (in vignette) 124

holistic integration (*see* integral life practice)

holotropic breathwork 50–51, 53, 211

Horney, Karen 11, 15

humanistic psychology xxiv, xxxi, 9, 11, 13, 15, 33–41, 53, 55, 75, 82, 117, 137, 138, 147, 185, 191, 210, (in vignette, 34, 37, 38, 39)

humility 84, 113, 166, 168, 175, 176, 177, 178–179, 233, 238, (in vignette, 233)

hygiène de vie (*see* life hygiene)
hypnagogic state 225

id 8, 12
I Ching 82–83
individual psychology 10, 14
individuation 9, 45, 46, 48,
    125–126, 222
Indus Valley civilization (*see* Harappan
    civilization)
Industrial Revolution 6
Ingersoll, Elliot 130, 131
Institute of Transpersonal Psychology
    (*see* Sophia University)
intake interview 187
integral (definition) 142, 163, (Sri
    Aurobindo, 143), (Ken Wilber, 143)
integral psychology xxv, xxvi, xxviii,
    9, 14, 15–16, 19, 24, 52, 53, 60, 87,
    92–95, 99, 111, 113, 117, 135, 138,
    140, 143, 145, 159, 183, 185–205,
    207, 208, (Sri Aurobindo, 92–95),
    (Sen, 111), (Wilber, 117–136),
    (dangers, 151)
integral life practice 173, (integral
    transformative practice, 126–128),
    (holistic integration, 126, 127)
integral transformative practice (ITP)
    (*see* integral life practice)
integral yoga 91, 95–101, 111, 143
integral yoga psychology (*see* integral
    psychology)
integral psychotherapy (*see* integral
    psychology)
integration (as therapeutic goal) 148–149
integrative/eclectic psychology 186
intuition 24, 30, 39, 42, 46, 49, 63, 100,
    121, 122, 126, 127, 138, 152, 156,
    163, 167, 177, 179, 187, 188, 207,
    208, 225, 227, 228, 237, 238, (in
    vignette, 172, 203)
Islam xxx, 3, 6, 60

Jainism xxx, 63, 75–76
James, William xxxi, 44–45, 117

Jin Shin Jyutsu 193, 228–229,
    (in vignette, 85)
Jnan Yoga 62, 68, 96, 98–99
journaling 50, 222–223 (in
    vignette 29)
Judaism xxix, 3, 5, 6, (mystical, 153)
Jung, Carl xxxi, 10–11, 14, 15, 44,
    45–47, 48, 74, 75, 117, 123, 133,
    134, 168

Kabat-Zinn, Jon 217
Kabbalah 153, 179
karma 62–63, 70, 112, 168, 188,
    192, 201–203, (ancestral, 73, 202),
    (Buddhism, 76), (collective, 198,
    201), (Jainism, 75–76)
karma yoga 62, 68, 96–98
kriya yoga xxii, 69
kundalini experience, awakening, crisis
    (*see* spiritual emergency)

Laszlo, Ervin 131
Leonard, George 131
libido 12, (Freud, 8), (Jung, 9)
life hygiene 40, 164, 173–176
lovingkindness 29, 81
LSD (Maslow, 44), (Grof,
    50–52)

Mahabharata 68, 165
Maharishi Patanjali (Yoga Sutras) xxx,
    62, 69–71, 75, 152, 237
manas 67
mantra 62, 73, 175, 191, 203, 233
Maslow, Abraham 33, 34–35, 42, 44,
    117, 123, 178
mastery 62, 63, 70, 74, 79, 126, 155,
    165, 171–173, 208, (breath, 210),
    (emotional, 215, 218, 221, 236),
    (self, 67, 69, 86, 132), (and control,
    171–173), (in vignette, 29, 172–173,
    219–220)
May, Rollo 33, 36–37
meditation xxii, xxiv, xxvii, 1, 40–41,
    42, 50, 53, 59, 63, 68–71, 75–80, 87,

106, 127, 140, 149, 174, 180, 182, 185, 193, 225, 230, (Buddhist, 76–77, 78–79, 156)

mental health (Indian view) 72–74

mental illness (*see* psychopathology)

mindfulness 127, 141, 193, 195, 208, 217, (meditation, 235–236), (in psychotherapy, 217–219, 227, 236–237), (in vignette, 29–30, 219–221)

mindfulness-based stress reduction (MBSR) 31

modernity xxv, 86, 120

modernization (challenges of) 72, 86

Mohammed, the Prophet xxx

The Mother (Mirra Alfassa) xxxi, 91, 92, 95, 98, 101, 113, 159, 194, 234

Muller, Max 64

Murphy, Michael 131

narcissism 9, 13, (spiritual, 156–157)

near-death experience (NDE) 23, 125

nervous system (cardiac coherence, 212), (parasympathetic, 31), (sympathetic, 212)

new age xxiii, xxiv, xxxi, 54, 149, 154, 183, 211

neurosis 9, 138, (Freud, 12), (Jung, 11), (Rank, 11)

Newbold House (*see* Findhorn Foundation)

nonduality 126

nonordinary states of consciousness/experience 24, 42, 43, 44, 50, 51, 52, 54, 55, 125, 130, 138

occult disturbance 191, 203–204, (possession, 73, 109, 203), (in vignette, 203–204)

occult phenomenon (*see* occult disturbance)

Oedipus complex 11

online therapy 238

ontomotivation 112

out-of-body experience (OBE) 23, 184

paganism xxix, 2

panic (in vignettes) 215–216

past-life recall 80, 201–202, (vignette, 80, 182, 200–201)

past life regression therapy 186

Paramahamsa Hariharananda xxii

Paramahansa Yogananda xxii, 59, 74, (Self-Realization Fellowship, 74)

Parsi (*see* Zoroastrianism)

Pavlov, Ivan 16

peak experiences 34, 35, 44, 54, 77, 85, 144, 148, 151

perennial philosophy 118, 120

person-centered dialogue 38, 209, 222, (in vignette, 79, 209)

phobia 16, (social, in vignette, 13)

Philo Judaeus (*see* Philo of Alexandria)

Philo of Alexandria xxx, 5, 210, 213

Piaget, Jean 122–123

Plato xxx, 4, 118

polytheism xxix, xxx, 2

positive psychology 35

possession (*see* occult disturbance)

postmodernity xxv, xxviii, 120

prana 129, 210, 211

pranayama 70, 71, 210

prayer 3, 60, 62, 156, 175, 193, 233, (in vignette, 233–234)

premonition 42, 49, 93, 199

pre-trans fallacy 125

psyche xxx, 4, 6, 8, 23, 50, 52, 59, 140, 224, 227, 230, 237, 238, (Chaudhari, 111), (Freud, 8, 15), (Grof, 50–51), (Indian view, 57, 60, 67, 72, 74, 212–213), (Jung, 10–11), (Sri Aurobindo, 114), (in vignette, 14, 34, 80, 173)

psychiatry xxxi, 7, 14, 20, 39, 43, 50–51, 73, 196, (in vignette, 200)

psychic being 54, 93, 101–102, 109–110

psychic transformation 101–102

psychoanalysis 16, 33, 37, 44, 45, 56, 57, 133, 148, (Freud, xxxi, 8–9, 10–11), (limitations, 12–15), (subconscious, 107), (in vignette, 13–14, 14), (case study, 25–30)
psychogenealogy 231
psychological disorders (views on) 7, 10, 15, 18, 20, 21, 22, 24, 130, (Indian view, 72–74), (Sri Aurobindo, 105–106), (spiritual, 55, 125)
psychology (of China, 82–85), (goals of, 146–150), (Indian psychology xxxi, 46, 61, 62, 69, 71–72, 82, 87)
psychology of religion 149
psychopathologies 73, (ADHD, 22), (anxiety, *see* anxiety), (bipolar, 17, 22, 200), (depression, *see* depression), (dissociation, *see* dissociation), (narcissism, *see* narcissism),
psychopharmacology xxxi, 20, (medication, 7, 20, 73, 138, 167), (CBT, 20), (limitations, 22–24), (in vignette, 21, 110)
psychosomatic illness 213, 217, (somatization, 193, 212)
psychosis 16, (Jung, 11), (psychoanalysis, 9), (in vignette, 200–204), (and spiritual emergency, 43, 51, 199)
psychosynthesis 47, 48–49, 181, 192, 227
psychotropic medication (*see* psychopharmacology)
PTSD 23, 223, (in vignette, 223)
purification xxii, 63, 67, 70, 99, 100, 144, 230, 233, (breath, 208), (mind, 56, 67, 71, 114), (Patanjali, 69, 70, 237), (psychosynthesis, 47–48), (in vignette, 108, 204), (of workspace, 174)

Ramakrishna Paramahamsa 74
Ram Dass 165, 218
Rank, Otto 11, 15
rational emotive behavior therapy 17

rebirth 52, 201, (Buddhism, 7, 76), (Vedas, 62)
rebirthing 211
reductionism/reductionist xxvii, 9, 14, 17, 20, 22, 25, 37, 44, 56, 72, 121, 137, 139, 149, 165, 172, 210
reincarnation 63, 73, 76, 109, 201
Renaissance (the) xxx, 6
repression of the sublime 175
Rig Veda (*see* the Vedas)
Rogers, Carl 29, 35–39, 117

sadhana 70, 102
samadhi 69, 70, 71, 94, 210
samskara 67, 720, (cellular/muscular memory, 173, 191, 192–193, 213)
sanatan dharma 62, 119
schizophrenia (*see* psychopathologies)
self-acceptance 147–148, 238, (in vignette, 220)
self-actualization xxvi, 18, 34, 35, 38, 55, 123, 138, 144, 167, 169, 176, 178, 189, 190, 207, 209, 222, (in vignette, 222)
self-esteem 10, 155, 175, 208, 217, (in vignette, 19, 34–35, 209)
self-sabotage 189, 190, 192, 197, 208, 222, (in vignette, 37, 226)
self-transcendence 35, 167, 178, 207
Sen, Indra 111
shadow 12–13, 86, 124, 126, 151, 154, 165, 171, 176, 184, 191, (in vignette, 124, 225–226)
shamanism xxxvi, xxix, 2
siddhis/spiritual powers 62, 64, 65, 70, 72, 94, 99, 102, 103, 113, 126, 150, 154, 165, 238, (in vignette, 80)
Sikhism xxx, 63
Skinner, B.F. 16–17
Skype (*see* online therapy)
Socrates xxx, 4, 163
spiral dynamics, 120
spiritual bypass (and meditation, 237)
spiritual emergency 51–52, 54, 125, 186, 203, 237, (kundalini awakening/

experience, 180), (and meditation,
237), (vignette, 198)
spiritual narcissism 157
spiritual discipline (*see* sadhana)
spiritual powers (*see* siddhis)
spiritual practice (*see* sadhana)
spirituality (dangers of 151–158),
(definition, 143–144)
Sri Aurobindo 91–115, (inconscient,
92, 97), (subconscient, 92–94,
107–108), (subliminal, 93, 101, 114),
(submental, 92), (superconscient,
93–94), (Supermind, 94–95, 100–101,
103–104, 108), (supramental, 96,
100–101, 103–104), (vital, 93, 95, 96,
98, 105, 106–109)
Sri Aurobindo Ashram xxv, 112
Steiner, Rudolph 39
Sufism xxx, 6, 60
supervision (therapeutic) 174, 177,
182–183
Supramental Transformation 103–104
Suzuki, Shunryu 78
synchronicity xxiv, 46
Swami Vivekananda xxxi, 74, 137

Tao Te Ching 84, 117
tai chi 53, (in vignette, 201)
Taoism xxx, 60, 78, 82, 83, 84–85
Therapeutae 6 (*see also* Philo of
Alexandria)
Tolle, Eckhart 112, (in vignette,
153)
touch 230
tradition (modern, postmodern)
72, 86–87
transcendence 35, 69, 70, 96, 111–112,
121, 123, 132, 137, 138, 140,
149–150, 153, 236, 237),
(premature, 153)
transference 11, 15, (in vignette, 25)
transformation 23, 43, 52, 54, 61, 74,
86, 94–95, 101–102, 109, 111, 112,
122, 126, 132, 133, 140, 141,
149–150, 153, 156, 169, 180, 199,
207, 211, 223, 237), (societal, 126),

transpersonal psychology 15, 33, 41–44,
47, 48, 50, 52, 53–56, 59, 112,
117–118, 137, 180, 211
trauma 11, 23, 73, 75, 107, 124, 212,
213, 218, 223, 231, 235, (in vignette,
201, 215, 224, 225)
Tzu, Lao xxx, 82, 84

The Upanishads 62, 65–68, 71, 75, 76

Vaughan, Frances 41, 52–53
The Vedas xxx, 62, 63–65, 67, 71, 118
Vedanta 65, 67, 68, 74
Vipassana 156, 169
Visuddhimaga 156
Vrinte, Joseph 140–141
vulnerability 2, 36, 155, 168, 178, 196,
221, (in vignette, 124, 128, 155,
215, 226)
Vygotsky, Lev 16, 122

Watson, John B. 16
Welwood, John 217–218
Wilber, Ken xxviii, xxxi, 39, 52,
114, 117–136, 142, 143, 144, 173,
(and Aurobindo, 138, 140–141,
190–191)
Wilhelm, Richard 46, 83
will 85–86, 106, 228
Woodworth, Robert S. 7
Wundt, Wilhelm xxxi, 7
wu wei 85

yoga (asana, 70, 71, 71, 075, 230),
(definition, 160n5), (therapy, 60, 180,
192, 230)
yoga of self-perfection 100–101
Yoga Sutras of Patanjali (*see* Maharishi
Patanjali)
yogic philosophy (Jung, 45)

Zarathustra xxx
zazen 78–79
Zen 60, 78–79, (Buddhism, 78–79,
78–79, 80), (koan, 78)
Zoroastrianism xxx

Lightning Source UK Ltd.
Milton Keynes UK
UKOW02n1648230117
292700UK00001B/13/P